CONTENTS

Rangers' 50 Flags

The Official Companion to Rangers' World Record-Breaking Journey to Fifty League Titles

Written by

Bob MacCallum

Edited by Douglas Russell

g

A Grange Publication

© 2003. Published by Grange Communications Ltd., Edinburgh, under licence from Rangers Football Club. Printed in the EU.

ISBN 1-902 704-64-9

INTRODUCTION

A LOOK AT SOME SIGNIFICANT LEAGUE CHAMPIONSHIPS

1890-91   The first Scottish League Championship and Rangers are joint Champions with Dumbarton.

1898-99   A world record - Rangers win EVERY league match.

1920-21   Bill Struth and Alan Morton's first season and only one league defeat.

1927-28   The Double won for the first time. Bob McPhail's first season.

1933-34   The Clean Sweep season. Arsenal are beaten in the unofficial British Championship.

1948-49   The first-ever Treble Season and the famous 'Iron Curtain' defence.

1952-53   Double Season with the League Title decided on goal difference.

1963-64   Scot Symon's Treble Season.

1975-76   Jock Wallace's first Treble Season.   First of the new Premier League.

1977-78   Jock Wallace's team become only the second side to win the Treble twice in three seasons.

1986-87   The Graeme Souness Revolution and the the club regains the title.

1992-93   Walter Smith's Treble Season includes 44 unbeaten matches.

1996-97   Richard Gough captains Rangers to Nine-In-A-Row.

1998-99   Dick Advocaat, first-ever foreign manager, wins the Treble.

PART ONE
THE TREBLE SEASON OF 2002-3

INTRODUCTION

Season 2002-3 was a truly memorable one for the club - not only was the League Championship regained, but various records were either equalled or extended. The most significant of these was the winning of the 50th Championship, a world record. Also, by completing the domestic treble, Rangers extended this record to 7, with Celtic (the only other club in Scotland to have achieved this feat) having managed it 3 times. Furthermore, by retaining the Scottish Cup, Rangers equalled our great rival's record of 31 wins. Meanwhile, the League Cup victory of last season brought that total to 23, almost double the number of wins by our nearest challengers, again, Celtic.

Rangers have always striven to be the best and, indeed, the first. Two seasons ago, UEFA recognised the wonderful achievement of its first member club to win 100 major trophies. Obviously, that total now stands at 105. Rangers were the first club to win the Scottish League Championship (jointly with Dumbarton in 1890-91), the first and only side to have won every league match in a season (1898-99), the first team to win the Premier Division (when it was devised in Season 75-76) and the first champions of the Scottish Premier League when it was constituted in 98-99. The following season, Rangers became the first club to win its league championship in 3 different centuries.

Furthermore, when the League Cup was inaugurated in Season 46-47, Rangers became the first winners and, two seasons later, the first club to complete the Treble. Finally, another oft-forgotten first is the fact that Rangers were the first British club to appear in the final of a European tournament.

However, these impressive statistics do not tell the whole story of what the club has achieved in Scotland since its players first kicked a ball against Callendar in 1872. In its 130 year history, Rangers have become a Scottish sporting institution. This has come about due to its ethos of excellence, hard work, determination, and team spirit - all qualities that stem from the Scottish nation itself.

This 'Rangers Spirit' was a factor in many a famous victory as was the dedication, loyalty and encouragement of Rangers supporters who can be found all over the world. Throughout the years, many wonderful players (both Scottish and foreign of all colours and creeds) have worn the light blue with distinction. From Season 2003-4 onwards, Rangers players will wear 5 stars above the crest on the Rangers shirt with each star representing 10 league championships. - a proud reminder of all those famous names over the decades whose contribution produced those stars. They are the REAL stars who will live in the memory forever.

This book not only charts Rangers' path to a world record 50 Championships, but also relives the events in one of their most dramatic and greatest seasons. In the first part, some of the most significant league championships from the 50 triumphs are examined, starting with our first under the management of William Wilton and ending with Dick Advocaat's Rangers in 1999. Then, in part 2, the 2002-3 Treble winning season under Alex McLeish is celebrated as Rangers set out on the quest for their next 50 titles.

THE YEARS OF THE LEAGUE CHAMPIONSHIP WINS

Key: Sc.C= Scottish Cup; L.C.= League Cup; G.C.=Glasgow Cup; Ch.C=Glasgow Charity Cup.

It should be noted that the Glasgow Cup and the Glasgow Charity Cup were treated seriously by all the Glasgow clubs well into the 1960s. Then, 6 teams competed for these trophies and all, bar Queen's Park, were usually in the top division in Scotland. The sides were: Rangers, Celtic, Partick Thistle, Clyde, Third Lanark and Queen's Park. In the early days of these competitions, other clubs competed such as Cowlairs, Pollokshaws and Northern.

Before the introduction of European football and the advent of the League Cup (after the Second World War), a team from Glasgow that won the double of League Championship and Scottish Cup plus the two aforementioned Glasgow tournaments couldn't do any better....as there was nothing else to be won!

1	*1890 - 91	28	*1952 - 53 Sc.C.
2	*1898 - 99	29	1955 - 56
3	1899 - 1900 G.C. Ch.C	30	1956 - 57 G.C. Ch.C.
		31	1958 - 59
4	1900 - 01 G.C.		
5	1901 - 02 G.C	32	1960 - 61 L.C.
6	1910 - 11 G.C Ch.C	33	1962 - 63 Sc.C.
7	1911 - 12 G.C	34	*1963 - 64 Sc.C. L.C.
8	1912 - 13 G.C.		
9	1917 - 18 G.C.	35	1974 - 75 G.C.
10	1919 - 20	36	*1975 - 76 Sc.C. L.C
		37	*1977 - 78 Sc.C. L.C.
11	*1920 - 21		
12	1922 - 23 G.C. Ch.C.	38	*1986 - 87 L.C.
13	1923 - 24 G.C	39	1988 - 89 L.C.
14	1924 - 25 G.C. Ch.C.	40	1989 - 90
15	1926 - 27		
16	*1927 - 28 Sc.C Ch.C.	41	1990 - 91 L.C.
17	1928 - 29 Ch.C.	42	1991 - 92 Sc.C.
18	1929 - 30 Sc.C G.C. Ch.C.	43	*1992 - 93 Sc.C. L.C.
		44	1993 - 94 L.C.
19	1930 - 31 Ch.C.	45	1994 - 95
20	1932 - 33 G.C Ch.C	46	1995 - 96 Sc.C.
21	*1933 - 34 Sc.C. G.C. Ch.C.	47	*1996 - 97 L.C.
22	1934 - 35 Sc.C.	48	*1998 - 99 Sc.C. L.C.
23	1936 - 37 G.C.	49	1999 - 2000 Sc.C.
24	1938 - 39 Ch.C.		
THE SECOND WORLD WAR		50	2002 - 2003 Sc.C. L.C.
25	1946 - 47 L.C. Ch.C.		
26	*1948 - 49 Sc.C. L.C.		
27	1949 - 50 Sc.C. G.C.		*Asterisk denotes featured title win.

THE 19TH CENTURY (1890-1900)

The start of the last decade of the 19th century saw the formation of the Scottish League. In the 10 years to the end of the century, Rangers won the league championship 3 times and were runners-up 3 times. The only club to eclipse this record were the fledgling Celtic who won the title 4 times. Formed in 1888 and 15 years younger than Rangers, they had embarked on a policy of seeking instant success by poaching some of the best players from the more established clubs especially fellow, self-proclaimed 'Irish-Catholic' club Hibernian of Edinburgh who had recently won the Scottish Cup.

Nevertheless, this was a successful period for Rangers. Apart from sharing the first league title with Dumbarton (one of the giants of the time), Rangers won their first Scottish Cup in 1893-94 by beating Celtic 3-1. Another 2 Scottish Cup triumphs were added before the next Championship victory in Season 1898-99. This was perhaps even more special than the first ever Championship since the side set a world record that could never be beaten - every league match was won!

Throughout this early period of league competition, some of the greatest Rangers players in history displayed their prowess. Most, but not all of them, were content to ply their trade at First Ibrox. For instance, in 1891-92, the tremendous full-back Donald Gow, a member of the first Championship-winning side, was transferred to Sunderland on terms of £70 down and £3 a week - big money in those days. Another 2 members of that team found their way to the English League with Wylie going to Everton and Hislop to Aston Villa. It would be almost a century before this trend of Scottish players moving to England (to 'better' themselves) would be reversed although it has to be said this process never happened that often at Rangers.

Despite Gow leaving, Rangers became stronger in the full-back department with the emergence of the legendary Jock Drummond

who would later be partnered by another colossus - Nicol Smith.
This full-back pairing is still, to this day, one of the finest ever to
play for Rangers. It was in this decade that some of Rangers' most
revered legends appeared in the light blue. Internationalists such
as Neilly Gibson and Jacky Robertson (who had played for Everton
and Southampton) plus brilliant international forwards such as
R.C.Hamilton, Alec Smith and John McPherson were at their peak.

In this section, the sides that won Rangers' first 2
Championships will be examined in some detail but a brief mention
must be made of the team that won the title in Season 1899-1900.
Fittingly, this side (having won all their league matches the previous
campaign) retained the title in the season that saw Rangers move
from their home of First Ibrox to the site of the present day stadium.
The flitting was virtually 'next door' and took place in December
1899 with Rangers half-way to holding on to their league title.
A wonderful 6-1 defeat of Kilmarnock was the last match at First
Ibrox. By the end of the season, Rangers would be 7 points ahead
of Celtic at the top of the table. When the team lost 3-2 at Parkhead
in January 1900, it was Rangers' first league defeat in almost 2
years. The side had not been beaten since February 1898 - 31 wins
and 4 draws in a 35 match sequence. A total of 66 points had been
amassed (out of a possible 70) and the team had scored 145 goals
whilst losing just 39. It is a record that still ranks with other Rangers
teams down the ages. That period was to be the second title in
a run of 'four-in-a-row' - until then, the most consecutive
Championships ever won.

RANGERS' FIRST LEAGUE CHAMPIONSHIP: 1890 - 91

Near the end of March 1890, a group of club football administrators
met at the Commercial Hotel in Glasgow to discuss the formation of
a Scottish Football League. Of the 14 established clubs invited to
attend, only Queen's Park and Clyde declined. This meeting had no
doubt been prompted by the fact that the game had been growing

fast and our English cousins had set up their own (now thriving) league, two seasons previously. The leading lights of the Scottish clubs agreed that a league was a necessity thus avoiding the fixture chaos of cup matches and the series of friendlies that, until then, had comprised the football calendar.

Apart from Clyde, regal Queen's Park (who had dominated the Scottish game since its inception) refused to become involved. Their main objection was that a league would lead to 'professionalism' which, to them and many others, was still a dirty word. Queen's Park, the embodiment of 'Corinthian Spirit', wanted no part in this new set-up and, although they joined by the end of the decade (due to an inability to arrange enough 'friendly' fixtures), they stubbornly remained an amateur club whose glory days were over once the Scottish Football League had been formed. It was no consolation to Queen's Park that they were eventually proved correct when clubs were allowed to become professional in 1893 - years after the leading English clubs had taken this step. Despite its title and claim to be a national league, all the clubs (bar Hearts) came from the Clydeside area where the heaviest concentration of population had taken to this new sport.

Of the 12 clubs attending that fateful meeting, only St Bernards were not elected to join the elite group. Thus Rangers, Abercorn, Cambuslang, Celtic, Cowlairs, Dumbarton, Hearts, Renton, St Mirren, Third Lanark, and Vale of Leven became the Founding Fathers of the Scottish League. The delegates agreed that their league should remain amateur and play under the auspices of the SFA, a proposal put forward by Rangers' President John Mellish who had attended the meeting with his Match Secretary William Wilton. Ironically, by the end of the decade, the clubs had turned professional and five of the founder members (Abercorn, Cambuslang, Cowlairs, Renton and Vale of Leven) had gone out of business.

Before the advent of legitimate professionalism, however, 'shamateurism' was rife amongst many of the clubs who made under the counter payments to their players. The SFA even set up a committee - the Professional Committee - to monitor the clubs and try to prevent payments being made. They could, and indeed did, ask for clubs' accounts to be submitted to them for inspection and, on one occasion, were told by a club that books could not be produced as they had been burnt in a fire! At least none tried that well-known schoolboy excuse for failure to deliver homework - the dog ate it! To show that the SFA had teeth and could, indeed, severely 'bite' any member club, Renton, after only 5 matches in the new league and one of the prime movers, were expelled for 'professionalism' and all points won or lost against them cancelled.

To put all this into its historical context, it should be remembered that, in the year these clubs were setting up their league, United States cavalrymen were massacring Native Americans at Wounded Knee. It's also interesting to note that Rangers had been playing football for a few years when General Custer made his Last Stand at Little Big Horn! In Victorian Scotland, the year before the formation of the league, the Forth Rail Bridge had been completed with its re-painting no doubt having already started! In fact, just over a year previously, Jack the Ripper had been terrorising the women of the East End of London. Still, in 1891, a more civilised occurrence took place - the invention of the zip fastener. Where would we be without it? Meantime, it was the formation of this new-fangled league that caught the imagination of most West of Scotland males at the start of that decade.

So, in what would turn out to be a momentous season in the history of The Rangers Football Club, the opening match saw them play their first league game at Ibrox against Hearts on August 16th, 1890 in front of 4,000 fans. The side for that first-ever league encounter was: Reid; Gow, Muir; Marshall, A.McCreadie, Mitchell; Wylie, Kerr, H.McCreadie, McPherson and Hislop. In a 5-2 home win, it was ironic that the honour of scoring their first league goal should go to a Hearts player (Adams) who put the ball into his own goal. The side that won this game would go on to be recognised as the first of the great Rangers teams.

The player who would become its star was John McPherson (the Beckham of his day) who had been brought from rival club Cowlairs by William Wilton to boost Rangers' chances of winning the first Scottish League Championship. In 12 seasons at Ibrox, this supreme footballer managed to play for Rangers in every position. He played in 3 Scottish Cup winning sides and helped bring 5 league titles to the club. He was also capped by Scotland on 8 occasions (4 times against England) as well as gaining 5 'League' caps. Both powerful and a tremendous dribbler, his 15 goals in 18 league games that season proved that he had an eye for goal. In fact, to this day, McPherson is still in the top 5 of Rangers goal scorers against Celtic. In recognition of his stalwart service to Rangers, he was eventually made a director of the club - not as rare an occurrence then as it is today.

Being an historic first league season, it's obvious that all sorts of 'firsts' would be established. Thus the team's first league defeat came at the hands of the then mighty Dumbarton who, with Rangers, would dominate this first league campaign. Rangers were defeated 5-1 at Boghead, even then tagged 'Fatal Boghead'. Was ever a football ground more aptly named? Even modern fans will remember the playing conditions that tended to be prevalent at that location - no matter what the season! In addition to being a good team, Dumbarton took advantage of their pitch and set the pace. When the league closed down in the middle of October (until January), it was Dumbarton who were in pole position (won 6, drawn 1) with Rangers in second place, having played 2 matches fewer. During this break, Rangers travelled to the North-East of England for a series of 3 friendlies against Newcastle, Middlesbrough and Sunderland, winning the first two and only losing the latter game.

In the course of their opening 5 league matches, Rangers' progress had been affected by circumstances outwith their control. For example, in game number three, their 4-1 victory over Renton was declared null and void after the SFA had expelled Renton from the league for professionalism. However, a year later, their league status was restored after the club having taken the authorities to court. After all, they were the self-appointed 'Champions of the World' after having beaten West Brom, the English FA Cup holders. The football world was indeed a small place in those days!

After the league break, came another significant 'first' - the first Old Firm match although it was not called that in those days. This took place at Celtic Park in March 1891 and ended in a 2-2 draw. If only those 12,000 fans who witnessed that game realised what lay ahead over the next 100 years! Indeed Celtic might have been challengers for the title but 4 points were deducted from their total early-on for fielding an ineligible player. At almost the half-way point in the league programme, it was Dumbarton who were setting the pace, having dropped only one point out of a possible 18. Then Rangers gained some unexpected help when Celtic drew 2-2 at Boghead. The title race was hotting up.

With only 6 matches left, Rangers were still adrift of 'The Sons of the Rock' and, after a 2-2 Parkhead draw, they played their final away game (beating Cowlairs 2-0) leaving them with the obvious advantage of 4 Ibrox games still remaining. On April 4th, Vale of Leven were beaten 4-0 before the crunch game - Dumbarton at Ibrox! Defeat would hand the title to 'The Sons' but, in front of 12,000 fans, Rangers pulled out all the stops and won 4-2. The great John McPherson scored one of those vital goals....in his first game since he had married. Funnily enough, he was now the only married man in the side. Having defeated their main rivals for the crown, Rangers now had 2 matches left and needed only 3 out of a possible 4 points to win the Championship.

The first of these games was against yet-to-become arch-rivals Celtic and, not for the last time in the club's history, the team in green put a spanner in the works. With the score 1-1, Celtic netted the winner near the end following a mistake by the Rangers keeper Reid. Rangers now needed to win their last game to simply tie with Dumbarton. Despite being badly hit by injury (where have we heard that before?) the brilliant 4-1 defeat of Third Lanark on May 9th

ensured that tie. Being a new organisation, such an eventuality had
never occurred. A play-off to decide the winners was ordered and
duly took place before 10,000 spectators at First Cathkin Park, the
home of Third Lanark.

Despite being 2-0 up at halftime, Rangers faltered and a great
rally from Dumbarton saw them claw the two goals back for the
match to end 2-2. Cue scratching of heads as to what should be
done now to determine the title's destination. Thankfully, nobody
suggested tossing a coin! When the League Committee convened
to consider the matter, it took the Chairman's casting vote to decide
that the Championship should be shared jointly. What a brave man!
Or was he really a coward? Or was he just showing the wisdom of
Solomon? Can you imagine such a scenario nowadays? Think of
the pressure and paranoia that would surround such a vote.
Apparently, if goal average or goal difference had been the deciding
factor, Dumbarton would have been declared Champions but the
rules had not incorporated these features so Joint Champions they
became with Rangers. Perhaps justice was done the following
season when 'The Sons' won the title outright whereas Rangers
would have to wait another 8 years before winning the league again.
Still, nothing could take away the glory from that inaugural season
of the Scottish League as Rangers amassed a total of 29 points,
losing only 2 matches - against Dumbarton and Celtic. How many
people could have imagined then that it would be the 21st century
before the club celebrated flag number 50?

LEAGUE CHAMPIONSHIP NUMBER 2:   1898 - 99

Rangers' second league title win also created a world record
that has never since been equalled. In fact, by its very nature, can
never be surpassed. This great Rangers side won every league
game it played that season. Admittedly, the league comprised of
only 10 teams and the total number of matches played was just 18
but it was still an incredible achievement to finish with a 100%

record. Consider how difficult it would be nowadays for any side, in any league in the world, to win 18 consecutive league games and you start to grasp the scope of the accomplishment. In 18 games, the Ibrox side scored 79 and lost 18 goals.

Rangers kicked off their season with a tremendous 6-2 home win over Partick Thistle in front of 7,000 fans whereas, by the final home game, some 30,000 fans were watching them beat Celtic 4-1. In this particular clash, captain R.C.Hamilton scored the first Old Firm Ne'er Day hat-trick. Hamilton would end the season top scorer with 21 league goals in a side that averaged more than 4 per game. In fact, Hamilton still makes the top 10 of Rangers' all-time league goal scorers. The title was actually won 5 games from the end of the league programme when Dundee were thrashed 7-0 at Ibrox. However, the record-clinching match came at Shawfield when Rangers beat Clyde 3-0. Second placed team, Hearts, were 10 points adrift.

One of the early turning points was match number six when Rangers went to Celtic Park and won 4-0 in front of a crowd of 46, 500. For once, Celtic caused Rangers no heartache in the league, only the cups. In fact, the team that came nearest to spoiling that 100% record turned out to be Hibs.

In the 11th match of the league programme, Rangers (who had lost to Queens Park in the Glasgow Cup Final the previous week) were in dire straits at Easter Road and, within 22 minutes, were down 2-0 with the Gers fans in the crowd of 10,000 wondering what had gone wrong. Naturally determined to keep their 100% record, the side changed tactics. Instead of the neat, short passing game, they altered their style to a more direct, long ball game thus attempting to get the ball into the opposition box more frequently. It started to work and they got a goal back just before half-time through Miller.

Then, one minute after the interval, Smith netted the equaliser. As if stung by losing their lead, Hibs went ahead again with Gemmell scoring his third of the game. Playing a skipper's part,

Hamilton again managed to grab an equaliser then, one minute from the end, showing that true Rangers' spirit, the winning goal was scored by Neil from a penalty. Apparently, a Hibs defender had grabbed Campbell by the shirt collar and tried to throw him to the ground like a wrestler. In those days, the penalty line extended right across the pitch. Can you imagine if that were the case nowadays?

When the return match with Hibs was played at Ibrox on Christmas Eve, the fans expected another titanic battle to be in store. How wrong they were! Within 20 minutes Rangers, playing superbly well, were 5 goals up. The match ended 10-0 which is still Hibs' record league defeat and Rangers' record league win to this day. In fact, if Campbell had not missed a late penalty, Rangers would have equalled the Scottish League's record win.

To create such a world record, a side needed to have fitness, skill, determination and, it has to be said, luck as well. Another factor was alluded to by club captain R.C.Hamilton in one of the tea parties that were always held after a game in Glasgow. He claimed that one of the most vital ingredients in Rangers winning every league game was the tremendous team spirit shown by all the players. Perhaps nobody embodied this more than Hamilton himself. After all, the season before, he had both played and scored in Rangers' winning Cup Final appearance against Kilmarnock - after sitting a three hour exam at Glasgow University that morning!

Probably, the quest for this record cost Rangers their chance of winning any of the cup tournaments. With Rangers attempting to lift the Scottish Cup for the third consecutive season (a feat still seldom accomplished) Celtic beat them 2-0 in the 1899 Final as well as in the Glasgow Charity Cup Final by the same score. Additionally, Queen's Park beat them 1-0 in the Glasgow Cup Final.

Still, even these setbacks could not diminish the feeling of tremendous success pervading Ibrox that season. Rangers players were now earning £3 a week - twice the rate of skilled workers such as joiners or plumbers - and the club made a profit of £1,200. Indeed, so successful had Rangers become that their turnover was rising year on year. As a result, at the end of this memorable season, the club members voted to become a limited liability company and, in May 1899, the club became Rangers Football Club Ltd. The first Board of Directors was appointed and James Henderson, who had been President of the club until then, became the first Chairman. He held this position until his death in 1912 having given the club many years of devoted service. The other crucial appointment made at that time was that of Manager and Secretary. The great William Wilton (who had been Match Secretary for 10 years) had no rivals for this post and, after resigning as Secretary to the Scottish League (a position he had held for 10 years) he became Rangers' first manager until his tragic death in 1920.

Rangers now set out to become the pre-eminent club in the country. As a further sign of this, by the end of that year, New Ibrox would have been built. It opened in December 1899 and was built to hold 85,000 spectators. The cost of the stadium was £24,000 and it was designed by Archibald Leitch, the architect who would become the doyen of football ground designers in Britain. Indeed, in 1928, he would design the Main Stand at Ibrox, now a listed building. At the turn of the century, The Rangers Football Club Ltd. was on its way.

A total of 16 players contributed to the team of World Record holders with 5 playing in all 18 games. Here is the full list:

PLAYER	POSITION	MATCHES
M.Dickie	Goalkeeper	18
N.Gibson	Right Half-back	18
R.G.Neil	Centre Half-back	18
R.C.Hamilton	Centre Forward	18
A.Smith	Outside Left	18
D.Crawford	Right / Left Back	17
J.Campbell	Outside Right / Left	16
J.Miller	Inside Left	16
J.McPherson	Inside Right	15
N.Smith	Right Back	13
D.Mitchell	Left Half-back	13
J.Drummond	Left Back	5
J.Miller (Elgin)	Left Half-back	5
A.Sharp	Inside Right	4
J.Wilkie	Inside Right / Left	3
J.Sharp	Outside Right	1

THE RESULTS OF THE LEAGUE PROGRAMME OF 1898-99

	HOME	AWAY
CELTIC	4-1	4-0
HEARTS	3-1	3-2
THIRD LANARK	4-1	3-2
ST MIRREN	3-2	3-1
HIBS	10-0	4-3
ST BERNARDS	5-2	2-0
CLYDE	8-0	3-0
DUNDEE	7-0	2-1
PARTICK THISTLE	6-2	5-0

THE EARLY 20TH CENTURY (1900-1918)

By the end of these 18 seasons, Rangers had won the league 6 more times. With only one Scottish Cup triumph (Hearts were beaten 2-0 after 2 replays in 1902-03) it had not been a great period in Rangers' history. Of course, everything is relative. At the time, the fans had not been too perturbed but they were not to know that the eras of Rangers' greatest success were still ahead.

It was during this period of Scottish football history that Rangers and Celtic justified their new nickname of 'The Old Firm' by dominating the Scottish scene. It was one of the few periods in history when Celtic created a better record than their neighbours. By the end of this era, Celtic had added 10 more league titles to their name and a further 6 Scottish Cups thereby holding the record of 14 league championships. In this period, their title wins came in two spells: one was a sequence of 'six-in-a-row' and the other 'four-in-a-row'. Not until the arrival of Jock Stein in the 1960s would the club have such a successful run again. A measure of the strength of the Old Firm's dominance can be seen in the fact that, during this period, only 2 teams (other than Rangers or Celtic) won the Championship. Third Lanark and Hibs were the teams in question in the period 1902-04! Indeed, from 1904, either Rangers or Celtic would end up Scottish Champions until Motherwell took the crown in Season 1931-32.

In tragic contrast to the highs of this era came the club's darkest hour - the first Ibrox Disaster of 1902. During a Scotland v England international, a section of the wooden terracing gave way causing the death of 25 people and injuring hundreds more. The consequence of this terrible event led to new safety measures being introduced to stadia so that, from then on, terracings would have solid earth foundations rather than wood.

On the football front, the 19th century had ended with a championship and the 20th century had started promisingly with the club winning the first 2 Championships of that era. The team's record for those seasons was:

	P	W	D	L	GF	GA	PTS
1899-1900	18	15	2	1	69	27	32
1900-01	20	17	1	2	60	25	35
1901-02	18	13	2	3	43	29	28

It took a remarkable comeback to win the 1901-02 title. With only 4 matches to play, Rangers were 5 points adrift of Celtic but, miraculously, Celtic lost 2 successive games then drew in their penultimate match. The Old Firm Ne'erday game at Parkhead was the fourth last match of the season and Celtic knew that the title came with victory. As sometimes happens, a controversial game took place with Rangers winning 4-2 but not before Celtic players had surrounded the referee protesting about the legality of 3 of the 4 Rangers goals. Indeed, one player (McMahon) was sent off because the referee thought that he had tried to trip him up when making his protest! Hardly surprisingly, the match ended in 'uproar' - as the papers of the day put it.

After the match, Celtic protested that the game had been stopped sooner than it should have been but when the matter came up before the appropriate League Committee, it turned out that Celtic had merely wanted to put the referee on the spot. When Mr Nisbet refused to answer the Committee's questions (which presumably impugned his honour) he was struck off the referees' roll. It was at the end of this campaign that striking legend John McPherson retired. However, by that time, Rangers had already found another goal scoring hero in the making - the legendary R.C.Hamilton.

If one particular year is to be singled out from this period, perhaps it should be 1911. In that year, Rangers played 51 games, losing only twice...and it was in the middle of a run of 'three-in-a-row' championships too. At the end of 1913, the great forward Tommy Cairns was signed but a more important addition to the staff around this time was the appointment of a certain Bill Struth as team trainer, a move that would benefit Rangers for decades to come.

Perhaps fittingly, the end of this era (that saw the end of the Great War) resulted in Rangers regaining the title in Season 1917-18 after Celtic had won the previous 4. To show that the nail-biting end to Season 2002-03 was nothing new in the annals of the Old Firm, that season's championship was also decided on the last day. With 4 matches left, champions Celtic were 2 points ahead of Rangers but a shock home defeat by Third Lanark saw Rangers back level with the Parkhead men. Level they stayed until the final games of the season. Both sides were at home with the likely outcome that 2 home victories would necessitate a play-off for the title since in those days neither goal average or goal difference was taken into account. Rangers played Clyde and Celtic faced Motherwell. In 2 tense affairs, the Rangers managed to win 2-1 at Ibrox but Celtic were held 1-1 at Parkhead sending the Championship Trophy across the city to Ibrox. It was Rangers' 9th league title.

Statistics for the years of those title triumphs:

	P	W	D	L	GF	GA	PTS
1910-11	34	23	6	5	90	34	52
1911-12	34	24	3	7	86	34	51
1912-13	34	24	5	5	76	41	53
1917-18	34	25	6	3	66	24	56

BETWEEN THE WARS (1919-1939)

In the 21 seasons prior to the Second World War, Rangers enjoyed a remarkable era under Bill Struth (who had become manager in 1920) that was unprecedented and would remain unmatched until recent times. In that period, Rangers won the league title 15 times with their greatest rivals Celtic managing only 5 championships and Motherwell the other one. From 1919 until 1929, Rangers won the championship 8 times whilst in the following decade, it was captured 7 times. With a genius of a manager and a host of players who would go on to become legends, Rangers dominated these two decades as no club had ever done before. This section examines 3 of the tremendous Light Blue sides that won the title: the first Struth side of 1920-21, the first double-winning team of 1927-28 and the first side to win everything, the team of 1933-34.

The 1920s saw the emergence of some truly great Rangers players such as Davie Meiklejohn, Alan Morton, Bob McPhail, Andy Cunningham, Dougie Gray, Jimmy Fleming, Tommy Muirhead and Sandy Archibald who, with many others, graced Ibrox and contributed to the continuing Rangers' success story. The league record for the championship wins of that era is as follows:

	P	W	D	L	GF	GA	PTS
1919-20	42	31	9	2	106	25	71
1920-21	42	35	6	1	91	24	76
1922-23	38	23	9	6	67	29	55
1923-24	38	25	9	4	72	22	59
1924-25	38	25	10	3	76	26	60
1926-27	38	23	10	5	85	41	56
1927-28	38	26	8	4	109	36	60
1928-29	38	30	7	1	107	32	67

It is worth noting the incredible consistency of the Rangers teams of this era and the fact that, in the final 2 Championship Seasons, over 100 league goals were scored.

In the 1930s, to the delight of Gers fans all over the world, this story was repeated. Many of the earlier heroes kept their place in the various sides but new blood, new legends were emerging all the time. Players such as keeper Jerry Dawson and defenders George Brown and Jimmy Simpson joined brilliant forwards like Jimmy Smith, Alex Venters, Torry Gillick in keeping Rangers at the top. Following is the league record for the championship wins during the 1930s:

	P	W	D	L	GF	GA	PTS
1929-30	38	28	4	6	94	32	60
1930-31	38	27	6	5	96	29	60
1932-33	38	26	10	2	113	43	62
1933-34	38	30	6	2	118	41	66
1934-35	38	25	5	8	96	46	55
1936-37	38	26	9	3	88	32	61
1938-39	38	25	9	4	112	55	59

Again, these figures for the decade reveal a wonderful consistency of performance with Bill Struth ensuring that his players produced both in terms of points accumulated and goals scored - over a century in three of the seasons detailed.

For particular scrutiny, the following 3 seasons will show just why Rangers were so dominant between both two World Wars.

LEAGUE CHAMPIONSHIP NUMBER 11: 1920 - 21

The Ibrox fans of the era debated whether this great Rangers team was actually superior to the one of 1889 - 90 that had won every league game played. By now the Scottish First Division consisted of 22 clubs with a 42 game programme now the order of the day. Despite this, Rangers only lost one match whilst drawing 6. Their points total was a new record of 76 (beating their own previous season's best by 5) with Celtic trailing the champions by 10 points.

A new manager, who would go on to become THE Rangers legend, was in place - Bill Struth. His elevation from team trainer to manager came about earlier than anticipated due to tragic circumstances. William Wilton, manager for 20 years, died in a boating accident at Gourock. Wilton had been enjoying himself with some friends on a yacht moored at the pier when a violent storm blew up. So dangerous did the storm seem that the party decided to evacuate the boat. Wilton was last to leave but as he tried to jump onto the pier, in the heavy swell, he lost his footing and fell into the swirling waters of the Clyde. He could not be rescued and drowned. This terrible tragedy could have had dire consequences for Rangers but for the fact that Wilton's replacement was already at the club and destined to become their greatest-ever manager.

Having won the previous season's championship by 3 points from Celtic, Rangers knew that their old rivals would again pose the greatest threat to their chances of retaining the title. Rangers' only defeat came at Ibrox on New Year's Day when, weakened by injuries, they lost 2-0 to the Parkhead side. Few of the happy Celtic fans in the crowd of 69,260 could have suspected their team's next Ne'er Day win at Ibrox would not be for another 62 years!

Before that defeat, however, this Rangers team had been mightily impressive racking up 44 points out of a possible 46 in their first 23 games. At that point, they were a massive 16 points ahead of Celtic and on their way to setting the new record. Apart from the manager, one of the main reasons for this was a player brought to the club by Struth before the season had started. Signed in June, this was Alan Morton's first season at Ibrox. Morton moved from the amateurs of Queen's Park, where he had been since 1913, for a signing-on fee of £3,000 - a huge amount of money in those days! Despite his elevation to Rangers (and a Beckham type wage of £60 a week), he remained a part-time mining engineer throughout his football career.

For many fans, Morton was simply the greatest living Rangers player until his death in 1971. When he retired in 1933 (having played 495 matches and scored 115 goals for the club), he was made a director and remained a most productive one for the rest of his days. He won 9 Championship Medals, 3 Scottish Cups and played against England 11 times. How the 'Auld Enemy' defenders must have hated the sight of him! It was after yet another tremendous, mesmerising performance against Scotland's southern neighbours that English sportswriter Ivan Sharpe dubbed him 'The Wee Blue Devil'. And no wonder! Here was a winger who had it all - skill, poise, quick reflexes and brilliant timing. All this no doubt due to the hours he practised as a boy, mastering the ball. Down the years, grateful Scots fans relished his tormenting of various English defenders especially when he was a member of the famous 'Wembley Wizards' team.

Famous nickname aside, he had another less well-known one - 'The Wee Society Man' - which stemmed no doubt from his immaculate appearance as he walked into Ibrox for training in his suit, wearing a bowler hat, leather gloves and carrying his trademark umbrella. His fastidious appearance reflected that of his manager who insisted on his players looking perfect in public as the Rangers image off the field was every bit as important. The huge painting of Alan Morton (in his Scotland jersey) that dominates the marble staircase inside Ibrox is an appropriate reminder of the legend.

If he was responsible for creating many of the 91 goals scored in the league that first season, another newcomer was instrumental in preventing goals at the other end. Goalkeeper Willie Robb was signed from a Junior side in time to start the new season with Morton and, considering the fact that he was replacing Rangers' famous English keeper Herbert Lock, 'the boy done good' as they say. Robb only conceded 24 goals in 42 league matches that season and did not miss a competitive match for 5 years!

Another defensive newcomer who joined Rangers in November was full back Billy 'Bucksy' McCandless. He formed a formidable full-back partnership with fellow Ulsterman Bert 'Daddy Long Legs' Manderson. Between them, they would play over 700 games for Rangers. That Rangers defence was certainly the bedrock of the side. The normal line-up would have been: Robb; Manderson, McCandless; Meiklejohn, Dixon, Walls. Spare a thought for James Walls who signed for Rangers in 1918 and hardly missed a game until Christmas Day 1920 when he broke his leg playing against Clyde at Shawfield, having scored earlier in the match. In those days, a leg break was a far more serious injury and, unfortunately, it basically ended his Ibrox career. Walls only played 2 games in the following 3 seasons as his time at the club fizzled out.

Luckily for Rangers, the player who effectively made the number six shirt his own the following season was the peerless Tommy Muirhead. For the 1920-21 period, however, he would share the vacated Walls' spot with James Bowie who became Rangers Chairman from 1934-47. Apart from that great defence, this championship-winning side had a forward line that still conjures up thoughts of thrilling victories. The usual line-up would have been: Archibald, Cunningham, Henderson, Cairns and Morton.

These front men gave Rangers many years of tremendous service. Perhaps the least well-known was Geordie Henderson, a prolific goal scorer who was much admired by the fans of the time. In Season 1920-21, he scored 21 goals in just 23 appearances and, over the next 4 seasons, hit a total of 90 league goals. It was Andy Cunningham, though, who was top scorer that first season with 24 league goals. This brilliant forward would go on to play 447 matches for Rangers and score 201 goals. He was ably assisted by Sandy Archibald who had the unenviable task of playing on the opposite wing from the great Morton. A wonderful winger in his own right, Archibald ended up playing 667 games for the club, scoring 162 goals in the process. And by the way, he helped Rangers win 13 League Championships!

The final piece of this attacking jigsaw was the inimitable Tommy Cairns who played 493 games in his Rangers' career and scored 160 goals as well as captaining the side for a spell. This brave, determined inside-forward had joined Rangers in 1913 and was immediately imbued with the 'Rangers Spirit' that saw him retrieve many a lost cause. The tragedy for Cairns was that despite an array of medals, he never did get his hands on that elusive Scottish Cup. Along with Manderson and Dixon, he retired at the end of Season 1926-27, the year before Rangers broke their Hampden hoodoo by winning the Cup for the first time in 25 years.

So they were the stars who brought Rangers their 11th Championship in 1920 - 21. An unexpected bonus came about at the end of that season. Rangers went to Copenhagen to play 3 friendlies, winning all of them. Apart from an increased reputation, they also brought back a new addition to their squad of talented players - Carl Hansen who was nicknamed 'The Little Shoemaker'. The following season, this legendary Dane became the first foreigner to score in an Old Firm game, remaining a popular player in the eyes of the fans.

LEAGUE CHAMPIONSHIP NUMBER 16: 1927 - 28

This was a tremendous season for Rangers - the club won the Double for the first time and equalled Celtic's record of 16 League Championships. This was to be Rangers' second league title in a run of 'five-in-a-row'. Half of the brilliant 1920 - 21 side (McCandless, Meiklejohn, Muirhead, Archibald, Cunningham and Morton) were still regulars. Moreover, these stars were augmented by players who would go on to become Rangers legends and / or record holders.

The side that played for most of the first half of the season was: T.Hamilton; Gray, McCandless; Muirhead, Meiklejohn, Craig; Archibald, Cunningham, Fleming, McPhail and Morton. Unfortunately, club captain Tommy Muirhead was injured in mid February (to be replaced by Buchanan) while R.Hamilton took over from Billy McCandless in December. The fans' sympathy certainly went to Muirhead who had signed from Hibs in 1917 for the sum of £20 and given Rangers sterling service throughout his career, eventually playing 352 matches and scoring 49 goals. His 'misfortune' was to see him miss the 1928 Cup Final when Rangers finally broke their Hampden Hoodoo.

Making his debut that season was the prince of goal scorers Bob McPhail whose record of 230 league goals would stand until a certain Ally McCoist overtook it in the 90s. Of course, that other prolific scorer, Jimmy Smith netted more but most experts exclude his 74 scored during the Second World War thus leaving Super Ally and McPhail as the top two.

McPhail was a big, strong, bustling centre-forward who, when he signed from Airdrie, already had a Scottish Cup winner's medal - which was more than could be said of any player in the side he was joining as it was 25 years since Rangers had won the Scottish Cup, despite 5 final appearances. That season he would play his part in destroying the cup hoodoo by scoring against Celtic in the final and going on to win 5 more winner's medals making him joint record holder, even today, with 7 medals. In 14 seasons, he would play 466 games for the club and score 281 goals, helping to win 9 league flags. With such a record it's ironic that his nickname was 'Greetin' Boab'!

However, although in that first season he forged a great partnership with Alan Morton and scored 17 goals, he was not top scorer at the club. That honour fell to Jimmy Fleming who was having the best season of his career to date. He almost doubled McPhail's tally, scoring 33 in the league and (in 45 matches) he scored 47 goals plus 40 the following season. Fleming still holds the club record for Scottish Cup goals with 44. It was an attacking arsenal of two great wingers (Archibald and Morton) supplying brilliant goal scorers such as McPhail and Fleming in addition to Andy Cunningham. All three are all still in the top 10 of Rangers' goal scorers and it is no wonder that this particular Rangers side was considered one of the most exciting ever.

If the attacking aspect of the team did not include enough riches, behind them could be seen true Rangers legends in the shape of David Meiklejohn and Dougie Gray. Include Muirhead, Hamilton in goal and Tom 'Tully' Craig (not the last ex-Celt to play for the Rangers) and you have a memorable line up.

Dougie Gray is the club's longest serving player. He played from 1925 until 1947, featuring in an incredible 667 league matches for the Light Blues. In all, he played a total of 940 matches for Rangers, winning 16 League Championships and 6 Scottish Cup medals. His legendary status can never be disputed. What a man to have at full back! And what a man to have at centre-half - the great Davie Meiklejohn, another player who with 490 league appearances still figures in Rangers all-time top 5. He played from 1919 to 1936, won 11 league titles, 5 Scottish Cups and scored 44 goals - a respectable haul for a centre-half. He was capped 15 times for Scotland with his finest hour coming at Hampden in 1931 when he skippered the Scots to a 2-0 victory over England, contributing greatly to the cause by having the legendary Everton striker Dixie Dean 'in his pocket' for the entire match!

Meiklejohn was a great reader of the game and a master tactician, not features we associate nowadays with the game in the 20s. He was Struth's lieutenant on the field and respected by everyone for his courage, strength and resolve. It was perhaps inevitable that he would become captain as he had played for Bellahouston Academy, not a free-kick away from Ibrox. His greatest test - and triumph - came during the famous 1928 Scottish Cup Final against Celtic.

Early in the game Rangers had their keeper Tom Hamilton to thank for keeping the score level when he made a miraculous save from a Connolly volley that had goal written all over it. That save maybe inspired his team-mates but, in the second half, it was Meiklejohn they had to thank for seeming to break the 25 year Scottish Cup hoodoo. A Morton cross was volleyed towards goal by Jimmy Fleming but was prevented from going into the net by the hand of Willie McStay. Or had it? It was a moot point whether the ball had crossed the line or not but the referee decided to award a penalty. With a side full of such great goal scorers as McPhail, Fleming and Cunningham, you would have thought that one of them would have volunteered to take the crucial penalty kick. However, captain courageous could not put that awesome responsibility on any of them so elected to take the kick himself. Ironically, he was only skippering the team that day due to the absence of Tommy Muirhead who had been injured earlier in the season.

With 120,000 fans at Hampden (then a British record) seemingly holding their breath, Meiklejohn stepped forward to face his destiny. He later admitted what a frightening prospect it was, realising that this could be a turning point not only in the final but in the history of Rangers. Cometh the hour, cometh the man, he blasted the ball past Celtic's legendary keeper (the ill-fated John Thompson), setting Rangers on the road to a 4-0 win. Afterwards, Meiklejohn was to say "We have done it at last. We can do it again." And Rangers did - they would go on to win the Scottish Cup 5 times in the next 8 years.

Alan Morton was to say of Meiklejohn years later - "He will go down in history as one of the greatest Rangers ever to wear the colours. No cause was ever lost when Davie was there behind you."

The league programme that season had started well for Rangers with a 10 game unbeaten run that surprisingly came to an end when they lost at Hampden to Queen's Park in October. Even then, the league was looking like a three horse race with Rangers, Motherwell and, not surprisingly, Celtic as the main contenders for the title. The team did not suffer another reverse until the New Year match at Celtic Park when a 70,000 crowd saw Jimmy McGrory score the only goal of the game. Still, at this point, they led Motherwell by one point and Celtic by 3. If Rangers had shown better form away from home that gap would have been wider but, ironically, it was when Motherwell beat them 2-0 at Ibrox in February that the league race was blown wide open. It began to look as if Celtic would be the team to win the Double that year.

Easter was a crucial spell in the league programme and this was when the fortunes of the two great rivals were reversed. In a three day period, Rangers won both their matches while Celtic lost both to Motherwell and Airdrie, allowing Rangers to enjoy a 3 point lead from having been a point behind. Then, 4 days after that famous Cup Final victory, Rangers beat Dundee away, leaving a win in their next game at home to Kilmarnock to clinch the title. This great side was not to be denied at the final hurdle and duly thrashed Killie 5-1, some 7 days after having broken their Scottish Cup hoodoo. It was a team that will always be remembered as one of the finest to grace Ibrox Stadium.

LEAGUE CHAMPIONSHIP NUMBER 21: 1933 - 34

Not for the first time, this was a season in which Rangers did the 'Clean Sweep' as it was called then. This side won all it could possibly win - including an unofficial British Championship. For a Glasgow team, the 'Clean Sweep' meant winning the League Championship, Scottish Cup, Glasgow Cup and Glasgow Charity Cup. What made their achievement all the more remarkable was that this side was disrupted by injury to key players. For instance, Bob McPhail missed a third of the league programme whilst Meiklejohn missed a quarter of the same schedule. Additionally, Alan Morton had retired at the end of the previous season (becoming a Director of the club) and it is obvious that this could have been a difficult time for the side

Probably one of the most decisive factors in the team's success was the fact that it had 4 tremendous goal scorers (all of whom would end up in the top 10 list of Rangers' greatest league scorers) - McPhail, Smith, Fleming and newcomer Alex Venters. Indeed, Venters was only signed in November from Cowdenbeath and an international player already. He was a brave, powerful, inside-forward who would amass a total (which included the war period) of 155 league goals for Rangers. That season, curtailed by injury, would see Bob McPhail 'only' score 22 league goals from 25 appearances. Meanwhile his strike partner, Jimmy Smith, would end up bagging 41 from 32 league matches.

Due to all the injuries, it is hard to name the first choice team that played that season but here is a version:

Dawson; Gray, McDonald; Meiklejohn, Simpson, Brown; Archibald /Main,Marshall, Smith, McPhail and Nicholson.

Additionally, Jimmy Fleming stood in for Smith while Venters stood in for McPhail. So, when the 2 top strikers were out, another 2 legendary ones replaced them. Not bad, eh?

Mention must be made here of that vastly under-rated goal scorer Jimmy Smith. This tremendous striker (as mentioned previously) scored 41 in the league in Season 33-34 but he also had scored 31 league goals the previous season and would claim 36, 31 and 31 respectively in the next three seasons. What would the present Rangers side give to have such a consistent scorer? Smith's Ibrox career total for league goals eventually came to 226 with an additional 74 being scored during the Second World War. Only Ally McCoist and Bob McPhail surpassed his total. It's safe to say that none of these three players' records will ever be broken now that the nature of football has changed forever.

Another important factor in this side's success was the defence. In goal was the 'Prince of Goalkeepers' Jerry Dawson who was considered Rangers' best-ever - until the appearance of one Andy Goram in the 1990s. Some fans who were lucky enough to have seen both, believe that Dawson was the best. Like Goram, he was not a tall, imposing keeper but more than made up for that by being brave with brilliant reflexes and a great sense of anticipation. His only weakness seemed to be in kicking a dead ball. No matter how hard he practiced, this was a skill he never quite mastered. Luckily, it was not that much of a handicap in a team that had quite a few defenders able to perform that particular function.

Dawson became the Scotland keeper in 1934 and held on to the position for 4 years. He played 271 matches for Rangers and was still around to take part in the famous Moscow Dynamo friendly at Ibrox in 1945 before being succeeded by another goalkeeping legend, Bobby Brown.

Ahead of Dawson in defence was Jimmy Simpson at centre-half. The father of 'Lisbon Lion' Ronnie, Simpson was a rock especially when Meiklejohn was injured. The other half-back was the skillful George Brown (a teacher by profession), one of those players who became a Director of the club. Another player in this side who had a 'profession' was James Marshall. He was a doctor working at Glasgow Royal and was, naturally, more frequently called 'Doc' Marshall. At the end of this season he was transferred to West Ham but not because he was seeking the fame or wealth of the English

League - it was simply a case of taking a medical position in London.

Although another Rangers great Torry Gillick was signed before the start of the campaign, he only played in 2 matches.

The side got off to a brilliant start by beating Airdrie 5-1 and then Ayr 9-1. Jimmy Smith scored 10 of these 14 goals. It was a taste of what the rest of the season would offer. Yet, by October, Rangers were 3 points behind Motherwell who had the greatest side in their history in the 30s and actually won the title in 1932. Indeed Motherwell defeated Rangers 2-1 at Fir Park in September and St Johnstone then beat the Ibrox men in November at Muirton but they were the only 2 defeats in any competition for Rangers during that season.

When Motherwell visited Ibrox at the end of January, it was already being billed as a league decider. Rangers knew they had to win and they did - 4-2. They continued to the end of the season undefeated and, in the third last match, clinched the title by beating Falkirk 3-1 at Brockville. Therefore, at the end of the 38 match programme, the Ibrox side were 4 points ahead of Motherwell, having taken 66 points and scored 118 goals. This was only one goal short of the Motherwell record created when they lifted the title in 1932.

As for the three cups, Clyde were beaten 2-0 in the Glasgow Cup Final and Celtic 1-0 in the Charity Cup Final. In the Scottish Cup competition, Rangers scored their highest number of goals in a match when they defeated Blairgowrie 14 - 2 (in round one) with Fleming claiming the club record with 9 goals. In the final, St Mirren were thrashed 5-0 at Hampden, the first of three consecutive victories in the tournament. This was, in itself, a tremendous feat as the last time any team had won the Cup in 3 consecutive seasons was back in 1882 when Queen's Park ruled the roost. In the early days of organised football in Scotland and in the first 10 years of the Scottish Cup, Queen's (twice) and Vale of Leven had triumphed on 3 successive occasions but this Rangers side was the first to repeat the deed.

In fact, apart from the great Rangers sides of the late 40s and early 60s, the only other club to have achieved this difficult task was Aberdeen in the 80s under Sir Alex Ferguson, no doubt a measure of that particular manager's prowess.

If winning everything in Scottish football in Season 33-34 was the cake, then the icing came when Rangers beat the mighty Arsenal. That September, the two greatest clubs in Britain played each other home and away (in the space of a week) to contest the unofficial 'British Championship'. Rangers won 2-0 at Ibrox then beat the 'Bank of England' club 3-1 at Highbury in London. This was a great achievement as Arsenal, managed by the legendary Herbert Chapman, were in the middle of a 'three-in-a-row' Championship run, a rare feat in England even to this day. Small wonder that the 1933- 34 Rangers outfit is still thought of as one of the club's finest.

POST WAR BLUES (1946- 59)

The Second World War had interrupted many Rangers players' careers (Willie Thornton for example) so when league football resumed in Season 46-47, it looked as if not much had changed as Rangers proceeded to win that first championship since Herr Hitler had disrupted Bill Struth's master plan more than rivals such as Celtic. Having said that, Rangers' conveyor belt of talented footballers continued as ever. Apart from some of the most famous defenders who ever played for the club, there were forwards of distinction such as Waddell, Thornton, Rutherford, Duncanson, Hubbard, Kitchenbrand and Billy Simpson. Of course, it was that famous defence that straddled the 40s and the 50s that will be forever remembered as 'The Iron Curtain'. Brown; Young, Shaw; McColl, Woodburn and Cox made up that most formidable barrier, the foundation of Rangers' success throughout that era.

Of the 13 championships contested in this period, Rangers won 7 of them. The club achieved the first Scottish Treble (the League

Cup had been added to the roll of national trophies) and completed the Double on 2 other occasions. The most unusual aspect of this time was that Celtic, in the main, were not the most serious contenders for the title. In fact, the best-ever Hibernian side, (containing the legendary 'Famous Five' forward line) won the title on 3 occasions with Celtic, Hearts and Aberdeen successful on one occasion each. In the middle of this period, Rangers also changed managers with Bill Struth stepping down (in 1954) at the age of 78. The great man had steered Rangers to an amazing 18 league championships, a record that will surely never be equalled. Former Ranger and Struth protégé Scot Symon took over and followed admirably in the footsteps of his old gaffer.

Below is the league record for the championships secured during that time:

	P	W	D	L	GF	GA	PTS
1946-47	30	21	4	5	76	26	46
1948-49	30	20	6	4	63	32	46
1949-50	30	22	6	2	58	26	50
1952-53	30	18	7	5	80	39	43
1955-56	34	22	8	4	85	27	52
1956-57	34	26	3	5	96	48	55
1958-59	34	21	8	5	92	51	50

LEAGUE CHAMPIONSHIP NUMBER 26: 1948 - 49

This brilliant Rangers team is revered for two things in particular - its 'Iron Curtain' defence and the fact that it was the first team in Scotland to win the Treble. In Season 1946-47, the League Cup was introduced to Scottish football thus providing a third major national trophy. As has so often been the case, Rangers were the first winners of this tournament beating Aberdeen 4-0 in the final. So the ultimate ambition in Scottish football was to win all three prizes of League Championship, Scottish Cup and League Cup with the

Glasgow and Charity Cups taking a back seat from now on.

However, the Rangers defence probably stayed in the fans' memory longer than the winning of the Treble or the 'Triple Crown' as it was called in those days. In the early post-war years, with the Cold War now started between the Soviet Union and the West, it had been Winston Churchill who had first coined the term 'iron curtain' to describe the Soviet bloc. This political term came to be applied to the Rangers defence because its individual parts held together as a unit and that unit was incredibly difficult to penetrate.

The men who made up this formidable barrier to opposing sides were: Brown; Young, Shaw; McColl, Woodburn and Cox. In this Treble season (in a 30 game league programme), this group played together in every game bar 5. George Young twice missed a match and 'Tiger' Shaw was missing on three occasions. Otherwise they played week in, week out as they would do for most of the following 4 seasons. Here was a group of players from the same mould - strong, determined, committed and very fit. Every one of them was 'captain' material and, in fact, all of them at various times captained Rangers and some, Scotland as well. Two of these players - Brown and McColl - later went on to become Scotland managers.

When Jerry Dawson retired, Rangers were extremely lucky to find Bobby Brown as his replacement. Brown might only have played 3 times for his country but after becoming the Scotland boss in 1967, he managed the international side for 27 matches. He eventually played nearly 300 games for the club. As a P.E.teacher, he played for amateurs Queen's Park after the War but when it came to leaving 'The Spiders', he could have gone to Manchester Utd as manager Matt Busby had a high opinion of him from earlier experiences. However, Brown chose to join Rangers and signed for them on the same day that the club brought-in stalwart Sammy Cox. A good-looking, blond-haired athlete, Brown became a great favourite with the fans and was recently honoured by being elected to the Rangers' Hall of Fame.

In front of him stood a group of defenders, seldom equalled since. The most legendary of these was a 'colossus of a man' George Young and not just because he was 6 foot 2 inches tall and 15 stone in weight. A true leader of men, 'Corky' could play at centre-half or right-back and dominate the field of play from either position. He gained his nickname from the fact that he carried a champagne cork in his pocket for luck. It certainly worked! He won 6 league titles, 4 Scottish Cups and 2 League Cups thus ensuring that he would never be short of a champagne cork! Until the arrival of Ally McCoist (again!), he was Rangers' most capped player with 53 appearances at national level. Incredibly, he captained Scotland against England on 8 occasions.

Prior to retiring at the end of an illustrious career, he even managed to play in Rangers' first two European Cup ties against Nice - the start of a new era. When Bill Struth was his manager, it seemed as if Young was his alter image on the field. He knew what his boss wanted and made sure that it was delivered. Ironically, he even played beside his next manager. When Scot Symon appeared at wing-half beside him, Young came to respect the player greatly and admitted that he had learned a lot about the game by playing with him. He fully expected Symon to become a great manager one day. Little did he realise that when that day arrived, it would be as his boss at Ibrox after successful spells at Preston and East Fife. So, for the last couple of years before retirement, Young played under Symon, a man he had respected as a player and now as a manager.

Young's full-back partner was another Rangers captain, Jock 'Tiger' Shaw. His nickname says it all. Today's so called hard men in football would be quaking in their boots if they had to face a defender such a Shaw. In that era, every side seemed to have an 'iron man' and, in a defence full of them, he exemplified the term. Although not a big player, he was as hard as nails and reliable, durable, unflappable with a fierce competitive spirit. No winger could pass him easily as his tackles crunched in on them.

'Uncompromising' was the diplomatic adjective used at the time to describe his style. During this momentous season, Shaw was actually 37 but his fitness was so great that he would play on until he was 42! He had signed for Rangers from Airdrie in 1938 and was almost an ever-present in the Championship-winning side that was disrupted by the Second World War. What a pity that the best years of his career were interrupted by the War. Having said that, his longevity allowed him to collect quite an array of medals by the time he'd finished playing in the 1950s.

The rest of 'The Iron Curtain' was equally impressive. Both wing-halves became Rangers greats. Ian McColl was a cultured player who would play over 500 games for the club. A civil engineer by trade, he showed brains as well as strength on the park. His passing ability was a vital ingredient in this Rangers side. A marvellous reader of the game and a thoughtful player, it was no surprise when he went on to manage Scotland during the first half of the 1960s. On the opposite side of the filed from McColl was Sammy Cox. Here was a man who captained both Rangers and Scotland, he was equally at home at left-back or left-half. Again, although not particularly big, he was strong, brave and a great tackler with more technical ability than most defensive players in those days. He was sharp and had a wonderful sense of anticipation and authority about him that few could match.

Of the final defensive piece, Willie Woodburn, more shall be said later in this book but he was the rock around whom the others played. So, there we have the most formidable defence in the long history of Rangers. However, there was much more to this treble-winning team. The first choice forward-line read: Waddell, Findlay, Thornton, Duncanson and Rutherford. Throughout the season, when injury intervened, Findlay would be replaced by Gillick, Paton or Williamson. With most of the plaudits being given to defensive set-up, it must have been quite galling for those forwards whose contribution was perhaps underestimated by the critics.

Willie Thornton, the centre-forward who would score 188 goals for the club (and become Assistant Manager in due course), once said, rather ruefully - "Of course, we did manage to score one or two." And how could it have been otherwise? Apart from the goal scoring talents and aerial ability of Thornton, this team had one of Rangers' greatest wingers, Willie Waddell on the right and another one, Eddie Rutherford on the left. At inside-forward the side could rely on the under-rated Willie Findlay, a lanky, athletic type who could create goals as well as score them. His mirror on the other side of the park was Jimmy Duncanson whose 22 goals against Celtic was a post-war record - until that man McCoist! Duncanson could even play on the left wing when required. He built up a great understanding with Thornton and, in this Treble season, he even scored 15 goals, assisting in many more.

When this brilliant Rangers side is analysed, it's easy to see the reasons for its success. Apart from a virtually impregnable defence, it had creative players who could also score in addition to two fast wingers and a prolific goal scorer. Considering the triumphs of that season, it's strange that it should have started so badly.

For the first 6 years after the war, the Championship would be shared equally between Rangers and Hibernian. In those days, the League Cup started with sections of 4 teams and, in 1948 - 49, Rangers found themselves drawn in a section consisting of Celtic, Hibs and Clyde - not the ideal start to a season! After two draws against Hibs and Clyde plus a defeat from Celtic in the first 3 matches, Rangers stared elimination in the face. However, a Celtic collapse (they lost their final 3 games whilst Rangers won their trio of matches) saw the Ibrox side into the next round. Eventually the Cup was won in March when Raith Rovers were defeated 2-0 and the first leg of the Treble was complete.

Meanwhile, in the league, things had not been much better. In the first 8 matches, it was a case of 3 victories, 2 defeats and and 3 draws. However, after their November defeat at Easter Road, it all changed. Apart from 2 losses at the beginning of January, Rangers never tasted defeat throughout the rest of the campaign. Although

Hibs had been the big rivals since the War, it was Dundee who became the main title challengers that season. Just as eventual victory in the League Cup had looked unlikely, so had a Championship win, especially after Dundee had beaten Rangers 3-1 at Dens Park in January. The teams were neck and neck.

Going into the final match, Dundee only needed to draw at Falkirk. The Bairns had lost their previous 4 league matches and had been eliminated in the first round of the Scottish Cup so Dundee didn't appear to have a difficult last game on their hands. But, as Jimmy Greaves used to say "It's a funny old game!" Falkirk beat the championship contenders 4-1 and, in the other game, Rangers (thanks to a penalty save by Brown and a Thornton hat-trick) beat Albion Rovers 4-1 to snatch the title.

The season was complete in April when Rangers beat Clyde 4-1 in front of 120,000 fans at Hampden to win the Scottish Cup and go down in history as the first-ever Treble winners.

LEAGUE CHAMPIONSHIP NUMBER 28: 1952 - 53

The Rangers team that achieved the Double was the last Championship-winning side under the direction of Bill Struth who would retire due to ill health at the end of the following season. After 34 years as manager of Rangers, he had won an incredible 25 league titles - half the number that this book celebrates. This team may not have been one of the club's finest ever but it still had those Ranger's qualities that brought about another title and Scottish Cup victory. For reasons that shall be made clear later, maybe it should have been renowned as the 227 team.

'The Iron Curtain' was coming to the end of its time and, indeed, a couple of members had been replaced already. Johnny Little took over from Jock Shaw as even tigers cannot go on forever! In goal, George Niven took the place of Bobby Brown. Thus, the first choice defence was: Niven; Young, Little; McColl, Woodburn and Cox. New left-back Little, although he had been born in Alberta Canada, even played for Scotland on one occasion. He was small, wiry and reliable without being outstanding. He would hold the position, however, for a few seasons until the appearance of Eric Caldow, a future captain of the club and true Rangers great.

George Niven was on the small side for a keeper but, then again, Rangers seem to have a tradition of goalkeepers who are not among the giants of their profession. Niven made up for his lack of stature by being an extremely agile great shot-stopper and had great reflexes with bravery in spades. The best example of his courage came in the Scottish Cup Final of that season against Aberdeen. In the first match, he had dived at the feet of an Aberdeen forward. Unlike the tragic Celt John Thomson who had died in such circumstances, Niven was lucky and only came out of the clash with a badly cut ear.

He was helped from the field with his head wrapped in towels, the blood visibly seeping through them. Since this was the era before substitutes, George Young took over in goal (for 18 minutes) as 4 stitches sealed the wound. How fortunate Rangers were that this giant of a player, in every sense, was there to fill the goal temporarily. The cheers of 129,000 fans resounded around Hampden that day when Niven returned, his head covered in bandages. By the way, for the replay (the first game ended 1-1), he was so determined to play that he wore a leather helmet for protection rather like the kind that the American grid-iron footballers used to wear in the early days of the game.

Ironically, Niven had not started the season as first choice keeper. In the first match of the season (a sectional League Cup tie at Tynecastle), Bobby Brown had been in goal. Hearts thrashed Rangers 5-0 with Brown having the proverbial footballer's nightmare. He did not play another game all season! Although Niven kept the jersey for that campaign and started the next, it was not quite the end for Brown. The following season, he played in the majority of league games before finally losing his place permanently. Niven was then recognised as the first choice keeper until the appearance of Billy Ritchie at the end of the decade.

Another member of the 'Iron Curtain' set-up who did not have long left to play (although he did not know it then) was the peerless centre-half, Willie Woodburn. 'Big Ben' would be banned 'sine die' by the SFA in 1954. Since his final ordering off had only been the fifth in a long career, this harsh sentence was not due to the number of his offences. It was rather because of the violence of his last one. In a match at Ibrox against Stirling Albion, Rangers were in complete control and winning 2-0. Woodburn, in a tackle with Paterson, crashed to the ground and twisted his leg. Known for having a rather short fuse, Woodburn once again lost his temper and lashed out by head-butting his opponent. Few expected this action to have such dire consequences.

His indefinite ban may have been a terrible injustice but Woodburn was coming to the end of his playing days anyway. The most dreadful aspect of this ban was probably the fact that it had soiled his reputation and taken away his dignity as a player. Many younger fans know of Woodburn's ban but how many realise what a wonderful centre-half he was? That is maybe the real tragedy of how his career at Ibrox ended. Certainly not the first or last Hearts fan to have joined Rangers, he signed in 1937 and proved to be one of the best defenders ever at Ibrox.

As a youngster, hours of practice had helped him become a two-footed player and, despite being a big lad, he was agile and athletic. He was certainly a dominant player and had that fierce sense of competitiveness that stood him in good stead but could also be his Achilles heel. As well as being excellent in the tackle, he was comfortable on the ball and capable of coming out of defence to spray passes to his forward players. In this respect, he was more like a modern central defender. Most observers thought him a stylish player but, due to the tragic ending of his career, that is a term that not many fans nowadays would have associated with this fine player. Perhaps the ultimate tribute to his prowess was the fact that the great George Young had to move to the right-back position in order to accommodate Woodburn at centre-half.

Although nearing the end of its era, it was as well Rangers still had the bulk of that famous defence because, in Season 52 - 53, the forwards certainly were not as exciting or as prolific as many of their forerunners had been. Again, the old guard was changing with Willie Waddell in the twilight of his career and partner Willie Thornton even nearer to the end of his time. Indeed after the League Cup sections were out of the way at the start of the season, Thornton only played another 4 league games. Add a handful the following season and his days at Ibrox were over.

The recognised forward line was: Waddell, Grierson, Simpson, Prentice and Hubbard.

In winning the title that season, Rangers 'only' scored 80 goals with the bulk of them coming from Grierson, Simpson and Prentice. The reigning Champions were Hibs and the Edinburgh outfit would come close to retaining the title thanks mainly to the brilliant 'Famous Five' forward line. That selection of Smith, Johnstone, Reilly, Turnbull and Ormond was certainly superior to the Rangers' forwards but, then again, the Gers still had their 'Iron Curtain' to help them win the points.

Billy Simpson was a genial, big, bustling Ulsterman. A modest, hardworking centre-forward, he won the hearts of the fans with his courage, industry and quite a few goals. He scored 21 goals in 21 league games that season and his energic commitment probably made many more.

Beside him, and by way of contrast, was inside-right Derek Grierson. Like so many Rangers players in the past, Grierson was destined to become a teacher. At only 5 foot 6, he was the antithesis of Simpson but bravery, determination and skill compensated for this relative lack of height. He scored 23 league goals plus 5 in the cups that season. The other inside-forward was John Prentice who signed from Hearts. Again, he was more in the mould of Grierson than Simpson and more a creator than scorer. His tally was 13 in all matches. Prentice was yet another Ranger who would manage Scotland in due course.

Perhaps the most famous and durable of the new forwards was Johnny Hubbard. From Pretoria, South Africa, Hubbard arrived at Ibrox in 1949 thanks to a former Hibs player who had written to the club recommending him and saying how keen the lad was to play for Rangers. Bill Struth arranged for the boy to travel but must have been disconcerted, to say the least, when he met this skinny, puny-looking, apprehensive lad at Ibrox. In his entire Rangers' career, Hubbard never weighed more than 8 stones 10 ounces. Despite appearances and having come such a long way, Rangers could hardly reject the boy out of hand. Struth took him out on to the field and ordered him to take a corner kick. The way Hubbard curled a lovely cross into the goal impressed him at once. He was then asked to run towards the manager, keeping the ball up with his head as he did so. This feat he did with a grace and effortless ease that convinced Struth they had been sent a gem. He was promptly taken up to the office and signed!

Johnny Hubbard was a totally different type of winger from Willie Waddell on the opposite flank. Hubbard had an elegance about him with great balance, timing and ball control. Somehow, he seemed to glide past his opponent using trickery and cunning rather than power or pace. In 10 years at the club, Hubbard would score 116 goals but he is best remembered for one particular feature of his game - taking penalty kicks. He is considered by older fans as THE penalty taker. His remarkable record of scoring 54 penalties out of a possible 57 will probably never be matched.

These were the players who would win yet another Double for Rangers that season. In the first 6 seasons after the War, Rangers and Hibernian shared the Championship with 3 titles each. With Hibs the reigning Champions, Rangers knew that this was the side they had to overcome if they were to regain the title. Traditionally slow starters, the season did not begin well for Rangers with 3 defeats in the opening 5 matches with both Celtic and the Leith outfit beating them in this spell. However, by the start of November, the ship had been steadied and Rangers never lost another league match until March.

After their final league game (Raith Rovers were beaten 4-1), Hibs had totalled 43 points from 30 matches. Rangers, with 2 games left, knew that they needed 2 wins to be sure of the title. The first step towards the ultimate goal was successful when they beat Dundee 3-1 at Ibrox, thanks to goals from Grierson (2) and Simpson. This encounter, incidentally, took place only 3 days after they had beaten Aberdeen 1-0 in the Scottish Cup Final replay. Then, 5 days later, the Light Blues headed for Palmerston to face Queen of the South, knowing then that a draw would be enough to secure the Championship.

The match was a tough one and the situation looked bad when the home team took the lead. Still, Rangers knew what they had to do so they simply rolled-up the sleeves and increased the pressure on the opposition. How apt that it was one of their veterans (a man who exemplified the Rangers spirit) who saved the day. With 15 minutes left, Willie Waddell went on one of his lung-bursting runs down the wing. He powered past two, then three defenders before unleashing a brilliant shot that crashed into the net. Rangers got their draw and won the league - on goal average. Rangers' goal average was 2.051 compared to Hibernian's 1.824 - a difference of 0.227. The next time Rangers would win the title in such a close arithmetical fashion would be Season 2002-3 when goal difference would be the deciding factor and Rangers would beat Celtic by ONE goal.

THOSE SWINGING SIXTIES (1960-64)

This decade began as if the Struth legacy would last forever. The first 4 years of the decade saw as fine a Rangers side as had ever strutted its stuff at Ibrox, including the arrival of British football's first 'popstar' footballer - the idol that was Jim Baxter. Slim Jim had done it all before a certain George Best began repeating the scenario in Manchester. Of course, it was not just a one man band and, at the time of writing, 8 members of the best side of those 4 years are currently in the Rangers' Hall of Fame: Bobby Shearer, Eric Caldow, John Greig, Jim Baxter, Willie Henderson, Jimmy Millar, Ralph Brand and Davie Wilson.

In the first 4 seasons of that decade, Rangers won the title 3 times, having been only stopped on the other occasion by the greatest ever Dundee side who were winners in 1961-62. In the first of those seasons, the League Cup was added to the Championship while the following season the 2 cup competitions were won as the title went to Dundee. The next campaign, the Double was achieved and, in the final title-winning season of the 60s, the Treble was completed. Who knows what might have happened if Jim Baxter had not left for pastures new - and Jock Stein had not become Celtic's manager?

The title-winning record for that decade read:

	P	W	D	L	GF	GA	PTS
1960-61	34	23	5	6	88	46	51
1962-63	34	25	7	2	94	28	57
1963-64	34	25	5	4	85	31	55

LEAGUE CHAMPIONSHIP NUMBER 34: 1963- 64

In the early 60's Rangers dominated domestic football. Manager Scot Symon (a protégé of Bill Struth) had taken over from the great man and built a side that won the league 3 times out of 4 and reached the final of the European Cup Winners' Cup. Although in 63-64 Rangers won the Treble (the club's second following a 15 year gap), most fans would have claimed that the side from the previous season was actually superior even though they had 'only' won the Double. That particular team was considered by many to have been the greatest Rangers team ever. Even after all this time, the names still trip off the tongue: Ritchie, Shearer, Caldow; Greig, McKinnon, Baxter; Henderson, McMillan, Millar, Brand and Wilson.

This is the side that probably reached its zenith the previous season when Celtic were demolished 3-0 in the Scottish Cup Final replay.

Manager Scot Symon (by the end of the Season 63-64) had utilised a total of 21 players, a much higher than normal number due to injuries. The Treble side of 63-64 was more often than not this side: Ritchie, Shearer, Provan; Greig, McKinnon, Baxter; Henderson, McLean, Forrest, Brand and Wilson.

Veteran Ian McMillan was used sparingly that season and played in only 10 league matches. His replacement was a totally different type of inside-right - George McLean. 'Dandy' had been signed from St Mirren in January 1963 for the then record sum of £26,500. Whereas McMillan was a slick passer of the ball with a cunning brain, McLean was more of a goal scorer who took on opponents as well as linking with the other forwards. The trouble with McLean was his erratic form which hit both highs and lows - and all in the same game sometimes! He would do something wonderful with the ball and then, at the end of it, seem to trip over it. He was an early version of Ted McMinn in the 1980s and certainly never did fulfil his undoubted potential at Ibrox.

The other major change was at left-back where Davie Provan had taken over from the injured Eric Caldow. Captain Caldow had broken his leg at the end of the previous season when captaining Scotland at Wembley. He was a classy left-back who was never ever booked in his entire career, partly due to the fact that being so fast himself, no winger would ever run past him. At 6 foot 2, Provan was a slim player, perhaps too tall and gangling to be a full-back. Central defence, which had been his original position, might have been a better place for him. He was, nevertheless, hardworking and reliable. The following season he even played at right-back to accommodate the return of Caldow although, after that period, he moved back over to the left and kept his place for a few seasons.

Another dramatic alteration to the Double side was the emergence of young gun Jim Forrest in place of the old warhorse Jimmy Millar. Forrest had signed as a schoolboy in 1960 but this was his first full season in the side. He was quick, agile and had a real eye for goals. When he was injured, Jimmy Millar was a straight replacement for him but Millar also played in the same team as him when others were injured or tactics dictated it. By the end of that season, Forrest had played in 24 league games as opposed to Millar's 22. Forrest would undoubtedly have played in more (and scored more goals) but he was injured at Pittodrie in March and missed the rest of the season.

Forrest was a prolific scorer and the next season he would score a club record of 57 goals, 40 of these before Christmas - and yes, Christmas was still in December in those days. By the end of his comparatively short Rangers career, Forrest had amassed an incredible 145 goals in only 164 games. Unfortunately, along with George McLean, he was made scapegoat for the disastrous Scottish Cup defeat at Berwick in 1967 and never played for the first team again.

Of the others in the side, some have become legends. Indeed more than half the 1963 side is included the Ibrox Hall of Fame: Shearer, Caldow, Greig, Baxter, Henderson and Brand.

Billy Ritchie was a great keeper, only kept out of the Scotland side at that time by the brilliance of Bill Brown of Spurs. Ritchie was an unassuming type of hero who did his job quietly but oh so effectively. He was brave, agile, superb in the air and a tremendous shot-stopper. He was utterly reliable and his team-mates had the utmost confidence in their last line of defence.

Skippering this side in place of the stricken Caldow was Bobby Shearer. His nickname - 'Captain Cutlass' - says it all. He took no prisoners. Here was a full back in the mould of Shaw, Young or Cox. What he lacked in speed, he gained in determination, timing and fierceness in the tackle and a will to win that made it so difficult for any opponent to get past him.

In central defence was Ronnie McKinnon, a centre-half good in the air as well as being quick and nimble on the ground. He was another reliable defender who went about his business quietly. In the early 60s he shared the Scotland position with Billy McNeill of Celtic. He may not have been the dominating, inspirational figure that the Celtic captain was but a very effective defender nonetheless.

Of course, McKinnon did not need to be inspirational because beside him was John Greig - the Legend, the Greatest Ranger. Greig could play anywhere in defence or midfield. He was a player who roamed all over the park, tackling at one end and unleashing great shots at the other. His passing passing skills were under-rated but, without being a Baxter, he was still a better distributor of the ball than many suggested. In the lean years that followed, it was often said that he carried the team on his back and, many the time, a shot from Greig saved the day.

With McLean in midfield was the genius Jim Baxter. What more needs to be said about 'Slim Jim'? At the time, he was probably the best player in Britain (bar none) and his artistry had been recognised all over Europe. He was simply the icon of Ibrox.

This side had two exceptional wingers - Willie Henderson and Davie Wilson. Henderson, in the opinion of some, was a better winger than Celtic's Jimmy Johnstone who came to prominence a few years later. Henderson was small but quick, brave and a bag of tricks. He could bamboozle any defender and it wasn't uncommon for him to beat two or three defenders before sending over the perfect ball for his forwards. On the other wing, Wilson had a lesser repertoire but could still beat his opponents by speed and guile. He made many openings too but was more capable of scoring goals than Henderson - indeed 157 goals for a winger who seldom took penalties was an impressive haul. A regular internationalist, he had shown his ability at the highest level and was popular with the fans.

Apart from the striking prowess of the newcomer Jim Forrest, Jimmy Millar was still playing for the majority of the season. Include his partner Ralph Brand as another scoring threat and it is easy to see why this Rangers side won everything that season. In the eyes of many older fans, Millar and Brand is still the best Rangers striking partnership even including McCoist and Hateley. Millar was tough, brave and, despite a lack of height, superb in the air as well as being a fine distributor of the ball. He scored 162 goals during his Rangers career but, probably, created as many again.

His partner Ralph Brand, another Edinburgh man, was strikingly different. Although equally brave (to be a successful striker you have to be), he was small and slight. He was very quick off the mark and constantly on the move and must have been a nightmare for defenders to mark. He also a thinker, a player ahead of his time in terms of how he thought about the game, how he did extra training after the regular sessions and how he looked after his body etc. The understanding he developed with Jimmy Millar has probably never been bettered. By the end of his Rangers' career, Ralph brand had scored 206 goals, many of them winning ones.

Is it any wonder that this side won the Treble considering with the great defence, a midfield genius, two brilliant wingers and a prolific striking partnership? In the league, Rangers did not lose a match until the end of November and, surprisingly, it was at home - to Hearts. This was a run of 13 league matches and 6 in the section of the League Cup. Rangers had actually beaten Celtic 3 times by then, including two 3-0 wins both home and away. Indeed, that term would see Rangers play Celtic 5 times and beat them 5 times. In fact, Rangers would only lose another 3 league games in total and one of those was the final match of the season after the title had been won. Rangers amassed 55 points to finish 6 ahead of Kilmarnock.

In the League Cup, which was played from August until October, they disposed of Celtic, Kilmarnock and Queen of the South in their section before seeing off East Fife and Berwick Rangers. Unfortunately, Davie Wilson broke his ankle in the semi-final with Berwick and did not return to the side until February, missing the final against Morton. A crowd of 105,907 watched Rangers demolish the team that would walk away with the Second Division title. The 5-0 score-line actually flattered Morton who could not cope with one particular family - Jim Forrest scored 4 goals that day while his cousin Alec Willoughby (who only got a rare start in the first team) scored the other one.

At the start of 1964 the Scottish Cup campaign began and Rangers sailed through the early rounds against Stenhousemuir, Duns and Partick Thistle before playing Celtic at Ibrox in the quarter-final - one of the few times in the past 40 years that Rangers have played Celtic at home in an Old Firm cup match! Having already lost to Rangers 4 times out of 4 that season, Celtic must have been dreading their visit to Ibrox. A 2-0 win for the Gers with goals from Forrest and Henderson (who scored after a brilliant solo run leaving half the Celtic side in his wake) justified their worst fears.

Dunfermline were eliminated at the semi-final stage, paving the way for a showdown with Dundee in a Scottish Cup final that proved to be a classic. Fans still talk about that game to this day. It was labelled 'Bert Slater's Final' by journalists afterwards because of the brilliant display by the Dundee keeper. For most of the first-half of this Hampden encounter, it had been Slater who had kept the score-line blank, defying some brilliant Rangers' forward play and winning the admiration of the 120,000 plus crowd. When Jimmy Millar finally scored 19 minutes from the end, most fans thought that Dundee's resistance had been broken but precisely one minute later, they equalised!

With only 2 minutes left on the clock, it then became 'Willie Henderson's Final' as the wee man created both the goals that won the cup for Rangers. First, Millar converted before Ralph Brand made sure of victory by scoring a third just one minute later. What a finish to a thrilling match!

It had been a thrilling season too for the Light Blue followers, watching players like Baxter, Henderson, Wilson, Miller and Brand at their peak and believing that much more was still to come from younger players such as Greig, McKinnon and Forrest. No wonder the side of the early 60s is still regularly recalled and the players' names recited with such delight! Few fans of that time, however, would have believed that 11 long years would pass before the league flag was flying over Ibrox again.

MODERN TIMES (1974-78)

Having suffered during the Celtic 'nine-in-a-row' period prior to this era, Rangers fans now entered one that would certainly alleviate some of their pain. Two Trebles were won in 3 seasons (emulating one of Jock Stein's feats) and something that has still never been repeated since the 1970s. The club won the last of the old First Division championships and, appropriately, the first of the new Premier League titles.

The emergence of Jock Wallace as manager saw Celtic's winning streak come to an end and, for the fans, was almost as pleasurable as watching a Rangers side once again capable of winning the title, having already tasted European success in the early 70s by winning the European Cup Winners' Cup.

Below are the statistics for those title-winning seasons:

	P	W	D	L	GF	GA	PTS
1974-75	34	25	6	3	85	33	56
1975-76	36	23	8	5	60	24	54
1977-78	36	24	7	5	76	39	55

LEAGUE CHAMPIONSHIP NUMBER 36: 1975-76

Mainly due to Jock Stein's Celtic having won 'nine-in-a-row', the previous season had seen the last contest for the old First Division Championship. Ironically, it wasn't a change of organisation that brought Celtic's run to a halt but Rangers themselves. After the longest gap in their history (and for the first time in 11 long years), Rangers, under the management of Jock Wallace, won the league by drawing with Hibs at Easter Road, 5 games from the end of the programme. So, Rangers had won the final First Division honour and, this season, would go on to win the first of the new Premier Division titles.

Jock Wallace had by now built a side with a winning blend. He had a team that showed skill, power, determination and tremendous fitness. Nobody could ever doubt the commitment of his players who all seemed to be imbued with that famous 'Rangers Spirit'. The foundation for this great side was the defence which would normally be: McCloy; Jardine, Forsyth, Jackson and Greig;

Keeper Stewart Kennedy, a Scottish internationalist, had held down the number one spot the previous season but Peter McCloy regained his place for this Treble-winning season although Kennedy did play a dozen league matches and in the final of the League Cup. Another international keeper, McCloy (tall at 6 foot 4) was obviously reliable in the air but he was also a good shot-stopper for such a big man. A bonus in his play was his ability to launch huge kicks directly into opponent's penalty area which had actually created quite a few goals. Rangers were indeed fortunate to have two such good goalkeepers as their last line of defence.

At full-back, there was the contrast of Sandy Jardine and John Greig. By now Greig was a veteran but he still played with an energy and commitment that belied his years. At left-back, his great tackling ability and ability to read the game, came to the fore although he still managed to go forward and join in attacks. Following a brilliant season, he was voted the sportswriters' 'Player of the Year'. Remarkably, he was the first player to have been awarded this twice with the initial honour coming his way 10 years previously.

On the right, Sandy Jardine was a cultured back whose supreme fitness enabled him to run up and down the wing for 90 minutes. Jardine's anticipation and great pace ensured that few wingers got past him easily and, when assisting in attack, these attributes (plus his accurate passing ability) made it possible for him to set up goals like a winger. He could also score - as a total of 77 for Rangers verified. Thanks partly to the Wallace fitness regime,

Jardine would play over 600 games for Rangers and then go on to play a few more years with Hearts. How he deserved his place in the Hall of Fame! When either of these defenders was injured, the versatile Alex Miller filled in more than competently. Because of a serious injury to Jardine halfway through the season, Miller actually started in 25 league matches.

In central defence, there were two players whose actual presence gave real steel to the defence. Tom Forsyth ('Jaws' for reasons identical to 'Tiger' - as in Shaw) was an immense defender. His tackling was fierce but fair and accurate. Though totally committed and fearless, he was mobile and could pass a ball well, no doubt due to the fact that he started his career at Motherwell as a midfield player. Beside him was Colin Jackson who, for years, had been understudy to Ronnie McKinnon. Jackson was a quick, mobile defender too but also superb in the air. This excellence was often put to good use at the opposite end of the park and he claimed some vital goals.

Having confirmed that this side was a powerful one, it must be admitted that most of its strength was at the back. From midfield onwards, skill and brains were the order of the day. That season, Tommy McLean and Alex McDonald were the midfield maestros with Johnny Hamilton joining them from November. Hamilton, an excellent passer although on the slow side, would only play for this season and the next before being seen as surplus to requirements. McLean and McDonald would continue for years to come.

Tommy McLean had more than one aspect to his game. He could, and sometimes did, play as a traditional winger, able to send pinpoint crosses into the box for the likes of Derek Johnstone. Alternatively, he could play in a deeper position and be a modern right-sided (or left) midfield man with a passing ability second to none. In contrast, Alex McDonald was all energy, determination and no little skill. Thanks to his incredible fitness, McDonald always seemed to cover every blade of grass, attacking and defending when necessary. For a small man he certainly never held back and showed no fear regardless of opponent. He could also pass and link well with his strikers. However, the extra ingredient making him special was the ability to get beyond his strikers and to run on the blind side of a defence, traits which allowed him to score so many vital goals. In all, he netted 94 times for Rangers - a tremendous strike total for any midfield man.

That year, Rangers began with Bobby McKean on the right (or left) wing and in the middle, the two Dereks - Johnstone and Parlane. McKean, who was to tragically die in a terrible accident a couple of years later, was a tricky winger and adept with both feet. Without being a traditional pacy wide man, he could still get past the full-back and deliver great cut-backs or crosses into the box for his strikers.

The number 9 jersey was initially worn by Derek Parlane whose time at Ibrox was coming to an end. By November, he would be replaced by young Martin Henderson, a player similar in style. Both these strikers were big, strong and full of running. They made sure that no defence could relax during a match. Parlane had done it all before and his many goals had made him a true hero to the Rangers fans. In 1974, he even scored Rangers' 6,000th league goal. In contrast, Henderson would only really feature in this successful season before moving on a couple of years later. Still, this campaign would see him contribute 13 goals in all competitions.

Finally, beside either of these two strikers was the jewel in Rangers' attack - Derek Johnstone. This man would play over 500 games for the club and score 210 goals. He would probably have scored even more if he had not spent years playing as a central defender! He had been called the John Charles of Scotland, a reference to that great Welsh player's ability to perform equally well as centre-forward or centre-half. Tom Forsyth said that Johnstone was the best header of a ball he had ever seen and fans have many memories of brilliant such goals - none more so than the header that won the League Cup in 1970 when, at the age of just 16, Johnstone had scored the winner against Celtic. This fairy tale start to his Rangers' career was to continue and Johnstone for years was a 'Roy of the Rovers' type hero, only being overtaken in later years by a certain Ally McCoist who really did live out a Boy's Own story.

This was the side that would win the Treble of 75-76. It had a great defence, creativity, industry and scoring prowess in midfield, with an exciting winger supplying two strikers who knew their way to goal. Add to this the fitness that would see them win many a game in the dying minutes plus determination and commitment (from the manager as well as his players) and it is easy to see why they were such a formidable team.

Rangers started the season brilliantly by cruising through their League Cup section, eliminating Motherwell (a force in Scotland that year), Airdrie and Clyde. By the time of the first league match at the end of August, they were ready to take on Celtic. In front of 69,594 fans (still a Premier Division record) a 2-1 Ibrox win was the perfect start and, indeed, Celtic would not beat Rangers at all that season. The Light Blues would win two and draw two in the league and defeat their greatest rivals in the League Cup Final.

Although Celtic had a three point lead at the turn of the year, a Derek Johnstone Old Firm winner at Ibrox reduced this and, after losing at Pittodrie at the start of December, Rangers were not beaten again in a run of 21 matches. The title was sewn up at Tannadice in the third last match. The honour of sealing the title went to Johnstone who actually scored in just 22 seconds - before his manager had even reached the dug-out!

A week later, Johnstone would replicate this feat in the Scottish Cup Final against Hearts when he got off to a somewhat slower start by scoring in...45 seconds, twice the time it had taken him to score at Tannadice!

The previous October, Rangers had won the League Cup by beating Celtic 1-0. Having disposed of Queen of the South and Montrose in the quarter and semi finals respectively, a much tougher task was expected against Celtic in the final. In a dour game, it looked as if one goal would be enough to settle it and, sure enough, that was the case. A flying header from Alex McDonald won the cup and the Treble was now a possibility.

By the time of the Scottish Cup Final in May, Rangers had won the other two trophies and the Treble awaited them. As it turned out, a comfortable victory followed when Hearts were beaten 3-1 and, once again (apart from the inevitable Johnstone), Alex McDonald scored in a final that season. However, perhaps the cup (and, in effect, the Treble) had been won in the March semi-final with Motherwell. At half-time, the Lanarkshire side, having played brilliantly, went in 2-0 ahead and were looking good. That Rangers' spirit, however, seemed to take over in the second half and the comeback began when Johnstone 'won' a penalty that was converted by Miller. DJ then went on to score another two goals himself on the night that the Treble was 'saved' and, mainly, by the talisman who hit 31 goals that season.

Rangers had lifted their first Treble in 11 years. Little did they realise that they would only have to wait a couple more for their next one.

LEAGUE CHAMPIONSHIP NUMBER 37: 1977-78

Basically, the same Rangers side that had won the Treble in Season 75-76 repeated that feat this season. In doing so, they equalled a record set by Jock Stein's Celtic in the 60s. These are the only two sides to have won two Trebles in three seasons - a record that still stands. The Rangers side from 75-76 was, in the main, still there but Jock Wallace had added 3 new players at the start of this campaign who would improve his team and make it even more exciting. Another slight change was the fact that Stewart Kennedy would be in goal for the bulk of the season, playing in 22 league matches as opposed to McCloy's 14. Ironically, when their roles had been reversed in season 75-76 (due to injury), McCloy had missed out on the League Cup Final. This season Kennedy again played in the League Cup Final but missed out on the Scottish Cup

Final. So, in both Treble seasons, McCloy gained a Scottish Cup medal and Kennedy a League Cup version.

The Rangers defence was still the immoveable force of: Kennedy; Jardine, Forsyth, Jackson and Greig; However, the rest of the side changed with the addition of three very skillful players. In midfield, Bobby Russell now complemented McDonald with McLean moving between right midfield and right wing while the front three consisted of Johnstone with a new strike partner in Gordon Smith. Last, and certainly not least, the marvellous Davie Cooper was on the left wing.

Midfield genius Bobby Russell was the find of the season. Signed from Shettleston Juniors, he played as if he had been a professional for years. Although slender and on the small side, he was not brushed off the ball easily and actually tackled quite well due to a quickness and anticipation that helped sneak the ball from an opponent. His main asset, of course, was his passing ability and vision. This cool, silky player could send the ball all over the park, supplying both wingers or sending perfectly weighted passes through the middle for the strikers. He reminded the fans of Jim Baxter and certainly had the same kind of influence on a game. Ironically, that wonderful first season was perhaps the peak of his Rangers' career.

Johnstone's new striking partner was Gordon Smith who had been signed from Kilmarnock as a winger. However, Jock Wallace saw him as a secondary striker to complement the talents of Derek Johnstone and played him just behind DJ. Having been a winger, Smith had skill in addition to pace and his intelligent running helped him both create and score many goals that season. He finally totalled 27 in all competitions. It has to be said that Johnstone benefited greatly by Smith's presence and his haul that season was an impressive 38 goals, earning him the 'Player of the Year' award from the Scottish Football Writers' Association. With these two strikers capable of scoring both in the air and on the ground, it is no wonder that the Treble was achieved again.

Add the genius of the immortal Davie Cooper on the left wing and it is manifestly evident this was a tremendous attacking team that could play entertaining as well as winning football. Cooper had an educated left foot similar to that of Jim Baxter in the way a ball was controlled and telling passes delivered. Of course, Cooper could use this talent and his amazing dribbling skill to lose any full-back without the need for blistering pace. His skill and vision (not to mention those thundering left foot shots!) would thrill all friends of Rangers for years.

This was, therefore, the 'normal' side that would win the Treble in Season 77-78:

Kennedy

Jardine, Forsyth, Jackson, Greig

Russell, McDonald

McLean, Johnstone, Smith, Cooper

This would prove to be Jock Stein's last season in charge at Celtic and their challenge for honours that season would be the weakest for years. Instead, Aberdeen would be Rangers' main rivals in both the league race and the Scottish Cup. Indeed, the Dons would beat Rangers 3 times out of 4 in the championship but still finish runners up and also lose to them in the Scottish Cup Final.

Surprisingly, Rangers got off to a terrible start in their league campaign with two defeats - by Aberdeen (at Pittodrie) and Hibs at Ibrox. Few could have envisaged a Treble triumph at that stage. In their League Cup early rounds, however, things were decidedly better - especially following a 6-1 Ibrox defeat of Aberdeen. In the next two rounds, Dunfermline and Forfar were taken care of before facing Celtic in the final. When played in March, that Hampden encounter was similar to the Old Firm clash in Rangers' previous Treble season. It was a hard-fought affair with tension too high to allow the talented players to express themselves properly. Goals from Cooper and Smith saw Rangers win 2-1 and take the first leg of another magic Treble.

Meanwhile, in the league, after their defeats in August, only Celtic and Aberdeen (twice) managed to beat the Light Blues. The Granite City side kept on the tails of Rangers right to the end of the season and, when it came to the final match, Rangers required full points in order to regain the Championship. That match was against Motherwell at Ibrox and a comfortable 2-0 victory (goals from Jackson and Smith) saw the title back in Govan.

The last mission for this great side was to win the Scottish Cup and complete the Treble for the second time in three seasons. There remained, though, the toughest barrier possible to be overcome -Aberdeen. Having defeated Rangers 4 times already, they must have fancied their chances of lifting the cup despite failing to pip Rangers for the title. What a let down it must have been when Rangers cruised to a very comfortable win - much easier than the 2-1 score-line suggests. Aberdeen just could not get going and Rangers' key players (such as Bobby Russell) all had brilliant games. The Dons' only goal was merely a consolation effort coming, as it did, in the final few minutes of the game. Few who were there will forget it. A mis-hit shot was scooped up into the air and McCloy, thinking the ball had gone over the bar, was left swinging from it before apparently being the last man in Hampden to notice that somehow the ball had actually squirmed into the net, instead of over the bar.

Even this bizarre ending could not spoil the ensuing party as the fans in blue celebrated yet another Treble win on the Hampden slopes.

THE SOUNESS REVOLUTION AND BEYOND (1986- 2003)

Eight seasons passed between Jock Wallace's final championship and Graeme Souness' first. It was one of the most barren spells in Rangers' history. In some ways, it was worse for Rangers fans than the Jock Stein 'nine-in-a-row' years when Celtic had pushed Rangers into second place for most of that era. This time, they were not even coming in second and, to make matters worse, it was not just Celtic beating them to the title. In this period Celtic won the league 4 times but Alex Ferguson's Aberdeen won it 3 times and Jim McLean's 'corner shop' side (Dundee United) even won it once. Rangers' position never seemed to rise above mediocre. Twice they came 5th (the club's lowest ever league position), three times they finished 4th and there was only one runners-up spot in that period.

Even the return of Jock Wallace as manager had failed to turn around the club's fortunes. Drastic action was called for and it was taken by the new majority shareholder Lawrence Malborough, the grandson of former Chairman John Lawrence. In truth, this astute businessman had only recognised the obvious: Rangers had more financial muscle than any other club in Scotland so it was about time that action was taken to regain the pre-eminent position.

Malborough appointed David Holmes as Chief Executive and gave him a free hand to examine the situation at Ibrox and come up with solutions. His main conclusion was that a change of manager was necessary but, even more startling, was his choice of successor to Wallace. Holmes pinned his hopes on Graeme Souness, Scotland captain and former Liverpool idol who was then plying his trade in Italy with Sampdoria. An Edinburgh man, Souness had had no connection with Rangers (or indeed Scottish football), having played in England since he left school. Many wondered if Souness really knew what he was letting himself in for when he accepted the position, especially since he would be under the added pressure of being the club's first player-manager.

Souness was not so much the proverbial breath of fresh air but more the hurricane that swept through Ibrox. By the end of his first season in charge, he had moved on a total of 15 players, mainly old hands who had outlived their usefulness to Rangers, as he saw it. More importantly, Souness' new recruiting policy really revolutionised the game - not only at Ibrox but eventually throughout the whole of Scottish football. He reversed the age old trend of Scotland's best players moving to England and began to buy English players with a proven pedigree. Various factors played a part in this strategy being effective: Souness' reputation and status in the game (backed up by Rangers' new determination to pay top wages) and the fact that English clubs were banned from playing in European competition at the time.

His first signing, striker Colin West from Watford (for a modest £200,000), barely caused a ripple but when he signed England goalkeeper Chris Woods from Norwich then England captain Terry Butcher from Ipswich, people started to take notice. The notion of England internationalists leaving their own league to play in Scotland was just mind-boggling. Later that season, names such as Graham Roberts and Jimmy Nicholl were added to the roster, confirming that Souness had set his sights high.

Of course, history shows that Souness was correct. He won the championship in his first season (as well as the League Cup) and was manager for practically 4, leaving for Liverpool with only a few games left of his final season. In his 4 terms, he took the title 3 times and, by the time he left, had facilitated the arrival of his friend David Murray as the new owner of the club. From then on, Rangers went from strength to strength. Souness' contribution to the 'new' Rangers should never be underestimated.

When the volatile manager left Ibrox, his successor was the steady Walter Smith whose astute management continued Rangers' run of title wins until the magical 'nine-in-a-row' was achieved in 1997 thus equalling Jock Stein's record that everybody had thought was unattainable in the modern game. Unfortunately, the holy grail of 'ten-in-a-row' could not be achieved despite the presence of brilliant footballers such as Laudrup, Gascoigne and Albertz.

Chairman David Murray had already been told by Smith of his intention to step down at the end of that campaign so he had already decided on his new manager, well before the season's climax. He shocked everybody by appointing Rangers' first foreign manager - Dick Advocaat, former Holland coach and manager of PSV Eindhoven. Advocaat arrived knowing that most of the side was being moved on and that new players, indeed practically a brand new team, would have to be assembled. Luckily for him, his Chairman was more than willing to spend the vast sums necessary to bring success back to the club.

Signings such as Numan, Van Bronckhorst, Amato, Klos, Hendry, Wallace, Kanchelskis, McCann and Reyna were blended into a fine side that won the Treble in Advocaat's first season before achieving the Double in his next. It seemed money well spent. However, when a new manager was deemed the next step in 2001, Hibernian's manager Alex McLeish was appointed and immediately brought dividends in the shape of the Scottish Cup and CIS League Cup. Last season, of course, the league championship was regained, making Rangers the first club in the world to have won its domestic title 50 times. The story of that season is chronicled in part two of this book but, first, a season from each of the three managers mentioned above is examined.

The Championship record for those years when Rangers won the title 13 times out of a possible 17 looks like this:

	P	W	D	L	GF	GA	PTS
1986-87	44	31	7	6	85	23	69
1988-89	36	26	4	6	62	26	56
1989-90	36	20	11	5	48	19	51
1990-91	36	24	7	5	62	23	55
1991-92	44	33	6	5	101	31	72
1992-93	44	33	7	4	97	35	73
1993-94	44	22	14	8	74	41	58
1994-95	36	20	9	7	60	35	69
1995-96	36	27	6	3	65	25	87
1996-97	36	25	5	6	85	33	80
1998-99	36	23	8	5	76	31	77
1999-00	36	28	6	2	96	26	90
2002-03	38	31	4	3	101	26	97

LEAGUE CHAMPIONSHIP NUMBER 38: 1986-87

As stated earlier, new manager Graeme Souness had set his sights high and wanted to regain the league championship in his first season. He persuaded Walter Smith to leave Dundee Utd to become his assistant as part of that quest. By signing English internationalists, Terry Butcher and Chris Woods (as well as other players plying their trade in England such as Graham Roberts, Colin West, Jimmy Nicholl, Jimmy Phillips and Neil Woods) he reaffirmed his ambitions. Allied to these newcomers, Souness also got the best out of existing Rangers such as Davie Cooper, Ally McCoist, Robert Fleck and Stuart Munro. He also showed that he was not afraid to play youngsters and local boys Ian Durrant and Derek Ferguson were given vital midfield roles.

The league campaign started with a disastrous 2-1 defeat at Easter Road with the new player-manager sent off for kicking Hibs forward (and ex-Celt) George McCluskey. In the third match, a home defeat by Dundee Utd was even harder to take. It had not been a smooth start for the rookie manager. However, by the end of

August, the tide was turning when Rangers played brilliantly against Celtic at Ibrox and won by an Ian Durrant goal to instill fresh belief in the side.

Nevertheless, by the end of November, Rangers were only 4th in the table and, although they had a game in hand, were 9 points behind leaders Celtic. At the start of the season, Souness had tried to sign Richard Gough from Dundee Utd but, understandably, Jim McLean would not sell his prize asset to a competitor. Souness was still searching for a vital piece of the jigsaw that he believed would give his side a chance of winning the title. In December, his temporary solution (as it turned out) was to sign tough-tackling defender Graham Roberts from Spurs for £450,000. Like all good managers, Souness had now assembled a formidable backbone to his team. His 'spine' saw Woods in goal with the two central defenders Butcher and Roberts. In midfield, it was Souness himself while at centre-forward there was Ally McCoist, a consistent scorer.

In Roberts' league debut at Ibrox against Dundee Utd on December 27th, he set up the second goal in Rangers 2-0 win and then the side went on a run of 19 unbeaten league matches including another great Ne'erday win over Celtic at Ibrox. With the snow trickling down, Rangers won 2-0 (going on 6!) thanks to goals from Fleck and McCoist with the play being orchestrated superbly by the manager. Rangers' next league defeat would be in April at Parkhead when Celtic gained their revenge by winning 3-1.

The team that seemed to be Souness' first choice, barring injuries, that season was:

Woods

McPherson, Roberts, Butcher, Munro

Ferguson, Souness, Durrant

Fleck, McCoist, Cooper

The defence was an obvious strength and the statistics confirmed this at the end of the campaign, showing that only 23 goals had been conceded in 44 league games. During that period, Chris Woods set a new British shut-out record when he (and his defence) went 1,095 minutes without losing a goal. 12 clean sheets took place before an Adrian Sprott goal for Hamilton at Ibrox, sensationally put Rangers out of the Scottish Cup in January.

Woods was a vital ingredient in the impregnability of that defence. He was big, strong, brave and commanding - easily the best Rangers goalkeeper since Billy Ritchie. For a big man, he was very quick and agile but could also deal confidently with cross balls. There is no doubt he would have gained many more England caps if it had not been for the presence of Peter Shilton, who was on his way to 100 caps plus.

Ahead of Woods, was veteran Irish international and former Manchester Utd player Jimmy Nicholl who started the season at right-back before Dave McPherson took over when Graham Roberts arrived in the December. McPherson was a lanky, awkward-looking defender and his best position was undoubtedly in central defence where he could use his height to best advantage. In contrast, Nicholl was a quick, hard-tackling, feisty player with great stamina who could run up and down the right flank all day. On the opposite side, Stuart Munro was competent, hardworking, consistent though hardly spectacular, a left-back who was one of the side's unsung heroes.

It was in central defence, however, that Rangers excelled. Roberts was smaller but stockier than his partner Terry Butcher. He was the typical 'hard man' of a team and his tackling could be ferocious but, in the main, fair. He had a temperament that meant he was happy to take knocks as well as give them. He seemed to fall in love with the club from the start and endeared himself to the Rangers' fans, especially the following season when, during an Old Firm match at Ibrox, he had gone in goal (after Woods had been sent-off) and when Rangers snatched a late equaliser near the end, he had 'conducted' the Rangers' 'choir' that was in full voice at the time!

Beside him was Terry Butcher, the new Rangers captain, who would eventually be elected to the Hall of Fame such was the importance of his contribution during his time at Ibrox. Taller than

Roberts, he was dominating in the air but, for a big man, also quick on the ground - a formidable barrier. His left foot, in particular, meant that he was a far better passer of the ball than he had been given credit for prior to his arrival in Scotland. He would often spread passes over 30 yards straight to his forwards on either side of the pitch. With organisational skills that were invaluable, Butcher's true grit inspired his team-mates in many difficult situations. It is fair to say that he probably turned out to be the manager's key acquisition.

In midfield, Souness himself was a real bonus. His vast experience enabled him to control the flow of a match with his vision and tremendous passing ability. He also had a powerful shot and his tackling could intimidate the fiercest of opponents. Unfortunately, his temperament meant that he fell foul of Scottish referees far too often. Beside him, 2 Scots youngsters with energy, enthusiasm and skill complemented their boss. Derek Ferguson was small (but not afraid to get stuck in) with passing ability that was a great asset to the side. In contrast, Ian Durrant could cover every blade of grass, pass the ball just as well and, more importantly, get ahead of his forwards into goal scoring positions from which he could convert chances.

Up front, veteran winger Davie Cooper regained some of his old form under Souness with his class coming to the fore now that he was surrounded by better players. To score the goals, legend-to-be Ally McCoist was assisted by Robert Fleck, a tough little character who would battle against much bigger opponents, link up well with the rest of the forwards and also show an instinct for scoring. He netted a respectable 19 league goals, a total that only paled in comparison to McCoist's 34 from that season.

In October, Souness had picked up his first Rangers' trophy after Celtic were beaten 2-1 in the League Cup Final and, as the season progressed, it looked more and more likely that the championship would join the League Cup in the Ibrox Trophy Room. In the penultimate match of the season Rangers were away to

Aberdeen at Pittodrie while Celtic took on Falkirk at home. A shock defeat at Parkhead for Celts meant that a draw would be enough for Rangers to clinch their first title in 9 years.

Another sending-off for the manager looked to have jeopardised Rangers' chances of securing the required result. However, a brilliantly headed goal by skipper Terry Butcher gave his side the lead and, although the Dons equalised later-on, Rangers held firm to gain that precious point. What an achievement for Graeme Souness. He had won the championship in his first season as a manager although nobody would surely have guessed that his assistant Walter Smith would emulate that feat when he succeeded his boss 3 years later!

LEAGUE CHAMPIONSHIP NUMBER 43: 1992-93

Season 1992-93 turned out to be one of the finest in the history of Rangers. Under the management of Walter Smith, the side not only won the Treble but was also only one goal away from a European Cup Final. The number 5 turned out to be significant - this was Rangers' 5th league title in a row, their 5th Treble and the title was won 5 games from the end of the season. Additionally, the club went on an unbeaten run of 44 matches which included European Cup games.

Furthermore, Rangers were slap bang in the middle of the 'nine-in-a-row' sequence and many fans would claim this was the season that the team peaked. In fact, the majority of the side would still be at Ibrox when the record-equalling 9th title was clinched in 1997. With the effects of injury and fatigue becoming more prevalent on a side in the modern game, it is obviously harder to identify a 'regular' team. Besides, Walter Smith had built up a large pool of players to deal with the injuries and suspensions which always crop up every season. It was just as well. Apart from the size of the squad, the versatility of some players was also invaluable. Guys like Stuart McCall played in midfield or right-back, a problem position that year. John Brown could also play in midfield as well as anywhere in the defence, but below is probably the 'normal' side that season.

Goram
McCall, Gough, McPherson, Robertson
Steven, Ferguson, Brown, Huistra
McCoist, Hateley

As mentioned earlier, the right-back spot was a problem and, although Scott Nisbet started off with the number 2 shirt, veteran Gary Stevens, McCall and even Steven Pressley also filled that position. In midfield, Ian Durrant and Alexei Mikhailichenko contributed in almost half the league games while, later in the season, young Neil Murray made quite a few appearances. The unluckiest player was perhaps big Scott Nisbet who was injured that season after having just started to make an impact. He never did recover his full fitness, eventually having to retire at the early age of 25 (due to a pelvic injury) at the end of the season.

Walter Smith had certainly constructed a formidable side. In goal was Andy Goram, recently voted the Best Rangers' Goalkeeper - ever! Few would disagree with that assessment. For a small man he could deal with crosses competently and was both agile and brave. He was also very good at the increasingly important, 'new' goalkeeping skill of controlling the ball with his feet following a pass-back. In any one-on-one situation, the fans' money would always be on Goram to make the block. The fact that he did become a hero to the fans really says it all as few keepers achieve this kind of distinction - of course, maybe his frequently outstanding displays against Celtic had something to do with that!

In central defence, club captain Richard Gough was as inspirational as all Rangers skippers are required to be. Superb in the air and almost unbeatable at the back, he also had the knack of frequently scoring vital goals at the other end. A great tackler and very mobile, he seemed to epitomise the modern defender with his organisational skills. Beside him, the tall figure of Davie McPherson was often under-rated. Like Gough, he was also good in the air but, for a big man, deceptively skillful on the ground when the ball was at his feet. Souness had transferred him to Hearts but Walter Smith brought him back to the club that he had supported all his life.

At left-back was David Robertson, signed from Aberdeen for just under £1 Million in 1991. Here was the modern full-back at his best. A natural left-sided player, he had great pace and was a tough tackler but, even better, he was a brilliant over-lapping player. Using his speed to set up attacks (and sometimes finish them off), he knew that if the move broke down he had the pace and stamina to get back and help defend any counter-attack.

The midfield area of this team included a tremendous variety of talents. Stuart McCall and Ian Ferguson were two ball-winners who could tackle, cover every blade of grass, pass the ball well and even score goals from long-range. With the tough-tackling and determination of defender John Brown (who could also shoot from distance), it was a forbidding barrier to any opposition. To complement those battlers in midfield were 3 players whose sublime skill and goal-scoring abilities added excitement to the side. Step forward Ian Durrant, Trevor Steven and Alexei Mikhailichenko.

Hall of Fame Ranger Durrant had recovered from the terrible knee injury that almost ruined his career and was once again the type of player coming from deep to run beyond the strikers and score vital goals. Allied to his passing ability and work-rate, Durrant's skill made him one of the club's most popular members. Another player whose skill could light up a game was Ukrainian international, Mikhailichenko. He perhaps did not show the commitment or work-rate of Durrant but he did have the ball control and skill to equal his team-mate. Only his rather laid-back approach prevented him from really becoming a Rangers superstar. Ironically, since he retired from playing, he became Assistant Coach to the great Lobanovsky at Dynamo Kiev and, when the great man died, he took over as Head Coach. Has it changed his rather relaxed approach to the beautiful game?

The other very talented midfielder in this side was English international Trevor Steven - an intelligent passing player who could run all day from area to area, head the ball well (for a relatively small and slightly-built man) and score great goals. He was truly the modern midfield ideal. Sadly a variety of injuries curtailed his contribution for too many of his seasons at Ibrox. Another player who contributed to the cause was Dale Gordon, a right-winger who could also fill the role of a right-sided midfielder. Although he scored the odd goal, he was more likely to create one by fine wing play. Without being the fastest of wingers, he could pass the opposition by guile more than anything and was always alert to the space opening up in front of him.

Up front, the normal trio was McCoist, Hateley and Huistra. Dutch left-winger Peter Huistra was another slight figure but he was pacey and could be relied on to get past defenders and supply his strikers with great service. His balance and skill were great advantages but it has to be said that he could be bullied out of a match by more ruthless defenders. Perhaps he was too delicate for the robust Scottish game.

The strikers benefiting from his crosses were the 2 players who perhaps formed the best Rangers' striking partnership since the days of Millar and Brand in the 1960s - Hateley and McCoist.

In the previous season, Ally McCoist (Rangers' most prolific ever striker) had been voted the sportswriters' 'Player of the Year' after having scored 41 goals in all competitions. He also won the Golden Boot for being Europe's top goal-scorer. McCoist was brave, confident, hard-working and an instinctive striker, always alert to a chance. His sense of anticipation and ability to go beyond defenders allowed him to score many a goal. A chirpy nature and self-confidence meant that he never hid during a game. If he missed 3 or 4 chances, it just did not get him down and he would always be there for the next one. In Season 92-93, 'Super' would score a total of 49 goals with 34 coming in the league. This total would surely have been greater if he had not missed the last 7 league games (and Scottish Cup Final) due to injury after breaking his leg in April playing for Scotland in Portugal. McCoist would play nearly 600 times for Rangers and his final tally of goals would be 355, making him Rangers' all-time top scorer.

In later years, McCoist's goal average probably increased due to the fact that his striking partner was Mark Hateley. 'Attila' was the perfect foil for McCoist. A powerful, 'traditional' centre-forward, Hateley (with his long hair flowing behind him) pressurised defences endlessly and terrorised them into making mistakes that would bring about goals. Superb in the air, he could be a target man when needed but he was so much more. For a big man, he was quick and nimble, linking well with the other players and spreading the play out to the wings or back to midfield. His time in Italy and France had provided him with great experience which he used to the full. Although a goal-scorer in his own right, he could not compete with McCoist who was simply the best. Still, that season, Hateley managed to score 29 times in all competitions with 21 of those being league goals. So, with nearly 80 between them, it is clear that these players developed a most profitable understanding, one that produced great dividends for the club that season.

Funnily enough, this wonderful season had not begun as if it was going to be the best in living memory. In the first league game, it had taken a McCoist goal (10 minutes from time) to defeat St Johnstone in a nervous opening match. After a routine 2-0 win against Airdrie at Ibrox 4 days later, it began to look anything but promising. A 0-0 draw at Easter Road, followed by a 4-3 defeat at Dens Park, meant that Rangers were more desperate than usual to win the first Old Firm game of the season. In the end, a 1-1 Ibrox draw was the best they could manage.

However, that was the turning point this particular season even although it was still only August. Following the Dundee defeat, Rangers went on a run of 44 games unbeaten in all competitions, including 8 European Cup matches. From August 15th at Dens Park, it took until March 20th the following year for Rangers to lose another game. Maybe not surprisingly, this came at Parkhead when Celtic won 2-1, just days after Rangers had played a gruelling European match against Brugges of Belgium. Sadly, that foreign adventure ended a few weeks later when Marseilles, rather than Rangers, qualified for the European Cup Final. In a 1-1 draw at Marseilles, one more goal would have seen the Ibrox club into the final of the first Champions' League instead of the French side.

By the end of February, in the league, Rangers were 11 points ahead of the field in the title race and, by then, had included two 1-0 victories over Celtic in their unbeaten run. In the fifth last match of the league programme, the title was secured at Broomfield when Airdrie went down 1-0. The honour of scoring the significant goal went to reserve striker Gary McSwegan who had taken the place of the injured Ally McCoist. Rangers only lost 4 league matches that season and 2 of these came after the match in which the Championship was sealed!

In the two cup competitions, Aberdeen were Rangers' victims losing by the same 2-1 score-line. In the League Cup Final at Hampden, goals from McCall (after a blunder by keeper Theo Snelders who would eventually become a Ranger) and an own goal from Gary Smith beat Aberdeen who played well enough without really looking capable of beating Rangers.

On Scottish Cup Final day, Parkhead was being utilised as Hampden was at long last being renovated. With McCoist out with a broken leg, the Dons may have thought that this might increase their chances of a cup win - they were sorely mistaken. Mark Hateley came to the fore and had a brilliant match, scoring the goal that put Rangers 2-0 up after young Neil Murray had notched the first. A tired Rangers side, at the end of an exhausting season, played out the game comfortably enough - until a late Aberdeen goal gave them some hope and ensured that the final few minutes of the game would be anything but comfortable for the Light Blues.

In the end however, Richard Gough went up to collect the Scottish Cup in the Main Stand at Parkhead and, as he held the trophy aloft, the Rangers fans no doubt took even more satisfaction than usual, seeing a Treble win being confirmed at the home of their deadliest rivals. Spare a thought for Ally McCoist here. He had played and scored in every round of the cup prior to this but missed out on a medal due to his injury. At least he took part in the celebrations, cavorting around on crutches with his team-mates.

LEAGUE CHAMPIONSHIP NUMBER 47: 1996-97

This was the season when Rangers achieved what, for many fans, was the impossible dream. Ever since Jock Stein's tenure as Celtic manager, Rangers fans had coveted 2 of his records that they wanted Rangers to emulate: winning the European Cup and securing the championship nine times in a row. This season saw the latter become reality. When Celtic's winning streak came to an end in 1974, few believed that it was possible for any club to ever repeat the feat. Indeed, league reconstruction would take place 2 seasons later in a bid to increase competition and prevent such domination ever again. Of course, as it turned out, Rangers deposed Celtic in the last of the old First Division championships anyway so Stein was defeated by his greatest rivals, rather than a change in the organisation of the league.

With the top league reduced to 10 full-time, totally professional clubs, playing each other 4 times a season (as opposed to a set-up of 18, some of whom were part-time, playing each other twice), it should have seen the end to any long sequences of title wins. Remarkably, by 1996, Rangers had managed to achieve 'eight-in-a-row'. Until the creation of Stein's Celtic, the best sequence of title triumphs had been 'six-in-a-row' which Celtic managed in the early part of the 20th Century. Rangers' best, incidentally, had been a series of 5.

When Stein's Celtic had attained their record, there was

obviously not the same pressure on the side after win number 7 had been achieved as they then moved into uncharted territory. However, for Rangers, with a target of nine to equal, the pressure had become more intense with each passing season. This 9th season would see a group of players under more severe pressure for a whole season than any other side anywhere in the world, at any time in the history of football. Rather unfairly, it seemed that, to some people, if Rangers failed to win this championship, the previous 8 would have therefore counted for nothing!

Unfortunately, 2 former great Rangers would not live to see the club's crowning achievement that season. Former captain and Scotland legend George Young and Treble-winning manager Jock Wallace both passed away during the course of the season. Both would have been as proud as any Rangers' fan when their club showed the finest of qualities in the quest for nine-in-a-row.

Such excellence would be needed as this championship was won in adversity, thanks to an incredible injury list throughout the season that cruelly disrupted the team's performances. Walter Smith stated that, at one point, out of a player complement of 58, he actually had 34 players injured or ill! It took all the managerial skills of Smith and assistant Archie Knox, as well as the determination, courage and skill of their players to win through in the end. Bill Struth would have been proud of them all.

An incredible 31 players were used by the manager - from veterans like Richard Gough and Stuart McCall to a very young Barry Ferguson who played in the final match of the season at Tynecastle. For most of the teams discussed in this book, it is possible to show a regular starting line-up or, at least, as regular as injuries allowed. However, for this team, that would be less possible than normal. Still, here is a version with the other significant players listed at the end.

Goram
Clelland, Gough, Bjorklund, Robertson
I.Ferguson, Gascoigne, Albertz
Miller/ Anderson/ Durie/ McCoist, Laudrup

Moore, Petric, McLaren and Shields played their part in defence while Durrant, McCall and McInnes helped out in midfield with Van Vossen, the ill-fated Rozental and, latterly, Hateley augmenting the forwards.

Only 2 new signings would be in place at the start of the campaign for that 9th title: German Jorg Albertz signed from Hamburg for £4 million and Swede Joachim Bjorklund signed from Italian club Vicenza, for nearly £3 million. By the end of this memorable season both would fondly be referred to by their respective nicknames of 'The Hammer' and 'Jocky'. These players would improve both the attacking midfield and defensive capabilities of the side.

Albertz, in particular, would become a Rangers legend, scoring many vital and spectacular goals with his explosive left foot. He was a tremendous passer of the ball and played brilliantly down the left side of the side. Indeed, at the start of the season, he had to fill in at left back for the injured David Robertson but, even this did not prevent him from showing his class and scoring long-range goals from the start of his Ibrox career. His first league season would see him notch 10 in total.

Bjorklund was certainly not the biggest, most physically imposing central defender in the league but his speed and anticipation usually saw him making tackles that nipped trouble in the bud. He also covered well for his fellow defenders (who had perhaps been overcome) and formed a formidable partnership with the inspirational Richard Gough. Bjorklund knew that his job was to defend and that was all he tried to do. Venturing into the opponents' half of the field would probably have given him a nose bleed!

The other new signing (arriving half-way through the season)

was a striker who seemed destined to take over from veteran
Ally McCoist. Chilean international Seb Rozental was an exciting
addition to the squad but unfortunately only played 2 games (one in
the Scottish Cup in January) before being injured and missing out
on the rest of the campaign. Nobody could have known that his
serious injury would dog him for the rest of his time at Ibrox or that
he would never really be able to compete for a first team place. But
it really was that kind of season in terms of woeful injury!

It was just as well that the club's 2 genuine world-class stars
performed outstandingly that season. Great Dane Brian Laudrup
played in all but 2 league matches and, by the end of the season,
had won the Sport writers' 'Player of the Year' award, his second in
3 years. The previous winner Paul Gascoigne (although not as
fabulously sensational this time round) played very well and scored,
as ever, some unbelievable goals. Sadly injury disrupted his form
when he missed 10 matches in February and March. Nevertheless,
he netted a respectable 13 goals compared to top scorer Laudrup
who netted 18 times, his best ever haul.

With these 2 inventive, creative players in the side, it must have
been a nightmare for opposing players. Laudrup had great pace,
dribbling skills, awareness, vision and a left foot that could shoot as
well as spray passes all over the park. Friends of Rangers will
always wonder what it might have been like if he had been in the
side when McCoist and Hateley had been at their peak.

As for 'Gazza', he also had that vision, awareness and passing
ability so necessary for a brilliant midfield player. But, like all the
greatest modern midfielders, he also had that ability to surge from
that area of the park, get ahead of his forwards and finish off moves
with sublime technique. His temperament was always suspect but
fans had come to realise that this was part of the territory with such
a charismatic genius.

So, for most of the season, Rangers had a top class spine of
Andy Goram in goal, Gough and Bjorklund in central defence,
Gazza and Albertz in midfield with Laudrup up front. It was the

foundation of Rangers' most memorable season.

The league campaign had started with 6 successive wins before Celtic were the visitors at Ibrox in the first Old Firm match. As in any season, the winner here would strike a tremendous psychological blow. Rangers played well and took the lead in the second half thanks to a towering Gough header from an Albertz corner. Missed chances, however, kept Celtic in the match and near the end, the Parkhead side almost equalised when a header smacked off Goram's bar. Ironically, Rangers swept up the park in a move that ended with another Albertz cross onto the head of Gazza who had typically run the length of the pitch. It was a vital victory.

As is usually the case, the Old Firm matches would turn out to be decisive in the race for the championship. For the first time ever in the Premier League, Rangers won all 4 Old Firm games. In November, a marvellous solo Laudrup goal in the east end of Glasgow secured the points and set up a great December in which 22 goals were scored in 7 games. By January 2nd, Celtic knew that they had to pull back something from their clash with Rangers at Ibrox. However, thanks to a quite astonishing free kick from Albertz and 2 goals near the end from substitute Erik Bo Andersen, Rangers won 3-1.

After 21 matches, Rangers had a 14 point lead over Celtic although their rivals had a couple of games in hand. Thus, two months later, in what appeared to be the final showdown of Celtic's 'Last Chance Saloon' took place at Parkhead on 16th March. A win for Rangers would virtually seal the title albeit not arithmetically. Brian Laudrup has said that before the game Archie Knox confirmed that this was the most important match in the club's history. Indeed, the man was not exaggerating!

The omens were not too auspicious as Celtic had knocked Rangers out of the Scottish Cup 10 days previously and injury would make the the Ibrox side's task harder. Goram, Gascoigne and Durie were all out while Gough was not really fit but, like a true leader, he played through the pain barrier because the team needed him. Even Goram's deputy Theo Snelders was injured so Welshman Andy Dibble (on loan) had to play. What a time and place to have to make your Rangers' debut! The injury situation was so bad that Walter Smith pulled a master-stroke by bringing back Mark Hateley from Queen's Park Rangers where he had gone the previous season. He knew that Hateley's physical presence (and reputation) would be vital in such a game.

So it proved, despite a sending off for the big man near the end of the clash. In a towsy match, a scrambled Laudrup goal won the points and, seemingly, the league. However, it was not to be as straightforward as maybe fans believed. By the time of the Monday May Bank Holiday, Rangers 'only' had to beat Motherwell at Ibrox to clinch the title. An astonishing 2-0 reverse set the nerves jangling again for players and fans alike. Rangers still needed one win from their remaining 2 away games at Tannadice and Tynecastle. Two days later, a Laudrup header from a Charlie Miller cross was enough to beat Dundee Utd and secure 'nine-in-a-row'. It sparked off the greatest celebrations, perhaps, in the history of the club with the fans already looking forward to the possibility of 'ten-in-a-row' title triumphs.

LEAGUE CHAMPIONSHIP NUMBER 48: 1998-99

Following the previous trophy-less season, few fans could have envisaged the club winning yet another Treble in Season 98-99, especially under the management of a new boss Dick Advocaat, who had become Rangers' first foreign manager. The previous year had been the last for Walter Smith and most of his 'nine-in-a-row' squad. The crushing disappointment of failing to achieve the magical 10 (and losing the Scottish Cup Final to Hearts) had left Rangers fans feeling pessimistic about the future. However, then came 'The Little General' as Advocaat came to be known.

A former Dutch National coach who had taken his country to the quarter-finals of the 94 World Cup, Advocaat had been tempted to leave his club PSV Eindhoven and start another revolution at Ibrox. Due to the changing of the old guard (who had left with Walter Smith), the new manager practically had to build a side from scratch and in a hurry. Gone from the previous season were legends and heroes such as McCoist, Gough, Laudrup, Goram and McCall. To replace the dear departed or other ageing stars, David Murray ensured that the necessary funds were made available and the manager set out on a spending spree the likes of which had never been seen in Rangers' long history. By the end of the season, Advocaat had spent over £30 million. His first target of regaining domestic dominance would be achieved and the secondary goal of improving the club's European performances would have begun.

As throughout the 90s, injuries and suspensions played a major part in the various team selections. Seldom could it be said that there was a 'regular' Rangers side. Therefore, rather than try to set this out, listed below are the various players who contributed to a tremendous season.

Incredibly, Rangers used 3 different goalkeepers: Charbonnier, Niemi and Klos - all different nationalities. In defence, the Walter Smith signings of Porrini, Amoruso, Moore and Vidmar remained while the new manager brought in Arthur Numan, Colin Hendry and the ill-fated Daniel Prodan. In midfield, some players from the previous regime played their part (the likes of Jorg Albertz, Ian Ferguson, Derek McInnes and Rino Gattuso) while young Barry Ferguson was given his head by Advocaat and allowed to blossom. Helping him was newcomer and Dutch international Giovanni Van Bronckhorst - one of the longest names in Rangers' history? American World Cup captain Claudio Reyna also joined the squad in April.

Up front, established Rangers forwards such as Jonatan Johannson and veteran Gordon Durie stayed on but were mainly used as substitutes for new signings Andrei Kanchelskis, Rod Wallace, Gabriel Amato, Stephane Guivar'ch and, eventually, Neil McCann.

Below is a full list of the Advocaat newcomers and their cost to the club:

Charbonnier	£1.2 million from Auxerre
Klos	£ 0.7 million from Borussia Dortmund
Hendry	£4 million from Blackburn Rovers
Numan	£4.5 million from PSV Eindhoven
Prodan	£2.2 million from Athletico Madrid
Van Bronckhorst	£5.25 million from Feyenoord
Reyna	£1.2 million from Wolfsburg
Kanchelskis	£5.5million from Fiorentina
Wallace	Free from Leeds
Amato	£4.2 million from Real Mallorca
McCann	£1.6 million from Hearts
Guivar'ch	£3.5 million from Newcastle

New keeper Lionel Charbonnier was a real character. Apart from being an art lover and artist, the Frenchman was both racehorse owner and trainer. He immediately struck up a rapport with the fans - not an easy thing to achieve considering that he was following in the footsteps of the legend that was Andy 'The Goalie' Goram. Very soon, the fans would be singing 'La Marseillaise' in tribute to him. Unfortunately, his Ibrox career was to be short-lived when he was injured in a UEFA Cup match at Ibrox against Bayer Leverkusen, the crack German side that Rangers eliminated. He did not play again that season and his career at Rangers was all but over although few realised this at the time.

For a while, he was replaced by Finnish keeper Anti Niemi who had been understudy to Goram. The big, blond Finn was popular enough with the fans despite having been the unfortunate goalkeeper in a 5-1 defeat by Celtic. He was, however, not popular enough with his manager. For some time Advocaat had been negotiating with Borussia Dortmund in an effort to buy Stefan Klos as he neared the end of his contract. Eventually, Advocaat's persistence paid off and, in December, the German joined the club.

If Charbonnier had been a flamboyant character, then Klos was his opposite. Reticent, efficient, unassuming, dedicated were just some of the adjectives that were applied to the newcomer. In the Rangers' tradition he was not a huge keeper who dominated his penalty box but he was cool, alert, agile, instinctive and a great shot-stopper. Once again the fans took to yet another new man between the posts and eventually his greatest tribute became his nickname 'Der Goalie'.

The defence in front of these keepers of course changed but, with injury and suspension, those who remained from the Smith era were still invaluable. Sergio Porrini, signed from Milan, was a solid back who tackled well and could be productive going forward even if he did not have the pace of a David Robertson. Lorenzo Amoruso, after suffering an injury that all but wiped out any appearance on the park in his first season, was like a new player in the side. He was big, powerful, self-confident and, as well as being good in the air, he could tackle on the ground. More than capable of starting attacks from the back, he loved to blast free-kicks from long-range. The one chink in his armour appeared to be that he thought he was a better player than maybe he was and occasionally his casual attitude resulted in errors and, sometimes, goals.

The player who changed most dramatically under the new manager was Australian Craig Moore. He had been at Ibrox for a few years and had never been one of the fans' favourite. In fairness, he had always considered central defence to be his best position but, often as not, Walter Smith played him at full-back or even in midfield where he had obviously looked like a fish out of water. However, in a very short space of time, Advocaat's coaching had turned him into a very competent central defender. It was a pity that, a few months into the season, he could not be dissuaded from joining Crystal Palace. Luckily, due to Palace's financial difficulties towards the end of the season, he came back to Ibrox where he has been a more than reliable performer ever since.

Dutch Internationalist Arthur Numan lit up Ibrox in the early months of the season before injury curtailed his appearances. Intelligent, quick and an excellent passer of the ball, Numan helped create much danger down the left flank. He was also a good tackler and read the game well. His injury-hit time, though, spoiled a good debut season for him.

When Scotland's captain Colin Hendry signed for the club, the pundits suggested it was for two reasons: firstly, he would add a 'Scottishness' to a side full of new foreigners and, secondly, he would captain the team. Hendry exemplified the 'Braveheart' image. Big, strong, blond, he was a brave, committed player who would give his all. An imposing barrier, he was a formidable player in the air and a fierce tackler. Still, Dick Advocaat had a surprise in store for the pundits as well as the fans - Hendry would not be captain of Rangers! Instead the Italian Amoruso, who had obviously impressed the manager, was named as skipper.

If Charbonnier's injury had been tragic, even more so had been that of Daniel Prodan. The Rumanian defender had been a brilliant player for years and the fans thought that he could be the ingredient that would make the defence impregnable. However, when Rangers signed him from Athletico Madrid, he had been injured but various medicals seemed to show that this would be no problem in the future. Sadly, Prodan never played one competitive match for the first team and a couple of years later eventually released. His case was reminiscent of another truly great defender whose career at Ibrox was wrecked due to injury - the Russian Oleg Kuznetsov.

As fans might have suspected from a manager who believed in playing a passing game, Advocaat's midfield, full of great players, was the strongest part of his side. He showed his faith in Barry Ferguson by making him a first choice and Ferguson, in turn, rewarded the manager by showing skill and a presence that belied his tender years. The player had become disillusioned and thinking of leaving Rangers but Advocaat helped change his mind and set him on the road to not one but two Sportswriters' 'Player of the

Year' awards - the youngest person ever to win that prestigious accolade twice.

Alongside this tremendous passer of the ball was another - Giovanni Van Bronckhorst. The Dutchman was a player of immense talent and energy who seemed to cover the entire pitch. For a relatively small man, he was an eager tackler but his biggest asset was the passing ability that could prise open defences. Allied to this, he could score spectacular goals. Talking of which, another team-mate was Jorg Albertz whose shooting had already become legendary down Ibrox way. The German was already an adopted Scot whose exciting forays into the opposition area and thunderous shots had won over the fans virtually from the first appearance at Ibrox. With a wonderful left foot for passing, it was easy to see how goals were created for the forwards.

In April, this splendid midfield would be supplemented by Claudio Reyna, an American who shared the the above qualities. Energetic, committed, a man who roamed all over the pitch, Reyna could tackle as well as attack and shoot.

What about the forwards who benefited from such midfield play? At that time, Ukrainian Kanchelskis was Rangers' most expensive signing. Although he seldom reached the heights attained a few years earlier with Manchester United, he was still a pacy winger who scored some valuable goals that season as well as making many more. On the left wing, Jonatan Johannson of Finland was a really quick winger who could even be played through the middle to take advantage of his devastating pace. Almost a forerunner of Peter Lovenkrands, he was capable of scoring goals from either position. Eventually, in December, he would be superseded by Neil McCann (bought from Hearts) and a Scottish cup winner against Rangers the previous season! He was also a quick, left-sided player who could pass defenders and deliver inviting crosses with the added bonus of being also a finisher.

In the middle, for most of the time, were Rod Wallace and Gabriel Amato. Wallace must have been the bargain 'buy' of the season - a rather misleading term considering the fact that he came from Leeds on a free transfer! The Yorkshire club had wanted him to stay but he had fancied a new challenge. Pound for pound, he was one of Dick Advocaat's best acquisitions. Despite his lack of size, the little striker was brave, alert and quick - qualities that helped him become the club's top scorer that season. Wallace also scored the winning goal in the Scottish Cup Final.

Finding a partner for him was a more difficult proposition. Argentinian Gabriel Amato had been signed from Spanish club Real Mallorca for that purpose but despite a creditable number of goals scored in La Liga, he never gave the impression of being an out-and-out striker. However, the fans did like him. An exciting, flair player, he seemed almost British in temperament, being strong and committed as well as delightfully skillful. Apart from scoring goals, he could set them up with his passing and ability to run at defenders, taking them on and opening up chances for others. Amato's only weakness seemed to be a lack of genuine pace that would have seen him flourish in the Premier League. He could get past opponents easily enough but could never quite get away from them.

In November, Advocaat signed another striker in Frenchman Stephane Guivar'ch. The player had failed to hit it off or settle at Newcastle and Rangers thought that a rescue mission would suit both parties. From the first sight of the player, it was obvious that he was a natural goal scorer. He had an eye for goal and a great technique that made scoring look easy. Unfortunately, he did not come across as the bravest or most hard-working striker ever seen at Ibrox - two qualities that are so essential in Scottish football. He may have been a brilliant poacher but seemed too easily intimidated by the 'hammer-throwers' (as Souness famously called them) in the league. He would eventually be shipped back to France once injury had made him even less willing to sweat blood for the cause.

Add to these players, the likes of Tony Vidmar, the Australian who would do a job anywhere in defence when required, veteran Ian Ferguson who was useful when fully fit, Rino Gattuso (soon to depart to Salernitana before ending up a Champions League winner with AC Milan) and Derek McInnes who was used for specific jobs in midfield. Dick Advocaat had built an excellent squad of players to take on the challenges ahead.

Having said that, the season started badly and the side went down 2-1 at Tynecastle in the opening league game. However, the way the team had played in the second-half had given the fans a glimpse at what was to come. Rangers then went on an unbeaten run of 17 matches beginning with a win at Ibrox against Motherwell. By the start of December, it was looking good. Rangers' biggest win had been in November - a 7-1 demolition of St Johnstone at McDiarmid Park when debutant Guivar'ch scored a brace.

Indeed, November had been an eventful time. Near the end of the month, Rangers had played 3 big matches within 8 days. The first of these had been the worst result of the season when Celtic won 5-1 at Parkhead. It had looked like a tough game from the outset as Jo Venglos' side seemed determined to pull Rangers back in the title race. However, Rangers' task was made impossible even before a third of the match had been played when referee Willie Young sent off Scott Wilson for a tackle that had probably merited a booking. Despite a great Van Bronckhorst free-kick goal to make it 1-3, Rangers did well to limit the damage to 5 that day. Apparently, in the Rangers' dressing room afterwards old stager Ian Ferguson had gone ballistic and attempted to 'explain' how a defeat this devastating would affect the fans and how it should also affect the players just the same way.

The following Tuesday, Rangers had drawn 1-1 with Italian giants Parma after playing quite well without getting the hoped for home result especially having knocked out Shelbourne, Paok Salonika, Beitar Jerusalem and Leverkusen on the route to this tie. Then, on the Sunday, the first trophy of the season was lifted by at the expense of the unfortunate St Johnstone in the League Cup Final (played at Celtic Park), making 'Paradise' a happier hunting ground than the week before. At least St Johnstone had the consolation of keeping the score respectable this time. A fairly routine 2-1 win was more important than the performance as goals from Albertz and Guivar'ch took the cup to Ibrox and ensured that the season was already an improvement on the previous one.

By the start of the next month, Rangers led the title chase with 30 points from 15 matches, Kilmarnock were second (two points adrift with a game more played) then Celtic next, 4 points behind Rangers and a game more played. In the New Year Old Firm game at Ibrox, full points were taken in a 2-1 win with Amato and Wallace scoring the vital goals. Rangers were now 10 points ahead of their old rivals. After that, the first winter shutdown in the history of Scottish football took place, giving players - and perhaps fans - a chance to recharge their batteries. Rangers took the players off to Florida for training and to keep their fitness levels up. It seemed to work as, in February, Rangers put together a great scoring run - knocking in 6 against Hamilton in the Scottish Cup, 6 against Dundee and 5 against Kilmarnock (at Rugby Park) to ensure that, by the end of the month, they were still 10 points ahead of Celtic.

The team remained unbeaten until the end of March when they lost to Dundee Utd. (the only home defeat) before losing a week later to St Johnstone who gained revenge for previous humiliations by winning at home. It was as close as Advocaat had been to a 'crisis' as it had been 5 years since Rangers had lost back-to-back matches. The side were now 6 points ahead of Celtic.

By the end of April, a great 3-1 defeat of Aberdeen at Ibrox meant a dream scenario as far as the fans were concerned. Rangers now had 69 points while Celtic had 62. A win against Celtic at Parkhead in their next match would give Rangers the title....and the club had never before clinched the championship at the home of their greatest rivals!

The possible explosiveness of the situation was perhaps recognised by the SFA who appointed Hugh Dallas, their best official, as referee. Unfortunately, a Sunday evening kick-off time of 6.30 had allowed the fans to drink for most of the day if they so desired. Bearing in mind what followed, too many had felt like it! Rangers started the better side and took the lead through Neil McCann after a sweeping move carved open the home side. Then Mahe of Celtic was sent off and things looked bleak for the home team. Before half-time, everything threatened to get out of hand: as Van Bronckhorst attempted to take a corner, he was pelted with coins. When Dallas went over, he was hit on the forehead by a coin and needed medical attention. A couple of Celtic fans even invaded the field of play seemingly in an attempt to get at the referee.

Once the mayhem had subsided and the ball sent into the box, a penalty was awarded and duly converted by Albertz who kept his head while many around seemed to be losing theirs. The second half was a calmer affair although, right at the end, Wallace and then Riseth of Celtic were sent off in separate incidents. Prior to this, Neil McCann had notched Rangers' third goal and sealed the championship to the delight of the few thousand lucky fans in blue who had managed to get tickets. When the final whistle was sounded, the Rangers players showed their delight by doing a mock Celtic huddle in the centre of the park much to the annoyance of those Celtic fans still in the stadium.

Having won the title at Parkhead, the only thing that could top that was winning the Treble by beating Celtic at Hampden the following month. The Scottish Cup Final was the first match to be played at the newly completed stadium so it was therefore fitting that it should be a contest between the Old Firm. Some pre-match talk centred on the previous match between the foes and the possibility of even more trouble. However, this proved to be unfounded and the events off the pitch were almost as tame as those on it.

In a rather lacklustre final, it looked as if one goal would be enough to settle it - Rangers, thanks to Rod Wallace, got that vital goal. Chances had been few and far between but the wee man took his gleefully and his strike not only won the Cup but also the Treble. Lorenzo Amoruso's pride was there for all to see as he lifted the trophy, the first foreign player to captain Rangers to a Treble.

With Alex McLeish's side winning the Treble in Season 2002-3, it meant that Rangers had accomplished this tremendous feat 3 times in 10 years, a wonderful achievement considering the fact that Celtic has only managed to win 3 Trebles in their entire history. Those 5 stars that have been added to the Rangers' shirts from Season 2003-4 onwards might signify that 50 league championships have been won, but more importantly, they will hopefully remind all Rangers fans of the great players and marvellous sides down the years who have given such joy.

PART TWO: SEASON 2002-3

AUGUST

In the run up to the first league matches of the new season, it was events off the field that dominated as the Old Firm clubs had been uncharacteristically quiet on the transfer front. Alex McLeish had only added £6 million Mikel Arteta from Barcelona and Kevin Muscat (on a 'Bosman' from Wolves) to his squad. Meanwhile, over at Celtic Park, Martin O'Neil was hoping that David Fernandez from Livingston would be a suitable replacement for the departed Lubo Moravcik. His only other signings were to strengthen his defence by adding Swedish international keeper Magnus Hedman from Coventry to the pool and Danish left back Ulrik Laursen from Hibs, only days before the start of the big kick off. O'Neil's total outlay was around £4.5 million but many wondered if this would be good enough to retain the Championship and progress in the Champions' League.

Sat. August 3, 2002
KILMARNOCK 1 RANGERS 1
(Arveladze)
Crowd: 13,972

Unfortunately, the season started with a whimper rather than a bang as the eagerly-awaited opening match of the season left Rangers fans feeling thoroughly deflated at Rugby Park. Wearing their new away kit of orange (sorry, tangerine!) tops, this was certainly no tangerine dream but more a case of Groundhog Day. In a repeat of so many games from the previous season, Rangers took the lead (through a header by Shota Arveladze) and proceeded to control the match. However, the vital second goal, which would have killed off Kilmarnock, failed to materialise despite several chances being created.

As the second-half wore on, Rangers' play became slower, showing less of the urgency of the first half and they began to give the ball away too easily. Eventually, with only ten minutes left, the inevitable happened when Killie equalised and two points were thrown away in the first match of the new campaign. The Rangers' fans really should have known better than to taunt Killie substitute Andy McLaren regarding his previous personal problems as it is almost a law of nature that the abused player will promptly bite you on the rear end. How McLaren must have enjoyed the moment when he took his chance after a corner kick had been handled badly by the visiting defence. Some claimed that Klos had been impeded in trying to deal with the initial corner but referee Kenny Clark was in no mood to be swayed by any protests.

How ironic that Clark should have been blamed by Killie boss Jim Jefferies for Rangers' goal when he gave a corner instead of awarding a goal kick. Jeffries declared that it was 'his only mistake' throughout the match. Obviously he had not seen the handball incident that should have given Rangers a penalty (with the score at 1-0) in the second-half. Most reporters claimed that it was 'a good shout' for a penalty but that Clark must have been unsighted.

At the end of the game, to make matters worse, the 'follow-followers' discovered that Celtic had beaten Dunfermline 2-1 at Parkhead thanks to two Larsson goals and a 'wonder save' from Rab Douglas in the dying minutes of the match. Groundhog Day, indeed.

The Rangers team: Klos, Ricksen, Moore, Amoruso, Numan, de Boer, Arteta, Ferguson, McCann, Arveladze and Lovenkrands.

Sat. August 10, 2002
RANGERS 3 DUNDEE 0
(de Boer, Arveladze, Lovenkrands)
Crowd: 47,004

The first home league game (against Dundee) saw an unexpected problem off the field when the Smartcard electronic turnstile system crashed leaving most of the fans locked outside the stadium. The game had to be delayed on three occasions, eventually forcing kick-off to take place almost 50 minutes late in order to allow most of the 47,000 fans time to enter the ground. Obviously, this was not the ideal preparation for the players waiting to get involved in the action. As new Dens manager Jim Duffy said afterwards "I won't use the late kick-off as an excuse but obviously it was frustrating having to give FOUR team talks - especially when NONE of them worked!"

Once again, Ibrox was bathed in sun and it seemed as if almost every fan was wearing one of those tangerine shirts. Since Rangers had started to manufacture them, minus the help of Nike, a healthy profit looked certain to justify their decision. A surprise for the fans, when the teams emerged from the tunnel, was the fact that Rangers were actually wearing their tangerine tops, allowing Dundee to keep to their normal dark blue. If it was designed as a marketing ploy by Rangers' management, they need not have bothered as most fans seemed to have taken a liking to the new strip within 4 days of it being available.

When the team was announced, it looked as if McLeish was, at last, going to support Flo with another striker - in the shape of Arveladze. However, once the game had started, it was obvious that the Georgian was staying out wide on the left with Ronald de Boer trying to support Flo by playing between the midfield and the strikers. Surprisingly, neither of the wingers from the first league game (Lovenkrands and McCann) started the match, with the latter not even on the bench.

After 12 minutes, de Boer glanced a header into the net from Arteta's corner but, just like the previous Saturday, Rangers (despite the lion's share of possession) could not find the second goal to kill off Dundee. Indeed, the away side had one great chance when they caught Rangers on the break but the shot was extravagantly chipped over the bar by the Spaniard Novo. Apart from a 10 minute spell in the second-half, however, Rangers rarely looked troubled which was just as well as Lorenzo Amoruso was not having one of his better days. In the second-half the Italian played with a big plaster above his eye but fans could have been forgiven for thinking that it was over his eye!

In contrast, Ronald de Boer was at his confident best. He continually performed magnificent turns, leaving a marker for dead and opening up the play ahead of him. Still, even he was being outshone by young Spaniard Mikel Arteta who went on to win the 'Man of the Match' award. Arteta had already become a big favourite with the fans and he produced yet another display of exciting, attacking football that augured well for the rest of the season. He was settling in well with Barry Ferguson, who also had a good game. With Ricksen supplying the 'dig' beside these skillful, attacking midfield men, this area of the team was looking good.

As the game progressed, Rangers' dominance created several good chances but these were either spurned (by a variety of players) or saved by Dundee's Argentinian keeper Speroni. However, with just over 20 minutes left, the match ended as a contest when Arveladze ran on to a deft lay-off from Flo and crashed the ball into the net. After the match, Jim Duffy complained that Flo "had used some of his experience to get up to a wee bit of mischief." He seemed to be suggesting that Flo had illegally held off the challenge from the Dundee defender who had been trying to pull him from behind while slipping the ball to the side for Arveladze to pounce.

A couple of minutes from time, there was a gloss on the score line when substitute Peter Lovenkrands ran on to a clever, defence-splitting pass from Arveladze and confidently planted the ball behind Speroni with some force. With a 3-0 win against opponents who had proved troublesome in the past (even at Ibrox), the fans left satisfied with their only grouse being about that, as yet, imperfect Smartcard system!

Mikel Arteta was pleased with the start he had made at Ibrox and his impact on the Ibrox fans. He sang just about everyone's praises. "From the day I came here, everyone has been so good to me and that has made it easy to play. I am learning English as quickly as I can because it's important to respect the country you live and play in. I am finding my game more and more each week and the reception I have had from the Rangers supporters each week has been fantastic." Sounded like his English was coming along nicely!

Team-mate Craig Moore also praised the youngster, "His technical ability is there for all to see. He's very talented and I feel he has adapted to things very quickly and very well."

Manager McLeish, thoroughly satisfied with the result and the performance, was nevertheless a realist. "The 90 minutes are never going to be perfect and there will be some anxiety but I felt our victory was totally deserved." That boy still has a lot to learn about Rangers! Their fans go to every game expecting the perfect 90 minutes".

The Rangers team: Klos, Muscat, Moore, Amoruso, Numan, Ricksen, de Boer, Ferguson, Arteta, Flo and Arveladze.

Sun. August 18, 2002
HIBS 2   RANGERS 4
(de Boer, Ferguson, Lovenkrands 2)
Crowd: 11,633

Rangers' next game, away to Hibs, convinced their fans that
this really was going to be Groundhog Season. Due to live television
coverage, the match was played on the Sunday and, thanks to a
5-0 thrashing of Dundee United the day before at Celtic Park,
Rangers started the game at Easter Road 5 points behind their
deadly rivals, with the season barely begun. They were playing
catch-up already and there was no room for error. But, with the
torrential rain pounding down before and during the game (making
the pitch quite treacherous in places), errors were something that
most fans expected to see.

The only change made by Alex McLeish from the previous
line-up was to include Lovenkrands in place of Flo who had a
'difficult' week in terms of going to speak to Sunderland regarding a
return to the Premiership. The mooted £6 million deal led to week-
long speculation whether or not he would be leaving Ibrox
immediately and, as that might have taken its toll, his manager was
taking no chances. He did, however, praise the player for his ability
to focus on Rangers' matters and be ready to play if required.

Rangers began well, taking charge of the game and, after only
6 minutes, surged into the lead. Hibs' midfielder Brebner gave the
ball away carelessly and the alert Arteta pounced. He moved
forward before sliding a pass to Lovenkrands on the left whose
accurate cut-back was side-footed into the net by Ronald de Boer.
From then on, it was all Rangers although it has to be said that Hibs
(still smarting from a 5-1 defeat by Hearts the week before) showed
great commitment, frequently thundering in on the Rangers' players.
Indeed, it was not long before ref. Hugh Dallas booked 4 of them.

A goal disallowed (for offside) plus some near misses that
followed seemed to have cost Rangers dearly when Townsley

equalised on the half-hour, poking in a shot from 6 yards after a
failed clearance by the Light Blue defence from a corner. Suddenly,
a game that had been totally controlled by Rangers was now
all square.

Thankfully, for all connected with the club, Rangers won a
penalty when Lovenkrands was pulled back by Hibernian's new
French defender Doumbe just prior to the interval. This rash act no
doubt left his manager Bobby Williamson doumbe-founded! Barry
Ferguson duly dispatched the penalty with ease and the visitors
went in at half-time with a deserved lead.

The second-half was all one-way traffic and, after only 5
minutes, the match was more or less won when German Matthias
Jack's mis-kicked clearance went straight to Fernando Ricksen.
His low cross fairly zipped across the goal mouth and was met by
Lovenkrands whose sharpness left the hapless Doumbe floundering
as the ball was pinged into the net from 6 yards. Later on, striker
Paco Luna was sent-off after receiving a second yellow card for
using a handling the ball into the Rangers' goal. Even the Hibs fans
knew there was no way back.

Rangers' fourth came when Lovenkrands ran on to a through
pass from Ferguson whose vision and ability enabled him to deliver
a first-time ball over the top of the Hibs defence. With the kind of
chance he just relishes, the young Dane slammed it past the
onrushing keeper with the outside of his foot. Almost on the final
whistle, young striker Garry O'Connor (an alleged Rangers' target)
fired home a consolation second goal that Klos got a hand to and
maybe should have saved. Still, most Rangers fans were not
complaining, having successfully negotiated what could have
been a difficult away match played in truly dreadful conditions.

*The Rangers team: Klos, Muscat, Moore, Amoruso, Numan,
Ricksen, Arteta, Ferguson, de Boer, Arveladze and Lovenkrands.*

By the time Rangers took on Aberdeen at Ibrox the following Sunday, they were 5 points adrift of Celtic who had narrowly won at Firhill the day before. For a change, it was a sunny summer Sunday with the only cloud on Rangers' horizon being the hamstring injury to Lorenzo Amoruso which may see him miss the next month of action. Young Bob Malcolm, who had almost left the club at the end of the previous season, was drafted in as cover for Amo.

Right from the start, it was obvious that the Dons had come to Ibrox with damage limitation in mind. Changed days, indeed, from the heyday of Sir Alex! With only D'Jaffo up front, manager Ebbe Skovdahl set out his team to flood the midfield and defend in depth. In 40 years of watching teams defend at Ibrox, rarely has side show so little ambition getting into the Rangers half of the field. For the older generation of Dons' fans, it must have been a most embarrassing situation.

The mainly young side, sticking to their task of defending in depth, showed great energy and commitment but were no threat whatsoever to Rangers' goal. Eventually, the opener arrived when Lovenkrands burst between two defenders, cut the ball across the face of the goal to be cleverly dummied by Arveladze. This fooled the defender behind him, leaving Ronald de Boer with an easy chance to sweep the ball into the net. It was now a question of how many.

Much of the remainder of the game was played at a less than frenetic pace as the visitors seemed quite content to lose by just one goal as Rangers, just like in previous matches, continued to squander numerous chances to kill-off their opponents. As it was, it took until the 77th minute before the match was finally tied up although the Dons had not threatened to attack Rangers prior to that anyway. Again, a ref was involved in controversy when he

97

awarded Rangers a penalty. The television evidence suggested that he made the wrong decision by giving handball against Kevin McNaughton who seemed to stop the ball crossing the goal line by using his chest and shoulder rather than arm. How odd to see Rangers getting the benefit of an incorrect decision!

The final 15 minutes or so fizzled out and a disappointing match came, mercifully, to an end. Aberdeen had finished fourth in the league the previous season so it was worrying that they could put up such a tame, defensive performance, leaving Stefan Klos without a save to make in the entire match. If sides like this would not (or could not) come to Ibrox and have a go, what chance would there be of lesser teams trying it? It did not bode well for the competitiveness of the league for the rest of the season.

The Rangers team: Klos, Muscat, Malcolm, Moore, Numan, Ricksen, Ferguson, Arteta, de Boer, Arveladze and Lovenkrands.

The following Friday saw Rangers' most expensive player ever, Tore Andre Flo, depart for the sunnier climes of Sunderland. The striker, who had cost a record £12 million pounds less than two years earlier, signed for the Weirside club the day before the new transfer window closed until Christmas. According to various reports, Rangers only recouped £6.75 or £8 million - depending on which source you believed. The Black Cats, who had Michael Mols training with them for a few days a couple of weeks previously, decided against signing the Dutchman, opting instead for Marcus Stewart of Ipswich.

The new FIFA-imposed transfer window system had been the subject of controversy. Fans and pundits alike could not make up their minds whether the new restrictive system would be beneficial to the game or not. Some believed that it would make a more level playing field for the smaller clubs, in that the richer ones would not be able to simply go out and buy a new player when hit with a string of injuries. On the other hand, the richer clubs would have a far bigger pool of players in the first place so surely injuries would affect the smaller clubs to a greater extent? Many thought that the new limitations may reveal the really good managers by forcing them into using their available resources and make the best of them. Another school of thought was that the inability to buy replacement players would force managers into using younger talent, hopefully Scots, already at the club. Thus, a new generation of players might get experience much earlier than they otherwise would have been the case.

However, the collapse of funding from television deals along with other factors, had led most clubs to make stringent economies with the result that many players found themselves without a club by the end of the close season. Some players were actually trying to put themselves in the 'shop window' by playing for nothing or taking a contract that was short term or for very low (comparatively speaking) wages. With a 4 month transfer embargo in place after the end of August, what was to happen to those players who had no club (therefore no job) but with a mortgage and family to take care of? Mutterings could be heard about challenging the new system under the terms of European employment law - how could it be morally right to keep 'workers' from finding a new employer by introducing an artificial and arbitrary deadline?

According to the hacks, Rangers had been trying to offload Flo since the arrival of Alex McLeish the year before. His weekly wage (reputed to be about £38,000) was a saving that the club were eager to make and it was obvious, from his team selections, that the genial striker was not his manager's ideal centre-forward. However, finding a club willing to offer the millions required was a difficult task bearing in mind the new financial restrictions that even most big club found themselves working under. It was accepted by everyone that Rangers would have to suffer a huge financial loss should they ever find a club willing to take on the Norwegian.

With barely 24 hours before the transfer window closed, Sunderland took the plunge and signed Flo. It was an accepted fact that McLeish would have to sell players at Ibrox before he could buy any new ones so the fans wondered if there would still be time for Rangers to find a replacement striker, someone who would fit into McLeish's grand scheme for the future. Having just sold the club's top scorer from the previous season, many 'follow-followers' were shocked to discover that no replacement would be signed. However, the fans did realise that the days of spending huge sums such as £12 million were over - probably for ever.

Flo's record, even in his short spell at Ibrox, proved that he was a goal-scorer. In 61 starts and 11 substitute appearances, he scored 38 times - a more than decent record. His critics in the press claimed, though, that he didn't score enough in the really big games, in European competition or against Celtic for example. Obviously, statistically, this was true but as Rangers had struggled at times to defeat even ordinary domestic opposition, most fans would have settled for him banging goals in against the Motherwells of this world.

Despite a goal scoring debut, Flo's career rather fizzled out at Ibrox once McLeish became manager. Flo's promise, when he scored on his debut against Celtic in their 5-1 Ibrox defeat, was never fulfilled. He scored plenty of goals - hat-tricks and doubles; clever goals and skillful goals but, for some, this was never enough. That missing power was always bemoaned. As some said, he was probably too nice to be the kind of centre forward that Rangers required in the Premier League set up.

Ironically, considering the 'charge' that he could not score in important matches or against the 'bigger' teams, Flo managed to score the equalising goal again Manchester United on his Sunderland debut! By doing this, he managed to keep his record intact by scoring on his debut for his three British clubs: Chelsea, Rangers and Sunderland. Who would have bet against this anyway?

SEPTEMBER

Sun. September 1, 2002
DUNFERMLINE 0 RANGERS 6
(Caniggia 3, Arteta, Ricksen, Ferguson)
Crowd: 8,948

The day after Flo made his successful Sunderland debut, Rangers were playing in yet another televised Sunday game - this time against Dunfermline at East End Park. However, for a change, Celtic were also playing that day so the only added pressure came from proving to everyone that they could score goals without Flo. An unexpected 6-0 drubbing of the home side suggested that was the case.

Echoes of the previous season, and before, could be found in the fact that, with barely a month of the new season gone, the injuries were mounting up. Apart from long-term absentee Michael Ball, also out were Amoruso, Nerlinger, McCann and now, in-form forward Peter Lovenkrands. Dunfermline, playing well, had been expected to provide tough opposition with former Ranger Scott Wilson making his debut against his old club.

The home side started brightly but and then the roof caved in. A mix up between Wilson and new colleague Bullen (in 12 minutes) allowed Caniggia to pounce on a through ball, round the exposed keeper and slot the ball into the net. It was Caniggia's first start of the season. Could he have been one of those players referred to by McLeish when discussing the exit of Flo and looking for a striker to push himself into the reckoning? If so, he took his manager's comments to heart and duly scored a hat-trick!

After the opening goal, it was one-way-traffic but keeper Ruitenbeek kept his side in the match with a string of great saves. Still, even he could do nothing to stop the brilliant 25 yard curler from Arteta that soared into the top left corner of his net. It was the young Spaniard's first goal for Rangers and he celebrated by running to the training staff in the dug-out. If that did not 'end' the match, a Fernando Ricksen shot from outside the box that thundered into the goal through a forest of players certainly did. By half-time, the total could easily have been 6 or 7 but Rangers' fans were happy with 3 at that point.

Into the second-half and it was pleasing to see that the visiting players were not taking their foot off the gas. They surged forward looking for more goals. Ten minutes into the half, Arveladze was denied a deserved goal when he was brought down by Scott Wilson. Barry Ferguson stepped up and confidently swept the penalty into the net for his third goal (all penalties) in 5 league games. Three minutes later, Caniggia thumped another in from close range following a cross that had not been cleared by the Pars defenders. Then ten minutes later, the little Argentinian completed his first hat-trick for the club by crashing in another shot after a goal mouth scramble with the Fifers at sixes and sevens - in this case, mainly sixes!

Rangers had other chances in the remainder of the match but, despite 13 shots on target, they could not increase their lead. Dunfermline manager Jimmy Calderwood summed up his feelings about the game. "It was men against boys," he said. "Rangers played tremendously well and we were poor."

Obviously, from the Ibrox perspective, things could not have gone much better. Maybe there would, indeed, be goal-scoring life at Rangers after Flo. The fans could only hope so. When the financial news emerged a few days later showing an increase in Rangers' debt, it was clear that McLeish would have to stand or fall with this pool of players

The Rangers team: Klos, Muscat, Moore, Malcolm, Numan, Ricksen, Ferguson, Arteta; Caniggia, de Boer and Arveladze.

There followed a week's break to allow the Euro 2004 qualifying match against Faroe Isles to take place. All the matches were then scheduled for the Wednesday (apart from Celtic's game at Fir Park which took place the night before) so, as for most of the season so far, the Gers were going to play catch-up. However, this time, there was a difference - because Motherwell had beaten Celtic (inflicting their first league defeat of 2002), it meant that if Rangers beat Hearts at Ibrox, they would leapfrog their oldest rivals and go to the top of the league, for the first time in over two years! The pressure was really on the side to achieve this and ensure that, forthwith, it would be Celtic trying to keep in touch with Rangers.

Wed. September 11, 2002
RANGERS 2 HEARTS 0
(Caniggia, Arveladze)
Crowd: 48,581

Apart from an injury to young Stephen Hughes (a damaged knee in training) all the internationalists who had been playing for their various countries came back unscathed. However, Peter Lovenkrands was still injured meaning the side that demolished Dunfermline (ten days before) took to the field on a lovely autumnal night in front of nearly 49,000 fans. Motherwell manager Terry Butcher, entering the Main Stand to spy on next opponents Hearts, received a special ovation from the fans, as much for his team's defeat of Celtic the night before as for his glittering career at Ibrox.

From the first whistle, the Rangers players looked up for it. Sweeping attacks down the right wing carved open the Hearts defence some 6 or 7 times in the opening 15 minutes but on each occasion the final pass just was not good enough or a defender would intercept with a last-ditch tackle or block a net-bound shot. It was disappointing that all this fine work had not resulted in a breakthrough although Hearts defended as if their lives depended upon it. Rangers' midfield was looking good with Barry Ferguson playing a captain's part, Ricksen sharing the defensive duties and Arteta, the most exciting player on the pitch. Meanwhile, at the back, Craig Moore was having his best game for sometime, taking care of the league's top scorer Mark de Vries, the huge Dutch striker who had started his Tynecastle career spectacularly by scoring 4 against city rivals Hibernian.

Although Hearts, expertly marshalled by ex-Ger Steven Pressley, were defending well, it was not the type of defensive performance that Rangers fans had come to expect from the Edinburgh side in recent seasons. Manager Craig Levein had obviously told his players to attack at every opportunity. However, it was Claudio Caniggia who scored the first goal of the game 5 minutes from half-time and it came from a move similar to so many in the earlier part of the game. This time, though, the cross from the right wing was perfect. Ronald de Boer made space out on the flank by getting past his marker to flight a tremendous ball across the 6 yard line. Caniggia showed bravery and alertness by diving low, getting his head to the ball before the defender who was the wrong side of him. The keeper had little chance from such close range and the Argentinian put Rangers on top of the league. Now it could only be snatched from them in the second-half.

Although Rangers continued to dominate after the break, their performance was not as convincing and Hearts came into the match more as an attacking force. Having said that, any likely danger came from deep crosses to the towering de Vries but, when this was successful on a couple of occasions, his headers went well over the bar - to the relief of the home fans. Hearts kept plugging gamely away gamely and, at no point, did Rangers fans or players feel that the three vital points would be safe until a second goal materialised.

Twelve minutes from time, home nerves were finally settled when the second goal duly arrived, clinching the points for Rangers. Substitute Billy Dodds made a great run down the left and, with only Caniggia in the middle of the box, tried to roll the ball in front of him. Unfortunately, he miskicked the ball ("sclaffed it" as Konterman might have said) and it slid behind Caniggia and the covering Hearts defenders. Fortunately, Shota Arveladze had not been in the box (where he should have been!) and he was simply able to run on to the loose ball as everyone else stood like statues. Rounding keeper Roddie McKenzie, he strolled forward another few yards and then tapped it into the empty net, unchallenged. At that point, Rangers knew they would be top of the pile that night.

Hearts toiled manfully right to the end but it was just before time before Klos had to make his only save of the evening, preventing a header from going over the line. When Mike McCurry's whistle sounded, the cheers from the Rangers crowd showed their delight at being back on top of the league - for the first time since May 2000.

The only drawback had been the injury to de Boer (a suspected broken toe) and a groin injury to Arthur Numan. Both were expected to miss the EUFA Cup match in the Czech Republic the following Tuesday but at least X-rays later proved that de Boer's toe had not been broken. Still, another two injured players had been added to the growing list.

Manager McLeish was obviously pleased with the result. "We are delighted to be at the top but the most important time to be there is after the last game in May." No Rangers fan would have disagreed with that sentiment! This was echoed by match-clincher Shota Arveladze, who said, "This is the first time since I came to the club that we have been top of the league. We have to continue to play well now in order to stay in front. It's a long competition and we know we'll have to work really hard to become champions." Under Alex McLeish, the players would not be allowed do anything else!

The Rangers team: Klos, Muscat, Malcolm, Moore, Numan, Ricksen, Ferguson, de Boer, Arteta, Arveladze and Caniggia.

The top of the table now looked like this:

	P	W	D	L	F	A	PTS
RANGERS	6	5	1	0	18	3	16
CELTIC	6	5	0	1	15	3	15
KILMARNOCK	6	3	2	1	8	8	11
HEARTS	6	2	3	1	10	8	9
DUNFERMLINE	6	3	0	3	11	14	9

Sat. September 14, 2002
LIVINGSTON 0 RANGERS 2
(Ross, Ferguson)
Crowd: 10,003

The following Saturday, Rangers proudly took the field at The City Ground, Livingston as league leaders. Everybody knew that victory here would not be an easy task as, on their last visit, they slumped to a 1-2 defeat. To make the pressure even more intense, Celtic had a home match against Hibs, currently struggling at the bottom end of the table and losing goals like the Titanic shipping water.

Rangers were without de Boer and Numan plus all the usual suspects with the exception of Lovenkrands who, returning from injury, found a place on the bench. The match turned out to be the type that Rangers' fans had suffered all too frequently the season before. It was a game of sweat and tears but no blood and precious little skill. A grim affair as Livingston, going through their worst spell since entering the top flight, tried to overcome the Ibrox side with sheer endeavour and muscle power. All their players scrapped and hustled, attempting to give the superior visitors no time on the ball to do any damage.

Most observers admitted that the turning point in the game came in the 57th minute with the dismissal of Livingston's midfielder Toure-Maman for a rash sliding tackle on Ricksen. His tackle was especially foolish considering the fact that he had been booked for a similar one on Craig Moore. A couple of minutes later, Rangers took the lead.

A typically incisive run through the middle by Barry Ferguson (followed by a defence-splitting pass inside the full back) allowed young Maurice Ross to take a touch with his left foot then, from about 12 yards, crack the ball low and hard past the diving Broto. It was his first goal for the club at any level. Everyone knew then that there was little way back for the home team, reduced to ten men. Nevertheless, it took until 4 minutes from time for the points to be truly safe when a Barry Ferguson penalty increased the lead as he smoothly stroked the ball in the other corner. It was Barry's fourth penalty goal in four attempts that season. He was getting to be quite an expert!

Afterwards, Alex McLeish recognised how tough a struggle the contest had been.

"Livi were fired up. They had their sleeves rolled up and made it extremely tough but we ground it out, and, credit to the players for that. There's no doubt that we've played much better so, to win the game, not being at our best, is a real plus."

So, although Celtic beat a poor Hibs 1-0 at Parkhead, Rangers remained at the top. Another plus was that there were no more injuries so, hopefully, the players could look forward to their UEFA Cup trip to Prague the following week.

Tues. September 17, 2002
VIKTORIA ZIZKOV 2 RANGERS 0
Crowd: 3,427

The following Tuesday saw the start of Rangers' EUFA Cup campaign. If their league programme had started badly with a draw at Rugby Park, then this was a disastrous beginning to their European adventures against the unknowns from Prague, Viktoria Zizkov. Acknowledged as only third best in the city behind Sparta and Slavia, the so-called minnows beat Rangers 2-0, leaving the

Ibrox club with a proverbial mountain to climb. Seemingly, in 46 years of playing in the three European competitions, they had never turned around a two goal deficit from a first leg away defeat.

So, when the match ended with no away goal, Rangers knew that the return leg was going to be a momentous task. Even if their key players were all fit and the side played well, it would only take one slip up to be eliminated at the first hurdle from Europe. The team could be three up (and looking great) but one header, one free-kick or defensive blunder was all it would take and it would be 'mission impossible' in reaching round two.

With 6 players already out injured, fans were hoping that Moore's pulled stomach muscle and Arteta's injury would not prevent them playing in the return leg. To overcome this deficit, it would only be possible if most of the regular stars were available and played to their potential. With the season still in its infancy, the injury 'jinx' was already causing concern amongst the fans.

The Rangers team: Klos, Muscat, Moore, Malcolm, Ross, Ricksen, Ferguson, de Boer, Caniggia, Arveladze and Lovenkrands.

A few days later, it was announced that Director of Football Dick Advocaat would be leaving the club in November. His contract had originally been scheduled to run until the end of the season but, apparently, it had been mutually agreed that it would be better for both parties if an earlier release was negotiated. Advocaat would thus be able to run the Dutch International team full-time, trying to steer them towards qualification for Euro 2004. For their part, Rangers would be saving a huge annual salary that some reckoned to be £1 million a year. This was seen as another example of the new cost cutting strategy and was welcomed by most fans.

So, within a year of being appointed to that new position, the former manager would be gone from Ibrox. Part of his remit seemed to have been the buying and selling of players but with the new transfer windows imposed by FIFA, there were only two spells in the year when this could be done so many fans wondered what else

Dick did to justify his salary. The newspapers were full of gossip about which players Rangers would attempt to move on in January with the opening of the transfer window. Names such as Dodds, Mols, McCann, Numan and even De Boer and Arveladze were being touted by the sporting press. Whatever the truth, Mr Advocaat was not going to be around to supervise any of it.

So, apart from the 5 trophies and, on the whole, more respectable showings in Europe, what was Advocaat's lasting legacy for the club? Most would agree that it was Murray Park, the state-of-the-art training and development centre at Milngavie. This centre was long-overdue and Advocaat not only persuaded David Murray to find the millions needed for building but also helped design the necessary facilities after having inspected the best that the major clubs in England had to offer. Buying big name players for millions was no longer an option for Rangers in the new financial climate so rearing their own Scottish players was a necessity. If Murray Park could start to produce a constant stream of talented youth who would eventually make their way into the first team, then the future of Rangers would be assured and, as a bonus, the Scottish International side might start to blossom again.

Sun. September 21, 2002
RANGERS 3 PARTICK THISTLE 0
(Lovenkrands, de Boer 2)
Crowd: 48,696

After the disappointment of Prague, Rangers returned to league duty with a home match against Partick Thistle. The game turned out to be a stroll in the autumn sun as Gers won the match in a canter, having scored the first goal in just two minutes. A Barry Ferguson free-kick into the box resulted in a scramble from which Ronald de Boer nicked the ball and hit a left foot shot from 8 yards out. Goalkeeper Arthur did well to parry the ball but it was merely knocked out a few yards for the onrushing Lovenkrands to tap into the unguarded goal.

Thereafter, it was the usual Rangers dominance in their quest for a second goal. To Thistle's credit, they were organised and stuck in (sometimes a bit too robustly) but seldom offered a real threat. Indeed, Klos had only one save to make throughout the entire match when he bravely dived at the feet of Mitchell a few minutes after the opening goal. The Firhill side stuck to their task and certainly looked no worse than the other teams who had visited Ibrox since the start of the campaign. Old Firm apart, they looked capable of holding their own with most sides in the season ahead.

In the 27th minute, the match, as a contest, was all over when de Boer scored the second. Maurice Ross, again playing at left-back, aimed a long throw into the box which was not dealt with properly by Thistle's defenders and bounced to the back post where de Boer (showing great awareness and athleticism) executed the perfect overhead kick from 8 yards that entered the bottom corner of the net.

Although Partick never gave up trying to get something out of the game, Arveladze missed a few chances and Arthur made some good stops until the 70th minute when the third goal was scored. This was perhaps the best move of the game. Ross threaded a pass through to Arteta, just inside the Thistle half. The Spaniard collected the ball and moved forward before seeing Lovenkrands making a run down the left wing. A beautifully-weighted pass, just inside the covering full-back, allowed the Dane to run past his marker and take the ball down the wing. His low, hard ball across the face of the goal was met by de Boer, making it look so simple, who angled his body and foot to steer the ball into the net. It emphasised once again the importance of that final ball.

After that, the most noteworthy occurrence was the appearance of substitute Michael Mols, ten minutes from time. The ill-fated Dutch striker received a standing ovation, reminding everyone that he is still the fans' favourite. Unfortunately, those last ten minutes were not long enough to make much of an impact. His manager had some words of encouragement for him afterwards. "Michael was never out of my plans and I know the fans love him. He was down the pecking order a bit but has shown a bigger appetite since Flo left and now needs to get past Arveladze and de Boer." A fit Michael Mols would probably delight the fans more than anything else so he knew he had the best wishes of them all every time he did appear.

Rangers increased their lead at the top to 4 points as it would be the next day before Celtic played their game at Dens Park. A added bonus was the fact that Amoruso returned after a month out with a hamstring injury and Craig Moore had recovered from his injury in Prague. These two players would be vital in the games ahead so hopefully they would remain fit for the rest of the season.

Once again, Mikel Areta excited the fans, showing what a classy player he had already become. He had been sorely missed in Prague a few days earlier and his ability to take defenders on and make incisive passes might just be the vital ingredient in helping to defeat the Czechs in the return leg at Ibrox. Arteta vied with de Boer for 'Man of the Match'. Afterwards, Arteta gave his first press conference without the aid of an interpreter. "People said I might struggle with the Scottish game but I know myself what I can do and I am very at home, even though you don't get much time on the ball. I am not as big as Amoruso but I feel I can handle myself."

Manager McLeish declared himself satisfied with the day's work. "It's fair to say we got a response from the players. We were criticised for our performance, or lack of it, in Prague, and it was deserved. Last Tuesday was frustrating and it was a severe kick up the backside for us. We have to keep applying ourselves game by game, task by task."

The Rangers team: Klos, Muscat, Moore, Amoruso, Ross, Ricksen, Ferguson, Arteta, de Boer, Arveladze and Lovenkrands.

Meanwhile, another live television appearance meant that Rangers' next match (Dundee United at Tannadice) would kick-off at twelve thirty thus giving the league leaders a chance to increase their lead over Celtic to four points. This game would be the start of an 8 day spell that would see the SPL leaders try to overcome a two goal deficit against Viktoria Zizkov at Ibrox on the Thursday before taking on Celtic (away) on the Sunday. Only superlative performances in each of these matches would see Rangers progress in Europe and increase their lead at the top.

Sun. September 28, 2002
DUNDEE UTD 0 RANGERS 3
(Amoruso, Ferguson, Arveladze)
Crowd: 10,013

The first of the hurdles (against Dundee Utd.) would be overcome with ease with most observers believing that this would be the easiest of the three games. From the start, Rangers seized the initiative and looked up for the match, putting thoughts of the two more vital matches on the back burner. During the first twenty minutes they came close to scoring on a number of occasions especially at set pieces when the United defence seemed to be very lax with their marking. Those early warnings went unheeded and, in 23 minutes, Lorenzo Amoruso angled a header into the net from a free-kick, brilliantly whipped in by Mikel Arteta who was having a great game in tandem with his partner Barry Ferguson.

A minute later, some slackness in the Rangers' defence could have presented United with an equaliser but the danger was smothered by Klos whose alertness allowed him to come out and dive at the feet of Scotland striker Steven Thompson. Having watched Arteta create the opening goal of the game, Barry Ferguson (on the stroke of half-time) decided to take action and promptly started and finished the goal that virtually tied up the three points. From just inside his own half, Ferguson looked up and delivered a great ball over the top of the opposition into the path of Ronald de Boer who was running through the inside right channel. The Dutchman caught the ball on the goal-line and turned to face the penalty box. With defenders rushing back frantically to cover their goal, de Boer took a couple of touches and waited patiently for the right moment. Then he slotted an accurate pass into the path of Ferguson (who had run half the length of the park) who met it perfectly, side-footing the ball high into the net.

The second-half was much of a non-event as Rangers did not have to move up a gear to keep control of the game, thinking, no doubt, of the two more important matches ahead of them. The most worrying aspect was that de Boer had limped off to be replaced by Caniggia. Indeed, it was the Argentinian who made the goal that really killed off any hopes of a United come-back. In the 73rd minute, he combined well with Arteta on the right wing before sending over a low, hard cross that was met by Arveladze. Gallacher, in goal, reacted well from close range, saving the initial shot but, as the ball was pushed out, the Georgian striker was first to react and bundled the ball over the line, giving the Rangers goals a neat symmetry in that each department of the side had contributed a goal.

Afterwards, Lorenzo Amoruso was more than pleased with the performance and his goal. "This result was ideal and we played well. I was pleased to get my goal as we had been practising it all week in training. It was a great ball from Mikel and I ran to the bench to celebrate because the gaffer had been winding me and Craig Moore up about not scoring." Bet you would not have done that with Dick Advocaat, Lorenzo! And, as for practising such moves in training - about time too, most fans would have concurred!

The Rangers team: Klos, Muscat, Moore, Amoruso, Ross, Ricksen, Ferguson, Arteta, de Boer, Arveladze and Lovenkrands.

OCTOBER

Thurs. October 3, 2002
RANGERS 3 VIKTORIA ZIZKOV 1
(McCann, de Boer 2)
Crowd: 47,646

The positive mentality demanded by Alex McLeish was in evidence the following Thursday. Not only were the players up for the match so was the crowd of almost 48,000. Unfortunately for Rangers, so too were Viktoria Zizkov. The Czechs surprised most people by being a lot better than they had been given credit for by the Scottish Press. Their players were big, strong, fast and very fit. Not only did they look organised but they were very quick to close Rangers down, making it hard for attacking players like Arteta, de Boer or Lovenkrands to find the space required and threaten their two goal lead. By starting Bert Konterman (for the first time this season) as a holding midfield player, it looked as if Alex McLeish was guarding against the dreaded away goal.

Rangers played very well throughout the match and made plenty of chances but, by the end of the 90 minutes, a 2-0 win meant that extra time had to be played. To be fair, most fans would have settled for that before the start of the match. When Rangers went 3-0 up in the first period everybody thought that the contest was over until the Czechs got their (undeserved) away goal. From then on, despite incredible pressure from Rangers, the visitors held out and when the final whistle sounded, the Rangers players collapsed collectively on the ground, realising that they were out of Europe in the first round.

Afterwards, a devastated Alex McLeish said, "It's obviously a sore one when you see what we squandered, the near things we had and the fact that their keeper had the game of his life. Also, Zizkov worked very hard and they deserve credit for that. Probably the defeat in Prague cost us overall."

The manager had three days to pick-up his players before

further battle against Celtic in the fight to be top of the league.

The Rangers team: Klos, Ricksen, Moore, Amoruso, Numan, Konterman, de Boer, Ferguson, Arteta, Arveladze and Lovenkrands.

Sun. October 6, 2002
CELTIC 3 RANGERS 3
(Arteta, de Boer, Arveladze)
Crowd: 59,027

Tribal hostilities recommenced in the east end of Glasgow on the Sunday. In a typically thrilling 3-3 draw, Rangers emerged the happier camp, hanging on to top spot in the table. The result and performance was a credit to the manager and his players considering the exertions of the previous Thursday which left the side with a few injuries as well as tired legs and minds.

Thankfully, those who had been struggling with injury made it and the only change from the European game was Konterman on the bench and Ross came at right back. Amazingly, it was the away team that started better as Rangers took control of the midfield with some lovely passing and possession play, keeping the action at the Celtic end of the pitch. For the first few minutes, the home side could hardly get a kick, in a constructive sense.

This period of play climaxed with a goal from Old Firm debutant Mikel Arteta. De Boer threaded a clever pass through Celtic defenders to Ricksen (just outside the area) and, as the Dutchman was about to shoot, a tackle saw the ball spin to the edge of the box where Valgaeren deflected it away from goal. The ball was met by Arteta(25 yards out) whose low, accurate shot should really have been saved by keeper Rab Douglas. However, inexplicably, the ball squirmed between his hands and ended up in the net. Joy for the Spaniard and his team-mates, despair for Douglas! Martin O'Neill, with typical understatement, was to say later of his keeper, "It was not his best day".

With this boost, Rangers controlled the match for the first 20 minutes before Celtic began to dominate. However, the home side really only looked dangerous from set pieces, especially free-kicks from just outside the Rangers' penalty box. As their midfield had faded, Rangers were trying to weather the Parkhead storm and reach the break still ahead but it was not to be and, 5 minutes from half-time, Henrik Larsson (who else?) came to the rescue of Celtic when he hit their equaliser.

The Rangers players greeted the half-time whistle with relief. More than relief must have been the emotions coming up the tunnel, though, as the BBC cameras, live, caught some kind of scuffle taking place between Rangers and Celtic players as they made their way to the dressing rooms.

As the sides emerged for the second-half, the main shock for Rangers fans was the presence of Bert Konterman in place of the injured Craig Moore. After only a couple of minutes, Neil McCann also replaced the injured Peter Lovenkrands whose contribution had been limited due to a few heavy challenges by the likes of Sylla, booked following a particularly bad one. In the 55th minute, Celtic took the lead when a corner (that could actually have been a free kick to Rangers) was headed home by Larsson, out-jumping his marker Arthur Numan. The home fans sensed that this was be the beginning of the end for Rangers.

They were not to know that Alex McLeish had instilled a new spirit within the team and they could come back from adversity. Within a minute, it was all square when de Boer headed the equaliser. An Amoruso pass down the left wing was missed by Sylla, marking McCann. The winger ran on to the ball and continued down the wing. Looking up, he flighted a perfect cross into the box and de Boer (who had eluded his marker Balde) headed past the flailing Douglas.

From then on, although Celtic had the majority of possession, the match was reasonably even with Rangers looking dangerous on the break. As ever, Celtic looked more likely to score from set pieces with one such free-kick from Thompson clipping the edge of the crossbar. Then, amazingly, it was Rangers who took the lead yet again with only 15 minutes of the game left. From around 30 yards out, Numan hit a shot that was low, accurate and swerving. Douglas got down but could not hold it. As the ball bounced away from him, Shota Arveladze got to it first and, from a couple of yards, the ball squirted into the Celtic net.

Cue desperate Celtic retaliation as their fans bayed for them to get back on even terms. Like the previous equaliser, this one was not long in coming. Again Rangers fans suggested that it had been Chris Sutton fouling Mo Ross and not vice versa when the referee awarded Celtic another free-kick. From a Thompson punt into the area, the ball bounced a couple of times off Balde and then Ferguson. Konterman should have cleared but he somehow ran beyond the ball, leaving the unmarked Sutton with the easiest of tasks - he simply cracked the ball into the goal from a few yards out.

Thus endeth the scoring but not the action, grit and excitement as both sides created half-chances to win the game. Game, however, seems too tame a word to describe such an event. It had been a gladiatorial battle that might just have kept Caligula happy let alone those English viewers who had tuned in to see the first-ever nationwide BBC broadcast of this most ancient of feuds, in full glory. Alex McLeish opined, "People would have loved it on television. It was a nice, wee relaxed game!"

After the dust settled - and, in the old days, that had been literally - Rangers were certainly the happier in terms of outcome since the draw had allowed them to remain top of the league with their unbeaten record intact. McLeish summed up the fans' views when he said, "My guys displayed a wonderful fighting spirit and they all showed tremendous application. They responded very well after Thursday night's disappointment. I'll probably watch the pictures later and be upset by the defending but it's not a bad result at the end of the day."

Ronald de Boer echoed the thoughts of his manager. "We gave them too much space and when we went ahead late on, maybe if we could have held on a couple of minutes more we could have gone on to take all three points. But they scored the equaliser quite quickly so we are disappointed but from the whole game we are glad we finished with a point. When you consider that we had to go all the way against Zizkov, which took a lot of energy out of us, it was a great effort and we showed a lot of commitment on the pitch."

The Rangers team: Klos, Ross, Moore, Amoruso, Numan, Ricksen, de Boer, Ferguson, Arteta, Arveladze and Lovenkrands.

Due to the continuation of Scotland's Euro 2004 campaign, a two week league break ensued. Amazingly, the whole country's morale seemed to be raised by an unexpected 2-0 win in Iceland followed by a 3-1 win in a friendly against Canada at Easter Road. This reaction suggested how Scotland's fortunes and expectations had declined in the preceding years.

Sat. October 19, 2002
RANGERS 3 MOTHERWELL 0
(Amoruso, Lovenkrands, de Boer)
Crowd: 49,376

In the next league game (against Motherwell at Ibrox), Mo Ross was given the right-back position in preference to Kevin Muscat. Despite confessions from Alex McLeish that Barry Ferguson was toiling with a persistent hip and pelvic injury that might need rest and special exercises to be cured, the skipper was chosen for this match. One player who had not recovered was Shota Arveladze who had been injured playing for Georgia earlier in the week. Veteran Caniggia took his place. The 'Well team was the only side to have beaten Celtic in the league so far but against Rangers, their most potent threat James McFadden was suspended, making the task in hand easier. The quest for all 3 points was made even easier by the fact that within 90 seconds of kick-off Rangers had scored.

Arthur Numan burst forward from the half-way line and fed the ball to Arteta on the left wing, just outside the penalty area. A dangerous cross into the box broke off Caniggia and a defender, just on the six yard line and fell near the lurking Amoruso (who was quicker than his marker to get to the loose ball) who hit it on the turn as if he was born to the manner. So, with the match barely started, Rangers were a goal up and the fans sat back naturally expecting more to follow.

However, it did not pan out that way. The leaders should have scored at least another couple as Lovenkrands and Arteta had goal-bound efforts deflected away by desperate defending before the base of the post stopped another Arteta shot. Meanwhile, Motherwell played their way into the match, defending well, keeping their shape, passing the ball about neatly and generally "showing great commitment" as a manager would have said.

In the second-half, Rangers gained more control and possession with Motherwell in the opposition box even less than during the first 45 minutes. Ricksen, in particular, was getting better and better and dominating the midfield. Despite quite a few chances, the all-important, clinching goal took until the 72nd minute. De Boer took a free kick from near the right corner flag, sending his pass to Arteta just inside the box. The Spaniard ran across the penalty area, using his left foot to control the ball while surrounded by 3 Motherwell defenders. He then wheeled round and took his opponents the other way, this time using his right foot to send an accurate chip into the six yard box. The alert Lovenkrands got between two markers to head flick the ball into the left hand corner of Woods' net.

The main focus of interest for the remainder of the match was the form of perennial favourite Michael Mols. Indeed, he showed some of his old touches and, in a couple of instances, might have scored if a team-mate had noted his run and fed the ball to him. With 15 minutes left, Partridge was sent-off by Alan Freeland for a wild lunge at Ricksen that, thankfully, did not cause any damage. Still, the away side kept their shape and showed great energy in keeping the final score respectable.

In the 90th minute, the third goal was scored by de Boer, Rangers top scorer so far this season. The instigator was Fernando Ricksen who, reaching the half-way line, swung a tremendous 40 yard cross-field pass to Lovenkrands on the left wing. The Dane controlled it instantly, cut into the box and dribbled past one defender. As the next one came towards him he shot at goal. Woods managed to block the shot but the ball spun out to the 6 yard line where de Boer just nicked in ahead of Lovenkrands (who had followed up his own shot) to guide it into the unguarded goal.

The Rangers team: Klos, Ross, Moore, Amoruso, Numan, Ricksen, de Boer, Ferguson, Arteta, Caniggia and Lovenkrands.

Thurs. October 24, 2002
HIBS 2 RANGERS 3
(Townsley og, Caniggia, Lovenkrands)
Crowd: 8,016

Before the next league game, Rangers had some CIS League Cup business to take care of. It was the 'big' teams' first foray in the competition that had given Alex McLeish his first Ibrox trophy. Rangers had been drawn against his old side at Easter Road with the match televised live by Channel 5. Having beaten Hibs 4-2 there earlier in the season, it might have looked a comfortable proposition but since then, the Edinburgh side had strung together 5 consecutive victories and were fifth in the league, just behind city rivals Hearts who many reckoned would finish third in the league.

Injury had already ruled out Craig Moore but a further shock injury rocked the team when Amoruso injured a calf muscle during the warm-up and had to be replaced by Bob Malcolm. So, instead of the normal central defence, Rangers lined up with Konterman partnering Malcolm and if the Gers fans were shivering at kick-off, it was not just because of the torrential rain that had been falling all day in Edinburgh.

As if sensing Rangers' weaker defence, the home side really went at them in the opening 5 minutes. Showing great energy and commitment, they forced the play and Rangers were looking decidedly rocky. It was no surprise when Hibs scored in the 6th minute, having already had a couple of shots at goal.

For the next ten minutes the Light Blues were on the rack as Hibs tried to increase their lead. Then, despite the dreadful conditions, Rangers started to get a grip of midfield, thanks mainly to Ferguson and Ricksen. Mikel Arteta was not looking like himself and was taken off (injured) to be replaced by Stephen Hughes. Still, Rangers were looking more and more like getting that vital goal and it duly arrived in the 22nd minute.

Ricksen sprayed a beautiful pass over the greasy ground inside a defender and on to the path of Ross who had galloped up the right wing. The youngster controlled it and cut back a dangerous low cross that defender Townsley could only slide into, poking it past his own keeper from close range. It was the bit of luck that Rangers needed. However, Townsley's night was to worsen when, three minutes later, he slipped when attempting to clear the ball. Ricksen, who was only a few yards away, showed great presence of mind to get his head to the ball, directing it inside to de Boer. The Dutchman made an instant, subtle pass into the path of Caniggia (who had beaten the offside trap) allowing him to simply chip the ball over the onrushing keeper Colgan. Rangers now looked to have the beating of the home side.

However, once again, things changed in the second-half when a determined and re-energised Hibs came out and, with great fighting spirit, pushed Rangers back. With 17 minutes left, yet another punt into the Rangers' area was knocked down by veteran Mixu Paatelainen to his striking partner O'Connor. He controlled the ball just inside the penalty box, side-stepped Konterman and lashed his shot past Klos. Rangers looked to be in serious trouble at this point.

Understandably, this goal sparked more effort from Rangers who had been sitting back too much. Once again, Ferguson took control of midfield and started more attacking moves. With only 11 minutes left, it was the Ibrox captain who began the move that led to the winning goal. He surged forward and slipped a lovely pass to Caniggia in the centre who turned and ran towards goal. The Argentinian then slid a great ball through the middle into the path of Lovenkrands. The winger, who in truth had done very little all night, made up for a poor game by hitting a first time shot perfectly, low and with pace, into the corner of the net.

Rangers were through to the quarter-finals despite a night of dreadful conditions, a fired-up Hibs and the absence of the 'spine' of the regular side: Moore, Amoruso, Arteta and Arveladze. And, what was their reward for such a good night's work? They were drawn away to Dunfermline (currently third in the league) in the next round, in two weeks time!

Worthy praise came the way of Fernando Ricksen from fellow Dutchman Konterman. "Fernando is playing so well just now. He's learned so much in the last two years and I'm so happy for him. When we played Motherwell last week, they targeted him. He was being kicked and they had several players booked as well as one sent off but Fernando kept his cool and did the same against Hibs." Meanwhile, Ricksen himself admitted to a new found control over his temperament. "There were a lot of tackles coming in but I can't react to them. These things happen and if I do react then it's only bad for the team so it's better to just get on with the game and try to make less of it."

The Rangers team: Klos, Ross, Malcolm, Konterman, Numan, Ricksen, de Boer, Ferguson, Arteta, Caniggia and Lovenkrands.

The next match took place three days later at Ibrox with Kilmarnock the SPL visitors. Killie and Celtic were the only sides to have stopped Rangers winning in the league so far and, presumably, Alex McLeish would have reminded his players of this fact prior to the game. By the end of the match, the headlines would be all about the return of Michael Mols who scored the first two goals and looked more like his pre-injury self. Also generating headlines was two goal skipper and 'Man of the Match' Barry Ferguson. However, most fans recognised the immense but under-rated performance of Fernando Ricksen who had a hand in 5 of the 6 goals.

After 5 minutes Rangers had control of the game when Mols scored the first goal, making it look so simple. Ricksen took a throw-in that found Mols inside the penalty area. With his trademark spin, the Dutch striker lost his marker Dindeleux, and instantly flashed a low shot off the near post and into the net. What a start! After this Lovenkrands and Hughes could have added to the score but for deflections or saves from Marshall in goal. Then, in 14 minutes, came Rangers' best goal of the season so far. Ross collected the ball deep in his own half and sent a pass up the right wing to de Boer, near the half-way line. He controlled it and turned it inside to Ricksen who sides-stepped his marker and sent a perfectly weighted pass down the wing (outside the full back) into the path of de Boer. The Dutchman then outstripped the defenders and, once inside the box, looked up before cutting the ball back in front of Mols (who had peeled off) leaving himself an easy side foot tap in for goal number two. Great work from the two front men but, of course, it had been Ricksen's pass that opened up the defence.

The build-up for the third goal started with a Hughes pass threaded through to the strong-running Ferguson who found de

Boer on the left wing who then cut inside the Killie box. As two defenders (one behind the other) barred his way, he came up with a stroke of genius to create a goal for himself. As he seemingly shaped up for a shot by moving to the right, the defenders moved in the same direction. Then, abruptly, he twisted to his left causing the defenders to do likewise. But, immediately, he changed direction again (too quickly this time for the defenders who must have felt that their legs were in knots) and curled an accurate shot low past the Killie men and into the far corner of the stranded Marshall's goal. It was a sublime piece of skill, reminiscent of Mark Walters at his very best.

Ten minutes from half-time goal number four arrived. Once again, it stemmed from the understanding that Ricksen has forged with Mols. Ricksen, on the right, slipped a lovely pass through to Mols inside the box. With his back to goal, the striker held the ball up and feinted to do one of his famous turns. Instead, he waited for the arrival of his captain who had burst through in support. A simple lay-off saw Ferguson take the ball away from his marker and crash the ball past Marshall to complete a brilliant piece of midfield play.

One minute from half-time, Kilmarnock scored when a free-kick was headed past Klos by Fulton - it was the first league goal Rangers had conceded in 6 matches at Ibrox this season. Still, to compensate, they had just watched perhaps the best 45 minutes of football played by Rangers for quite a few seasons.

The second-half could only be an anti-climax. De Boer was kept in the dressing room with Caniggia taking his place. In the 67th minute, a Ricksen corner was effortlessly headed into the goal by Craig Moore (returning from injury) and, 4 minutes later, Ferguson converted a penalty after ref Willie Young had spotted Kris Boyd elbowing Ricksen in the face as he moved for a Caniggia cross. So Fernando had, inadvertently, 'made' another goal! Despite a few additional chances, no more goals were added to the tally.

It had been an entertaining performance by Rangers against a woeful away team. Despite the absence of Amoruso, Arteta,

Arveladze, McCann, Nerlinger and Ball, Rangers had turned in a scintillating display. The biggest bonus was perhaps the return of Michael Mols, starting his first match under McLeish in 6 months. Mikey's confidence must have been boosted by his two goals as well as his all round play, linking smoothly with his team-mates, holding the ball up well and showing great strength and determination despite some rough treatment from the opposition.

Another bonus was the continued appearance of Maurice Ross who seemed to grow in stature with every match and the re-emergence of young Stephen Hughes whose many fine skillful touches, and shots at goal, had the crowd applauding. The watching Berti Vogts must have taken great heart from seeing these Scots youngsters playing so well alongside Barry Ferguson.

Alex McLeish must also have been heartened by the performance of Mols. The manager claimed, "Everyone linked up well and I was delighted by the partnership of Mols and de Boer. Michael did the sort of things I expect from him. Not just his goals but his link up play and keeping of the ball was also excellent. If he plays this type of football every week then he will have a future at this club." The player himself, while happy about his scoring return to action, was cautious. "My deal with Rangers finishes at the end of this season and who knows what may happen. I feel strong and good but I have to get to the next stage. I have to be involved on a regular basis. It's nice to be back after a holiday." And so say all of us!

The Rangers team: Klos, Ross, Malcolm, Moore, Numan, Ricksen, de Boer, Ferguson, Hughes, Mols and Lovenkrands.

After almost one third of the league programme, Rangers were still the only undefeated side and the top of the table looked like this:

	P	W	D	L	F	A	PTS
RANGERS	12	10	2	0	38	7	32
CELTIC	12	10	1	1	33	8	31
DUNFERMLINE	12	6	1	5	22	25	19
HIBS	12	6	0	6	17	19	18
HEARTS	12	4	5	3	21	17	17

NOVEMBER

Sat. November 2, 2002
DUNDEE 0 RANGERS 3
(Malcolm, Lovenkrands, Moore)
Crowd: 10,124

For Rangers' trip to Dens Park, Lorenzo Amoruso was still out and he had been joined by Maurice Ross (hurt in training) so Kevin Muscat came into the side and Malcolm retained his place in central defence. On the brighter side, Mikel Arteta returned from injury.

Dundee usually give Rangers a torrid time at Dens and this match started in much the same fashion. In the first minute, a long ball through the middle caught out the Gers' defence with Nacho Novo running on to it. Klos had to come out of his area but Novo ran round him and trundled the ball towards the exposed goal. However, great defending from Craig Moore saw the Australian chase back and, with a sliding interception, deflect the ball away from goal. It went straight to Novo but Moore was there again to block for a second time before clearing his lines. It could so easily have been a disastrous start.

Rangers got their act together and started to look dangerous. A corner from the left, taken by Arteta, was met by the head of Moore whose effort crashed off the bar to land at the feet of Bob Malcolm. The young defender calmly swept the ball into the net from 6 yards out. This 30th minute goal might have been seen as the turning point of the match but that, in fact, came a minute before the interval when referee Ian Fyfe, had no choice but to send off Dundee central defender Khizanishvili for a professional foul on Ronald de Boer.

Five minutes into the second-half and the game was effectively over when Rangers scored the second, crucial goal. Arteta took a pass on the right wing and made a run to the bye line. Peter Lovenkrands, who had gained a yard on his marker to get in front of him, met the delivery and cleverly headed the ball to his left into the net.

Rangers, with the extra man, dominated the rest of the match (as you would expect) but they had to wait until 11 minutes from time to notch the third goal. Again this came from an Arteta corner whose cross was headed down and forcefully into the goal by Moore from about 6 yards out. For once, Speroni could do nothing about it. Nobody was more delighted than the big Aussie as it was his second goal in successive matches.

After the match, another happy Rangers defender was Bob Malcolm who, having to compete with Moore and Amoruso, was realistic about his chances of regular games. "I could have moved in the summer but it was not in my mind to leave Rangers. I know Craig Moore and Lorenzo are going to be first choice but players are always going to get injured and it's up to me to take the chance when it comes along. I just want to play my part." As for his opening goal, he said, "It's so long since I scored that I can't even remember the date but it's a good feeling and a good time to score for Rangers."

It was a creditable result indeed considering the fact that Rangers had been minus Amo, Ross, Ball, Nerlinger, Arveladze, and McCann. 'Man of the Match' Barry Ferguson was also carrying an injury and was substituted in the second half as was Arthur Numan with an ankle knock. The result meant that this was the 8th consecutive match in which Rangers had scored 3 or more goals. Manager McLeish, obviously pleased, said, "When we manage to get in front in games the team is driving on and the experienced players are trying to breed that winning mentality into the younger players. Winning games is always the most important thing but if we can play good football and score goals into the bargain then that is always a bonus." At this point in the season, it was a bonus that the Ibrox fans hoped would continue indefinitely.

The Rangers team: Klos, Muscat, Malcolm, Moore, Numan, Ricksen, de Boer, Ferguson, Arteta, Mols and Lovenkrands.

Thurs. November 7, 2002
DUNFERMLINE 0 RANGERS 1
(Caniggia)
Crowd: 8,415

The three goals per game run ended at the very next hurdle, the CIS quarter-final tie against Dunfermline at East End Park. In the event, Rangers fans were just happy to have won this match and reach yet another semi-final at Hampden. As if jinxed in this competition, both Amoruso and Moore were injured as they had been for the Hibs match in the previous round. Deputising were Malcolm and Konterman - not every fan's ideal partnership! Another blow was the absence of Ronald de Boer, top scorer at Ibrox so far this season. On the brighter side, Arveladze was fit enough to be on the bench.

Overall, it was a poor game with very few chances or goal mouth thrills in the 90 minutes.Dunfermline, probably mindful of their 6-0 thrashing earlier in the season, got stuck in, giving Rangers as little space and time as possible. Even so, Barry Ferguson had another great game chasing and harrying the opposition when they had the ball and spraying passes around in attack.

Arteta was a target for some rough tactics but Fernando Ricksen was possibly Dunfermline Public Enemy Number One! It appeared that every Pars player wanted to have a go at him, maybe in the hope that he would lose his temper and be booked. As it

Picture Gallery

A powerful clearance from George Young.

The inimitable "Slim" Jim Baxter.

The legendary Willie Waddell, in his playing days.

The Premier League Trophy.

Mark Hateley salutes number six of nine-in-a-row.

More Championship success.

The 1990 squad line up following another successful season.

Terry Butcher leads the team in an impromptu celebratory song.

Captain Terry Butcher, manager Graeme Souness and
chairman David Holmes witness the unfurling of another League Flag at Ibrox.

An emotional "King" Richard lifts the League Trophy.

Ibrox from the tunnel.

The kids join in the celebrations.

Super Ally.

Walter Smith celebrates with Jonas Thern.

Treble champs in 1999.

Happy days once more for Gough and his team mates.

A jubilant Walter Smith salutes the fans.

Millenium champions.

Smiling for the cameras . . .

Amoruso cradles the new SPL Trophy in 1999.

The world-famous Ibrox Trophy Room.

Bill Struth presides over The Trophy Room.

The 50th title dream is realised.

turned out, two Dunfermline players were booked for wild tackles on Fernando within the first 15 minutes of the game! Throughout all this, Ricksen admirably kept his cool and refused to get involved, a fact that seemed to rile the home fans who booed his every touch.

In a turgid first half, Rangers came close twice but efforts from Mols and Arteta were saved by keeper Ruitenbeek. Apart from that, there was very little by way of thrills in either penalty box, despite the presence of Bert Konterman!

For a spell half-way through the second period, Dunfermline started to put real pressure on the Rangers' goal and had a strong claim for a penalty when Numan barged into Nicholson. After this, two good saves from Stefan Klos kept the match at 0-0. One save, especially, was worthy of note as a Crawford pile-driver looked net-bound only for the German to get a strong hand to it and knock it away.

Then, as is often the case, Rangers went up the other end of the park and scored what turned out to be the winning goal. Ricksen tried to make progress up the right touchline but Barry Nicholson desperately fouled him. Arteta took the free-kick and Caniggia (on for Mols by now) got ahead of two defenders to head the ball down from just in front of the penalty spot. Ruitenbeek dived to his left, got a hand to the ball but only succeeded in knocking it into the net off his post. With only 11 minutes left, the Pars had very little time to save the match and, as it turned out, did not make any chances and Rangers held on comfortably to ease themselves into the semi-finals.

Perhaps the most delighted player after the game was substitute and match-winner, Claudio Caniggia whose contract was due to expire at the end of the season. He said "Dunfermline bring me luck because I have now scored four times against them this season. I want to start every game but the manager makes the decisions and I won't complain."

The Rangers team: Klos, Ross, Malcolm, Konterman, Numan, Ricksen, Hughes, Ferguson, Arteta, Mols and Lovenkrands.

The following day, the transformation in the career of Fernando Ricksen seemed complete when he was awarded the SPL Player of the Month award for October. After almost two seasons of being vilified and scorned by sections of the press (combined with various misfortunes on and off the pitch), he had matured into a vital component in the Rangers' midfield. Alex McLeish, on arriving at Ibrox, had recognised that a midfield ball-winner with some dig was needed to improve his side. Fernando was given the chance to make the position his own and, from then on, his performances improved by the game.

His temperament, thanks to the constant guidance of his manager, had improved immensely and he was no longer getting involved with opponents. He was breaking down opponents' moves in midfield and surging forward up the right flank, creating chances or having a shot. He also had a quickness about him and the stamina to cover the entire pitch for 90 minutes, without seeming to tire. Testimony to his excellent form might have been the number of wild fouls that were being perpetrated on him now by players who obviously viewed him as a danger to their side. Having Ricksen in such fine form allowed Arteta, Ferguson and de Boer to be the creative force in the Rangers side and might just have saved Alex McLeish forking out big money for a hard-tackling midfielder.

His manager had nothing but admiration for the player. "It's great to see the way Fernando has turned it around. No-one is perfect. We are all human and at the end of the day, he's developed as a person. He is great to work with and very enthusiastic. If you dish it out you have to take it and Fernando has learned that. He's getting older and maturing. He is also a fixture in the Holland team and you don't get to be that unless you're performing and right now he is playing at a very high level."

The next league encounter saw Hibs at Ibrox, having run
Rangers close just a couple of weeks previously in the CIS Cup
clash at Easter Road. Before this match, boss Bobby Williamson
was claiming in most of the papers that the Old Firm sides get the
benefit of refereeing decisions when they play at home. He was
pleading for "fairness", hoping that the referee, Mike McCurry,
would not be intimidated by the Ibrox crowd. Rangers, as usual,
had their injury problems. Although Lorenzo Amoruso came back
into the side after a two week lay-off, Moore was still missing along
with de Boer and Lovenkrands and the usual suspects. In this
game, Rangers fans would see Dr Rangers and Mr Rangers as the
two halves of the match just could not have been more different.

The first-half was definitely preferable and team that played
free-flowing, skillful, exciting, dominating football. Indeed, in the first
ten minutes before the opening goal, they could have scored three
times. The Hibs defence was carved open again and again,
especially down the right wing where Ross and Ricksen (in particular)
were getting to the bye-line, ably abetted by Ferguson and Arteta.
Mols missed a good opportunity as did Arveladze whose effort
could have been the goal of the season.

However, the opener arrived in the 11th minute. Yet another
great passing move down the right wing involving Arveladze,
Ferguson and Ricksen saw the Dutchman clear as he raced for the
bye-line. He swept the ball accurately across the face of the goal
where Michael Mols, from a few yards out, crashed it home via the
underside of the bar. Cue the crowd's special celebrations when
Mols scores.

Further chances followed as Rangers sought to put daylight
between them and Hibs. However, a variety of circumstances kept

the score to just one. Nevertheless, it was inevitable that a second goal would come and, in 35th minutes, it did. In similar fashion to the first goal, Barry Ferguson's precise pass found Ricksen running into space on the right hand side of the penalty box. Instead of spraying the ball across the goal, Fernando had a shot himself. His effort smacked into Colgan who did well but the ball spilled out from the keeper. Caniggia had a go at putting it into the net but failed. All seemed lost as the ball went behind Arveladze but the striker rescued the situation by cutely back-heeling the ball just inside the post from a yard or so out.

Until half-time, Rangers continued to control the match but could not add to their goal tally. Then, right at the interval, the comfortable gap was reduced when McManus scored. Colgan punted the ball upfield from the edge of his area in a seemingly harmless manner. However, Paatelainen outjumped Bob Malcolm to send the ball further down the middle into the Rangers' box. With all the players watching the course of the ball and Klos coming towards it, McManus merely flicked the ball over the keeper and into the net. It was a silly goal to have lost...and from a nothing situation. No wonder most of the 48,000 fans were silent in their amazement. Instead of being 5 or 6 goals ahead, it was 2-1. The expression 'a funny old game' came to mind.

In the second-half, it was Mr Rangers as the team seemed to let Hibs take control. Of course, Rangers' rhythm was not helped by the fact that Amoruso (who had not really looked totally fit from the start) had to go off with a recurrence of his calf injury early-on. Bert Konterman took his place and many fans started to watch through their fingers. Then Arteta (who had looked troubled by a back problem for much of the game) had to be replaced by Hughes, followed by Latapy who came on for Caniggia also suffering from a sore back.

Although Hibs had the best of the second-half, they did not really create clear-cut openings. Indeed, Klos had only one save to make (but what a save!) from a 20 yard Garry O'Connor pile-driver.

Apart from this, the most dangerous thing that happened came via a Rangers player! Luna sent a long punt to the back post and, as Konterman and Paatelainen rose, the ball seemed to be headed backwards for a corner kick. The Hibs players, however, were adamant that it had been a handball with Bert Konterman the culprit. Luna, protesting for a penalty rather too vehemently for the ref's liking, ended up being yellow carded. Despite the visitors' claims later in the press, the television pictures, even in slow motion, were not conclusive.

After this controversy, the game continued as before although, in the last 5 minutes, Rangers almost scored the crucial third goal but spurned 3 other chances, the nearest being a Barry Ferguson free-kick that crashed off the bar.

The Rangers team: Klos, Ross, Malcolm, Amoruso, Numan, Ricksen, Ferguson, Arteta, Caniggia, Mols and Arveladze.

Sat. November 16, 2002
ABERDEEN 2 RANGERS 2
(Numan, Ferguson)
Crowd: 14,915

The next league game was at Pittodrie. Rangers played very well in the first-half, totally outclassing the Dons and should have gone in at half-time with the match well and truly won instead of with just a mere one goal lead. Then, in the second-half, Aberdeen found new spirit and belief and almost won the game.

As usual, injuries played a big part in Rangers' line-up for this vital game. The central defensive partnership of Moore and Amoruso was absent as were the exciting Arteta, Lovenkrands and Caniggia. On the plus side, de Boer returned and long-term casualties McCann and Nerlinger found a place on the bench. In fact, it was the German's first involvement in a squad since the start of the season. Despite a 7-0 thrashing two weeks before at Parkhead, Rangers knew that Aberdeen would pull out all the stops to damage their championship hopes although it certainly dld nol seem to be the case throughout the first 45 minutes.

Before Rangers opened the scoring, quite a few chances were squandered. Finally, in the 24th minute, Rangers actually managed to put the ball in the net. Coming in from the left wing, de Boer, as he reached the penalty area, cut the ball back to the edge of the box where Arthur Numan controlled with his right foot before steering the ball low (through a ruck of defenders) into the bottom right-hand corner of the net. Those of a blue persuasion at Pittodrie looked forward to an avalanche of goals. Instead, more misses reared their ugly heads.

Despite the disappointment of not having finished off the Dons in the first 45 minutes, few Rangers fans in the crowd could have envisaged the turnaround in fortunes that was to take place. Right from the re-start, the Dons played with a new energy, belief and commitment. Darren Young hit a thunderbolt that was net-bound until the diving Klos saved Rangers' skin with a tremendous stop, pushing the ball away for a corner kick. Unfortunately, the reprieve was short-lived as the Dons scored from the resultant corner when a Mike header squirmed into the net between Latapy and the back post.

Things went from bad to worse when Aberdeen took the lead in the 74th minute, thanks to another headed goal and by one of the smallest players on the pitch! Mackie, running in on the back post and totally unmarked, placed a precise header against the balance of Klos into the far corner of the net. Luckily, the Dons didn't have the ascendancy for long as, within 4 minutes, the equaliser arrived from the penalty spot. After all the controversy about penalties in the previous couple of weeks, perhaps it was just as well that this was the proverbial 'stonewaller' that even the most fervent home supporters could not have argued over.

De Boer collected the ball half way inside the opposition half and spotted a Ricksen run as the player surged towards the Dons' box. He then threaded a tremendous pass between two Aberdeen defenders. This took Ricksen into the box and, as he neared the 6 yard line (with only the keeper ahead of him), defender McGuire, sliding in from behind, clicked his ankles to bring him down.

Ice cool Barry Ferguson slotted the penalty kick to the right of the goalkeeper. It was his 8th goal of the season - 6 of them from the penalty spot. How ironic that the one penalty he missed had proved to be the most crucial - the one in Prague against Zizkov with the score at 1-0. As it was, a draw was enough to send Celtic (for the first time in two months) top of the league next day when they beat Partick Thistle 4-0. Rangers fans could only look forward to the Old Firm game at Ibrox (in three weeks time) when they would get the chance to regain that coveted spot at the top.

Alex McLeish best summed up his side's performance. "We played some fantastic stuff in the first half and scored a good goal. But we were wasteful in front of goal and paid for that. The players have been on a great run and deserve credit for that but there is huge pressure on them to win every game. And, sometimes, days like Saturday will happen." Maurice Ross also called it correctly when he said, "We've got to take it on the chin but it was very disappointing not to win after we'd dominated for 45 minutes. We'll just have to redouble our efforts and try to get back on another winning run. But credit to Aberdeen for the way they battled back. They always seem to go that extra mile against us."

Sat. November 23, 2002
RANGERS 3 DUNFERMLINE 0
(McCann, Mols, Arveladze)
Crowd: 48,431

Rangers next match was at home to Dunfermline - their third meeting of the season already! The absence of Maurice Ross (injured in Scotland's midweek 2-0 defeat by Portugal) meant a recall for Australian Kevin Muscat. Another surprise injury victim was Ronald de Boer. While Amoruso, Lovenkrands, Nerlinger and

Ball all remained on the injured list, the latest casualty during the week had been Bert Konterman who was to have key-hole surgery on a knee cartilage that would result in him being out for at least a month. On the other hand, Arteta and Moore returned to the team.

Dunfermline started well enough at Ibrox. It was obvious that they were well organised, had a game plan with every player showing great commitment. Rangers also started well but could not create the chances that might have been expected (given their domination and attacking superiority) mainly due to the hard work of the Dunfermline players and their ability to get the whole team behind the ball when Rangers were in possession. Thus, Rangers found themselves having to play through the entire Dunfermline side when attacking.

Rangers only really created three chances in this half but Ricksen and Arveladze (twice) failed to convert. The second-half started with Rangers driving forward and it was not long before the Pars would be down and out, thanks to a Rangers goal and a Dunfermline sending off. An Arveladze corner on the right saw McCann come short and take control of the ball just inside the junction of the 18 yard box. He turned, unmarked, sending a brilliant curling shot into the goal off the far side post. It was reminiscent of a goal scored by the current Dundee Utd manager Ian McCall at Ibrox when he was a young Ranger, playing with the likes of Ray Wilkins and Mark Hateley.

A couple of minutes later and the visitors knew they had to climb Everest to get a result. Substitute Sean Kilgannon was sent off only minutes after coming on! Muscat, sliding in on him from behind, thankfully missed him but, as the ball flew away and play continued, Kilgannon kicked Muscat as he was on the ground. Referee Underhill had no option but to send him off.

The decisive second goal was not long in arriving. Muscat, driving in towards to box, hit a ten yard pass along the ground to Mols who had his back to goal and a defender, Gus McPherson, right behind him. Mols did his famous dummy and turn, leaving the defender for dead, before smacking a left-foot shot past Stillie. It was what the Ibrox crowd had been hoping for throughout the match and it had come at last.

It had taken Rangers 20 minutes to increase the gap to two goals but, within two minutes, it was three! A typical Arteta attacking run saw him surge between three opponents. He passed at the perfect time to Mols on the right, near the 18 yard line. Mols' first time pass, across the face of the area, saw Arveladze meet it without even breaking his stride and slip the ball home. A sweeping move, from Rangers' half of the field, that needed only two passes and a shot for a goal. Back on top of the league again - well at least for 24 hours before Celtic played their next match - at Livingston. Despite the fact that Rangers remained a point behind their deadly rivals the following day, it was pointed out that this had been Rangers' best start to a league campaign for 35 years.

Alex McLeish was satisfied with the day's work. "I thought we came across with one of our best performances of the season so far. We've had injuries and at times have had to chase games but our work rate and attitude is exceptional." If only most of the injured players could get back to fitness, the Rangers fans could really start to look forward to a happy new year.

The Rangers team: Klos, Muscat, Malcolm, Moore, Numan, Ricksen, Arteta, Ferguson, Arveladze, Mols and McCann.

DECEMBER

Sat. August 3, 2002
HEARTS 0 RANGERS 4
(Ricksen 2, Ferguson, Hughes)
Crowd: 12,156

A tough test awaited Rangers in their next league encounter at Tynecastle. Two changes were made from the previous week's side - de Boer returned in place of Mols (who moved to the bench) and Amoruso teamed up again with Moore at the heart of the defence.

Rangers played well from the beginning and had the home team on the back foot. In fact, for most of the first hour, it seemed a carbon copy of their previous few encounters with the Gorgie Road outfit - total superiority, keeping the opposition away from Klos but missing chance after chance to tie up the game in the first-half. So, in the first 45 minutes Rangers had done everything but score. They had dominated, made plenty of chances and never looked in any trouble with Hearts' top scorer de Vries 'in the pocket' of Amoruso and Klos, a spectator. The only other talking point was the battle between McCann and Hearts right-back Alan Maybury. Both had been booked and it was obvious that this had not cooled their ardour for each other. Indeed, every time McCann received a pass with his back to goal, the young defender came from behind with either a good tackle or a foul. Most fans realised that one (or both) might end up taking an early bath if the fouls and retaliation continued in the second half.

The second period started in a similar fashion with Rangers missing more chances. The breakthrough came when Ricksen netted the opener. Maybury, ahead of McCann at the corner flag, turned with the ball and progressed up the touchline, all the while holding the chasing McCann off by extending his arm across his face. When he turned infield, he used his other arm to hold off the Ranger. Instead of blowing for a foul, Hugh Dallas let play continue. The persistent McCann eventually robbed the Hearts defender and supplied Numan. From the edge of the box, his cross was headed away by McKenna before Ricksen, on the 18 yard line, hit a first time shot that was deflected into the net by Austin McCann

A few minutes later the match was virtually over when Maybury was sent off. Standing just outside his own box, Neil McCann laid a pass off to Barry Ferguson but Maybury, with a late tackle, followed through and caught him with his trailing leg. As McCann went up in the air, everybody knew the consequences and Dallas had no option but to show a second yellow card. Despite being reduced to ten men, Hearts fought on and Rangers continued to miss chances that would seal the points.

The match was finally put beyond Hearts when Austin McCann fouled substitute Michael Mols and gave away a penalty. Barry Ferguson duly added another penalty goal to his tally, sending McKenzie the wrong way.

The third goal came when Arveladze did a nice step-over to beat a defender, reached the by-line and chipped the ball back to the 6 yard line where Ricksen, jumping ahead of his marker, nodded the ball down and just inside the near post. Number four, in injury time, stemmed from another perceptive Ronald de Boer pass. The Dutchman picked out substitute Stephen Hughes on the edge of the box and the youngster controlled the ball before sending an accurate right foot shot across the body of McKenzie whose fingers got a touch but could not prevent the ball entering the net.

The final whistle could not come soon enough for either the Hearts players or their fans. Most spectators realised that the damage could have been so much worse. Despite Ricksen getting the award from the BBC commentators, Barry Ferguson was 'Man of the Match'. He was everywhere - tackling, passing, controlling the play and looking every inch a Rangers captain. Considering the fact that he was not 100% fit and could only train for part of the week, his performance once again had been inspirational. Manager McLeish was in no doubt as to the value of his captain. "I felt that Barry ran the show. It's still the case of wrapping him in cotton wool. He didn't train until last Friday because of the injury he's carrying. I have to rule out resting him because we have massive matches but he is inspirational, his form has been fantastic. I think he's frustrated by the injury but, generally, his spirit has been great and he's happy with the way things have been going just now and the way he's developing as a player."

Ferguson's form, the team in general and the return to the defence of Moore and Amoruso meant that the fans were looking forward to the following Saturday's Old Firm game at Ibrox. A win, preceded by a home win against Livingston on the Wednesday, would see the Ibrox men top the league again.

The Rangers team: Klos, Muscat, Moore, Amoruso, Numan, Ricksen, Ferguson, Arteta, de Boer, Arveladze and McCann.

Wed. December 4, 2002
RANGERS 4 LIVINGSTON 3
(Ferguson, Arveladze 3)
Crowd: 45,992

The Wednesday before the Old Firm meeting at Ibrox saw Rangers play host to Livingston. While most towns around the country were switching on their Christmas lights, Rangers players were switching themselves off - once they went 4-0 up! It was the Dr Rangers / Mr Rangers syndrome again although, it has to be said, this time there was some excuse for it.

The one serious blow to the team selection was the absence of Arteta due to a hamstring injury he had picked-up at Tynecastle so Mols came in to replace him. The better news was that Lovenkrands, Ross and Nerlinger were on the bench, all having recovered from injuries of varying degrees.

Rangers almost got off to the perfect start when, in the first few seconds, a Mols' pass split the defence, leaving Ronald de Boer one on one with goalkeeper Broto, soon to play for Celtic against Rangers. Unfortunately, as on too many occasions, the forward failed to chip the ball over the keeper (or round him) and his shot simply hit off Broto's legs before being scrambled to safety.

Within the next 18 minutes, the Ibrox side were three goals up and Livingston, dead and buried - except most fans had forgotten that, in a previous incarnation, Livi had played in the old Commonwealth Games stadium under the name of Lazarus Thistle. Barry Ferguson started the rout with an expertly taken free-kick (from 25 yards) that bent round the defensive wall. It was gratifying to see that the captain's prowess in this area was growing with every game. Indeed, the hardest part of Ferguson's job was to keep

Lorenzo Amoruso from having a crack at it. The bold Amo seemed to be now resigned to the idea that he was in the vicinity merely as a decoy.

Arveladze, who had shown great movement operating from the right flank to the centre, notched goal number two a couple of minutes later when he buried a Neil McCann cross into the net with a diving, glancing header. Then, on 18 minutes, the same player headed another goal, rising ahead of his marker to net a Ricksen corner from the left. After that, it was obvious that Shota was eager for a hat-trick as, on a few occasions, he had wild shots at goal when it would have been more productive in passing to a better positioned team-mate. The match continued from this point with Rangers playing perhaps their best football of the season but making sure that Livingston posed no threat whatsoever to Klos.

Instead of going up the tunnel 6 or 7 goals ahead, Rangers went in 'only' three up. Still, they had played some great football and the 46,000 fans were more than pleased - apart from the hundred or so Livi fans stuck under the television screen. It was then that the home fans started to speculate who might not re-emerge for the second-half as the manager looked towards Saturday's Old Firm game. But McLeish surprised many by sending out the same players. Within two minutes Arveladze had succeeded in completing his first Rangers' hat-trick with the best goal so far. De Boer took a pass on the right wing and headed for goal. From outside the box, he delivered a perfectly-weighted pass across the edge of the 18 yard line. Mols took two defenders out of the game by dummying the ball as Arveladze ran in behind him. The Georgian transferred the ball from right foot to left while progressing into the box and, from some 16 yards, curled a low left foot shot just inside the post.

Livingston struck what most thought would be only a consolation goal a few minutes later. They were awarded a free-kick and, from 30 yards, substitute Zarate curled a belter round the wall and into the postage stamp area, leaving Klos with no chance.

Thereafter, the match proceeded as before with Rangers spurning chance after chance and Livi looking no more dangerous than before. However, it turned out to be the away side's substitutes who would make their mark. Within a minute, in a breakaway, substitute Barry Wilson finished off a good move by cracking a 20 yard shot in the net and, from then on, it was all downhill - for Rangers!

Fifteen minutes from time ex-Ranger Gary Bollan was sent off for his second bookable offence and that should have signalled the end of the Livi comeback. Instead, it was Rangers who looked like the beaten side. Most of the players seemed to have switched off, thinking that the game was already won. Instead of a victorious thrashing, the Ibrox faithful now consoled themselves with thoughts of a 4-2 victory.

Then, with three minutes to go, Zarate scored a third for the visitors. Suddenly the last couple of minutes became a nerve-wracking ordeal for the home fans as Rangers started to look more and more anxious. Thankfully, any disaster was averted and the whistle went to sighs of relief rather than delight. What had looked like being a record win had ended up being 'a damn close-run thing' as the Duke of Wellington might have said. Further disappointment was the news from Easter Road that Celtic had scored a late winner to stay one point ahead at the top of the table.

Afterwards Alex McLeish was more philosophical about events than the tabloids would have had the fans believe. "It was sloppy stuff in the second half and we switched off at 4-0. How many do you need to put the opposition away?"

A happier Ranger was Shota Arveladze who had missed some sitters in recent games about which he was as philosophical as his boss. "If you don't miss you will never score. If you miss then maybe you will score the next time."

The Rangers team: Klos, Muscat, Moore, Amoruso, Numan, de Boer, Ricksen, Ferguson, McCann, Arveladze and Mols.

Sat. December 7, 2002
RANGERS 3   CELTIC 2
(Moore, de Boer, Mols)
Crowd: 49,874

In the run-up to the Old Firm confrontation at Ibrox, early newspaper talk was of Celtic's striking 'crisis'. Both Sutton and Larsson had missed the match at Easter Road (Sutton with a hip knock and Larsson due to a virus) and the stories circulated that they were 'very doubtful' for the game at Ibrox. Also, a few Celtic players had taken knocks against Hibs and one newspaper even put forward the notion that half the Celtic defence might be missing!

Ronald de Boer added fuel to the already stoked fire when he gave his views on the respective sides. He was only stating what Rangers fans, especially, thought of their team as opposed to Celtic's. "The Old Firm have had quite different styles of play in the past couple of years. We are very much a footballing team whereas Celtic have their own qualities which, in perspective, are very effective. The style they use is different from us but you have to respect both ways of playing as there are many ways in which a team can play productive football."

By match day, Rangers had suffered a major injury blow with the news that Mikel Arteta had torn a hamstring and would be out of action until after the winter break. Meanwhile, the Celtic injury worries came to nothing as they all declared themselves fit to take part in this crunch game, as it was being labelled.

The home fans knew that if their team won, they would leapfrog Celtic to the top of the league and be ahead by two points. As the match began, they were confident but, 18 seconds after kick-off, they began to wonder if they had been deluding themselves! This was how long it took Celtic to score with Sutton claiming the fastest goal in the history of Old Firm games - 114 years of matches! No Rangers player had even touched of the ball before it entered the net. Such a stunned silence from the Rangers fans had not been 'heard' at Ibrox in the ten years since Gary McAllister volleyed Leeds' first minute goal in that famous Champions League encounter.

It had all been ridiculously simple. From kick-off, the ball had been passed back to left-back Laursen who simply sent a huge punt to the edge of the Rangers' penalty box. Unchallenged, Hartson jumped and chested the ball down to Larsson who, in turn, chipped forward to Agathe. From Agathe to Hartson, it ended up being bundled in by Sutton. Rangers should have equalised in the 5th minute. Following a goal mouth scrap, Barry Ferguson headed the ball over the Celtic defenders to Arveladze who was only 6 yards from goal. Agathe, lingering near the post, had played both him and Mols onside. With only keeper Douglas to beat, Arveladze screwed his shot past the post and the Celtic fans behind that goal breathed again.

Ironically, within three minutes, Rangers had equalised. From a Ricksen corner on the left, Moore timed his run perfectly, met the cross a split second before the Celtic keeper (and Amoruso) and saw his header fairly crash into the back of the Celtic net. Rangers then seemed to gain the upper hand and began to play their passing game.

In their best period of the game, they went ahead in the 35th minute. Out on the left touchline, just inside the Celtic half, Mols slipped the ball between two Celtic players into the path of McCann. The winger ran towards the box, cutting in-field. Balde came across to tackle but McCann forced his way past and, from the edge of the box, chipped a perfect cross to the 6 yard line where de Boer, arriving at speed, volleyed the ball high into the net with the side of his foot. The Rangers' celebrations had barely died down, however, when Celtic almost equalised.

From a corner on the left, Hartson out-jumped both substitute Bob Malcolm and Moore but fortunately, Stefan Klos was alert and he tipped the effort over the bar. It was to be the first of what turned out to be match-winning saves from the German. In the 40th minute, Ferguson took a pass from an Amoruso free-kick and sent the ball wide right to Ricksen, just inside the Celtic half. The bold Fernando weaved past two or three Celtic players before sending a pass into the box for Arveladze. Prodding the ball sideways across the area, it hit off Valgaeren before landing in the path of Michael Mols who gleefully smacked it past Douglas from 6 yards. The Rangers legions were delirious. What a turnaround - and all in the first-half!

As expected, with the start of the second-half, Celtic put severe pressure on the Rangers' goal. Rangers just could not keep possession and were giving the ball away very cheaply, allowing Celtic to maintain their pressure and build a head of steam. A Thompson thunderbolt from outside the box was swerving towards the top corner when Klos, at full stretch, dived to his right to tip the ball past for a corner. It might just have been the save of the season! However, Rangers' reprieve was only temporary and, a few minutes later, Celtic did indeed get their second goal when a one-two between Larsson and Hartson ended with the Welshman giving Klos no chance.

The final half-hour was nail-biting stuff for the Rangers fans. Having said that, Klos did not have another save to make and, for all their possession, Celtic failed to create any more good chances. In fact, once Lovenkrands replaced Arveladze, it looked as if Rangers might catch Celtic out with a speedy breakaway. At various points, McCann, de Boer, Lovenkrands and Ricksen motored past their marker into the heart of the Celtic box but their final pass was either poor or non-existent. One more goal would have eased the tension and allow the home fans to breathe a bit easier but it was not to be. With the sound of the final whistle, Rangers were back at the top of the league and Alex McLeish could celebrate a terrific first year in charge at Ibrox. In the calendar year, his side had lost three matches - two in Europe (Rotterdam and Prague) and the other in Livingston, West Lothian. He had confronted Celtic 6 times (winning three and drawing three) lifting two cups in the process. The papers were now talking about Eck having a hex on Martin O'Neill.

Afterwards Craig Moore, obviously pleased by the win and his contribution, said "that was certainly one of the most enjoyable Old Firm games I've played in although I don't know about it being my best performance. But I'm pleased to have played my part in scoring the equaliser in what was a very important win for us. The second half wasn't pretty. It developed into a bit of a battle - we were happy to defend and try and sneak one on the counter-attack. There is a feeling of confidence at the club at the moment, winning games does that, and we're pleased with the way it's going but we must keep focused on the next game. At the moment we are not even talking about winning the league. There are a lot of games to go."

Alex McLeish also praised his defender and the rest of the team. "Craig was outstanding. He is a real threat in the box, the way he times his runs and climbs high. We got an early equaliser which was really important but you have to give the players credit for going at their throats. The character of this team came to the fore." On his record in his year in charge of Rangers, McLeish said "I've improved as a manager in the last year but what's happened hasn't proved anything. The show goes on and I want as much success as possible. My family have been tremendously supportive as have all the staff at the club. We've stuck together whenever there have been adverse results. A lot of people felt that I was a managerial rookie but I felt confident I could do the job."

The Rangers team: Klos, Ross, Moore, Amoruso, Numan, de Boer, Ricksen, Ferguson, McCann, Arveladze and Mols.

With exactly half of the league fixtures played, the top of the table now looked like this:

	P	W	D	L	F	A	PTS
RANGERS	19	16	3	0	59	15	51
CELTIC	19	16	1	2	54	12	49
DUNFERMLINE	19	9	3	7	34	38	30
HEARTS	19	7	6	6	28	29	27
HIBS	19	8	2	9	26	28	26

Rangers' run of three consecutive home matches ended the following Saturday with a game against Dundee United. After that, they would be on the road to play Thistle, Motherwell and Kilmarnock so a 100% Ibrox record was essential. Illness and injury changed the line-up yet again. With Numan out, Muscat filled in at left-back forcing Ricksen to deputise at right-back for the still missing Maurice Ross. McCann and Caniggia were also out of action as well as Arteta. With one exception, this weekend turned out to be a good one for Rangers.

The opening goal came thanks to a stunning free-kick by the skipper. From 25 yards out (with Amoruso lingering as if about to blast the ball), Barry Ferguson bent a wonderful free-kick over the wall and into the keeper's top right-hand corner. Scotland fringe-keeper Paul Gallacher had no chance but, then again, neither would any other keeper as the delivery was so accurate.

It was ten minutes into the second-half before it looked as if Rangers had wrapped up the three points when Barry Ferguson scored his second goal. Young United defender Mark Wilson hesitated when he received a pass practically on the centre spot. Ferguson, who had been the Rangers' best player in the first half, pressurised, tackled then dispossessed him. With no other defender between him and the goalkeeper, Ferguson raced forward. The complication was that, as Ferguson started his run, Ronald de Boer was running back towards his own goal from just inside the opponents' half. Immediately, the linesman flagged but referee Stuart Dougal, quite rightly, waved play on as de Boer was not interfering with play or seeking to gain an advantage. Inside the area, Ferguson steadied himself for a shot and, with a defender ready to tackle, managed to clip his effort past the keeper into the corner of the goal.

That should have been end of contest but, then four minutes later, Ricksen was ordered-off for a foul on Charlie Miller. From post-match comments, it was clear that both Alex McLeish and Tannadice manager Paul Heggarty, who both viewed the incident at close hand, thought that it had been a harsh decision. From then on, former Ibrox favourite Miller was mercilessly booed every time he touched the ball but, strangely enough, this seemed to inspire him and he proceeded to play better than before the incident - another factor that did not endear him to the Ibrox faithful.

So, with half an hour left, Rangers were a man short but had the advantage of a two goal cushion. However, despite their numerical advantage, the away side only had one real chance to score and this was saved by Klos.

Ten minutes from time, the match took another unexpected turn when Jim McIntyre, the United forward, was sent off for aiming a kick at Shota Arveladze. With 4 minutes left, Ferguson completed his first-ever hat-trick for Rangers with a penalty kick. A sweeping move saw Lovenkrands pick up the ball outside the opposition area, turn back and lay-off to substitute Nerlinger. His first-time pass found Arveladze who ran into the box, trying to make an angle for his shot but McCracken tackled clumsily and gave no protest when a penalty was awarded. Ferguson stepped up and cracked the ball to the keeper's right. No wonder the young captain (and the fans) celebrated - it had been a unique hat-trick of brilliant free-kick, solo run with exquisite finish and text book penalty. These goals, plus his all-round game, ensured an undisputed 'Man of the Match' award.

Apart from Ricksen's sending off (and subsequent suspension), it had been a good day's work for Rangers. The situation was even better 24 hours later when Celtic could only draw at Rugby Park and thus trail Rangers by four points in the title race. However, with three difficult away matches to come, players and their fans knew that there was still a long way to go still in the fight for the Championship.

Perhaps the happiest player was Barry Ferguson who said "I'm just happy to have got another three points in the bag. We desperately want to go into the break at the top. It was nice to get a hat-trick but I have to admit I was a bit surprised. But the gaffer has encouraged me to get forward at the right times and as a midfielder you must weigh in with goals. United made it tough but we dug in and got another win. At this stage of the season, that's all that matters."

The Rangers team: Klos, Ricksen, Moore, Amoruso, Muscat, Hughes, de Boer, Ferguson, Lovenkrands, Arveladze and Mols.

By the start of the following week, it seemed safe to say that Fernando Ricksen was the unhappiest man at Ibrox. Due to his disciplinary record, he received a further two match ban on top of the automatic next game ban for his ordering off. This meant that of the four remaining games before the winter break, he would miss three.

Sun. December 22, 2002
PARTICK THISTLE 1 RANGERS 2
(Mols, de Boer)
Crowd: 10,022

For the first of the three vital away matches at Firhill, the injury list had lengthened. Out were: Numan, Ross, Ricksen, Arteta, McCann, Arveladze, in addition to the longer term injured players Konterman and Ball. This led to two youngsters - Andrew Hutton (defender) and Steven McLean (striker) - being involved.

Virtually from the start, Thistle looked organised and hungry for the ball as they harried their high-flying visitors all over the park. In 7 minutes they were rewarded when Alex Burns scored the opening goal. From a neutral point of view, this was exactly what was needed but from the Rangers' viewpoint, the last thing they wanted. Now they had to chase the game against a hard-working, home side with ten men behind the ball whenever Rangers were in possession.

The first half was undeniably forgettable with only Barry

Ferguson showing the necessary commitment, work-rate and guile to possibly salvage the situation. Most of the rest were lamentable, especially Russell Latapy who was taken-off by his manager before half-time. Thistle were content to deny Rangers space, passing the ball about without really looking threatening.

As expected, right from the start of the second-half, Rangers upped their game and were denied an equaliser on three occasions by Kenny Arthur in goal. Then, 20 minutes from the end, Mols made the breakthrough. Muscat, attacking through the centre as the Thistle players retreated, released Caniggia on the right who was just inside the penalty box. Moving towards the bye-line, he crossed to the back post where De Boer, with his back to goal and a defender behind him, brought the ball down with his right foot before flicking it up in the air again and heading to Lovenkrands just outside the area. The Dane then fired a shot that Arthur managed to get both hands to but could not hold before Mols finally managed to thrash it into the goal with his left boot. The tide, previously turning in Rangers' favour, was now in full flow. A couple of minutes later and it threatened to flood Thistle when striker Gerry Britton was sent-off after what seemed like an accidental clash with Muscat in the Thistle penalty area.

(Incidentally, a few days later, Britton received an early Christmas present when the referee Underhill reviewed the video evidence and reduced the red card to yellow. Everyone agreed that justice had been done.)

Most of the fans now knew that Rangers could pull the game out of the fire and take all three points against ten men. With 11 minutes left, the inevitable happened and Rangers scored what proved to be the winning goal. A Caniggia corner on the right found substitute Steven McLean at the back post. The youngster's downward header was deflected away from goal but was met on the half-volley by Ronald de Boer. His low shot went through a couple of defenders before Peter Lovenkrands had a swipe as it neared the goal. Luckily, he missed it and the ball found its way into the net to put Rangers in front. With just over ten minutes left, the match looked over - but not quite.

Rangers had Klos to thank for securing all three points. An attack through the middle saw the defence being cut wide open, leaving Hardie with a clear shot at goal. However, the German came off his line and, getting a hand to the ball, turned it past for a corner. It was probably his only real save of the game...but how vital!

Rangers hung on for the three valuable points, with the home team considering themselves very unlucky. To a certain extent, they were right. They had performed well and fought hard, were organised and committed, denying Rangers the time and space to play their usual flowing game. However, when the statistics are examined, it should be noted that Rangers had 59% of the possession whilst having 16 shots at goal (8 on target) as opposed to the home side's 10 at goal and only 4 on target. But, of course, everybody knows that old saying about statistics and lies!

Michael Mols was probably one of the most relieved of the Rangers players having missed a few chances during the game. He admitted afterwards, "It looked very much like it would be one of those days. Chances to score were very rare and, when that ball came to me, it was a vital moment. You're thinking, 'If I score, we're back in this' but I snatched at it. It's always in your mind then that it's going to be costly and I feared it would be for us. You know that in a battle like yesterday, if you can get one goal to make it 1-1 then the whole team gets a lift and you're in the ascendancy and there's a good chance you'll get a second. So, there were a lot of bad thoughts in my head when I missed that chance. Thankfully, I got another opportunity and I took it. Then Ronald scored and we were just happy to get out with the three points."

The Rangers team: Klos, Hutton, Moore, Amoruso, Muscat, Hughes, Ferguson, Latapy, de Boer, Mols and Lovenkrands.

Thurs. December 26, 2002
MOTHERWELL 1   RANGERS 0
Crowd: 11,234

For the traditional Boxing Day match, Rangers travelled to Motherwell to take on the club at the bottom of the league but the only one (apart from Rangers) that had managed to beat Celtic in the league. If the Thistle clash had almost been 'one of those games' then this contest at Fir Park turned out to be just that. From the previous game, Hughes, Latapy and Hutton were replaced by Malcolm, Caniggia and Ricksen who would serve the other two games of his suspension after this game.

The omens did not bode well as, in the absence of a white Christmas, rain had been teeming down for most of the day. Fir Park had one of the worst playing surface in the top division with the Main Stand side, in parts, looking like a ploughed field. As expected, the home team werte ready for this match right from the start. It looked like they had all been watching a video of the Thistle game and knew what was required. Of course, nobody would have expected anything less of a Terry Butcher team. Although Rangers dominated possession as usual, there were chances at both ends with the better ones coming the way of the home side.

Despite a few chances, Klos had not a real save to make - unlike his opposite number, the young French keeper Dubourdeau. At the end of a fine Rangers' move, Mols was presented with an unchallenged header but, lacking in power and the keeper dived to his left and held the effort. Lovenkrands wasted another chance when he blasted a shot high over the bar from just inside the box. Then the keeper made a great save from Ricksen whose low, 18 yard shot was turned round the post. A few minutes later, Muscat hit a sure fire 'goal' from 12 yards but Dubourdeau fisted it over the bar with his left hand. Despite chances at both ends, it was still 0-0 at the break.

From the start of the second period, Rangers showed an

improvement although still not firing on all cylinders. The bulk of the chances again fell to them but various players could not capitalise.

Ironically, it was the home side that took the lead. A free kick was punted into the Rangers' penalty area and, with the ball still high in the air, Motherwell striker Lehman jumped far too early, barging into the back of Amoruso who was about to go for the descending ball. Although referee Willie Young had an unhindered, close view of the situation, he did not blow for the expected foul. The ball bounced behind both men and Pearson, jumping between Muscat and Moore, headed the ball across to the 6 yard line where McFadden arrived before Klos and prodded it into the net.

After the goal, Rangers threw caution to the wind in an effort to equalise. As a result, quite a few chances were created but none taken due to poor finishing, stout defending and great goalkeeping. A typical 30 yard Amoruso thunderbolt swerved low towards the goal but was pushed away by the keeper. Then a tremendous, sweeping move (full of one touch passing and great movement) saw de Boer flick an exquisite pass, just outside the 6 yard box, into the path of Muscat but, unfortunately, his clever chip did not have enough on it. It would have been one of the goals of the season.

The equaliser looked certain when Lovenkrands got a pass inside the very crowded box and, by transferring the ball to his left foot, made space for a shot. It looked like a winner but a slight deflection took it inches past the post for a corner. Then, in added-on time, a great Lovenkrands cross was met by Billy Dodds, unchallenged towards the back post. His header looked net-bound until Dubourdeau dived to his right and, at full stretch, palmed the ball for another corner. It was the save of the game, winning his side all three points. The young Frenchman was later named 'Man of the Match' with nobody disputing that accolade. After the match, Dirk Lehman admitted that he had fouled Amoruso in the lead up to the winning goal. His manager Terry Butcher admitted, "Dirk said it was a foul. As Lady Luck would have it, it wasn't given."

In truth, Rangers had not played as well as they were capable of doing but they should have at least managed a draw considering the number of squandered chances. It was their first league defeat of the season and, in fact, only their second domestic defeat in the year 2002, the other one coming in May at Livingston. It was also the first time the side had failed to score in 44 domestic matches. With Celtic beating Hearts at Parkhead (thus drawing to within a point), it had not been a happy Boxing Day. Manager McLeish was realistic in his summing-up of the game. "I'm not going to make any excuses for the way we played. We lacked inspiration in certain areas of the field. We were ordinary and I'll be looking for a reaction from my players against Kilmarnock. Our final touch and delivery was poor and we were guilty of careless finishing. We have been on a phenomenal run in the league for a long time but now we must try and start things over again."

The Rangers team: Klos, Malcolm, Moore, Amoruso, Muscat, Ricksen, Ferguson, de Boer, Caniggia, Mols and Lovenkrands.

Sun. December 29, 2002
KILMARNOCK 0 RANGERS 1
(Lovenkrands)
Crowd: 13,396

The following Sunday at Kilmarnock, Alex McLeish got the reaction he had asked for from his players. Right from the whistle, they took control and had the home side on the back foot from the beginning. However, the 1-0 win turned out to be another nervy affair after Rangers had gone ahead as early as the 24th minute. Despite numerous chances to kill the game, Rangers just could not put away a second goal that would have made their trip to Ayrshire so much more comfortable for all concerned.

Despite having the bulk of possession (and ensuring that Kilmarnock did not get to close to Klos), first-half chances were few and far between. When the opening goal arrived, it was a beauty - from inception to finish. De Boer collected the ball in his own half and swivelled round to face the opposition goal. Seeing Peter Lovenkrands making a run out on the left flank, he hit a 50 yard pass into the path of the dynamic Dane who left his marker trailing in his wake. Bearing down on goal, he transferred the ball to his left foot in the area and, from a tight angle, lashed a powerful shot between the diving Marshall and his near post. A clinical finish to match that initial decisive pass. From that point, Rangers controlled the match with even more ease although their slim lead meant that they could never quite be satisfied.

Everyone expected the home side to change their style and tactics after the break and this proved to be the case. Kilmarnock became more aggressive and attack-minded, obviously having decided to give it a go and, if they were to lose in front of their own fans, they would go down fighting. Rangers, it must be said, still had the majority of the possession and, only twice, did Killie come near to getting an equaliser. Meanwhile, with Jefferies men pressing, Rangers were finding more space and Caniggia (on for the injured Arveladze) was exploiting the freedom of the right wing. In the final 20 minutes, Rangers should have put the game well beyond Kilmarnock but there was no more scoring.

When the whistle blew (ending the final league match of year 2002), Rangers were a point ahead of Celtic at the top of the table. It had been quite a turn around from the same time last year when Celtic were so far ahead in the league race that the title had been all but done and dusted. In the meantime, Rangers had won both Scottish and CIS League Cups, played Celtic 6 times (remaining unbeaten) and held the top spot in the SPL. Throughout the whole year, McLeish's Rangers had only lost four matches - all away games. Two had been in Europe with the others being at Livingston and Motherwell. It was certainly an admirable record but most recognised that only the return of the Championship to Ibrox would give McLeish the final seal of approval from the Rangers fans.

After the match, the manager recognised that the side still had work to do in order to maintain its lead at the top. "There's no doubt we were a bit nervy in the second half when we created real chances. We were wasteful. We missed chances and we didn't quite manage to put the game out of Kilmarnock's reach and that's something we will work on this week. We have to do a bit of shooting and heading practice. The players are even more frustrated than I am and that's a positive as far as I'm concerned. Overall, I have to be delighted. The target was to win three points and that is what we achieved."

The Rangers team: Klos, Ross, Moore, Amoruso, Musca, Malcolm, Ferguson, de Boer, Lovenkrands, Mols and Arveladze.

JANUARY 2003

Thurs. January 2, 2003
RANGERS 3 DUNDEE 1
(Ferguson, de Boer, Thompson)
Crowd: 49,112

Even before Hogmanay had dawned, a change would take place in terms of players in and out at Ibrox. It was announced that on New Year's Day, with the re-opening of the transfer window, the saga of Billy Dodds' return to Tannadice would come to an end with him signing for the club that had seen his best years. At the age of 33, he had been out of the picture at Ibrox for over a year but had always done his best whenever called upon - which was not very often. He knew he was returning to a club at the foot of the league (with a relegation battle in hand) but he relished the prospect and vowed to give it his best when he signed a two and a half year contract.

The other part of this transfer deal, with no fee involved, saw young Scottish international striker Steven Thompson move to Ibrox on the same day. The 24 year old would have been out of contract at the end of the season and had already intimated to the Tannadice club that he would not be signing a new contract. By agreeing to let him go at the start of the New Year, Dundee United got what they wanted - Dodds - and Rangers got Thompson. Despite the fact that Thompson had established himself as a favourite of international manager Berti Vogts, the striker still had a lot to prove as his goal scoring record at Tannadice had been nothing to concern opposition fans. However, he was big, strong and a bustling type of hit man and this was a piece of the jigsaw that McLeish and the Rangers fans had been looking for since the club had come under new management. The hope was that by playing in a far superior team (who created more chances), Thompson would show that he was capable of scoring his fair share. He might even get the chance against his former derby rivals, Dundee, before the winter shut down.

Rangers entered 2003 at the top of the league but, as the fans poured into Ibrox for the match against Dundee, they wondered if their happy new year would last for, at least, another 90 minutes, allowing their favourites to go into the winter break still number one. The team which ended the match against Kilmarnock started this one as Arveladze was still injured. Thompson had to be content with a place on the bench.

It was the Rangers captain who broke the deadlock in the 20th minute. Ferguson had looked to be the one player performing at the top of his game when he scored the first goal. De Boer collected the ball deep in midfield and moved up the right, towards the penalty box and then delivered a great pass into the middle of the area for the advancing pair of Caniggia and Ferguson. The ball hit off Caniggia's legs and fell into the path of the strong-running Ferguson who took it forward and chipped past Speroni from the penalty spot. It was the sort of goal that the fans were becoming accustomed to from their captain in the past year.

As per usual, the fans sat back, expecting the game to be killed off. However, only three minutes had elapsed before Dundee managed an unlikely equaliser. Until that point, they had played well, moving the ball about confidently and running cleverly into space without actually threatening. So the goal was certainly a shocker.

This setback merely increased Rangers' efforts although

de Boer missed an absolute sitter. However, his blushes were spared when the same player scored just before the interval. In an exciting, sweeping move, Mols gathered possession just inside the opposition half, managing to shrug off a couple of defenders. His pass to Lovenkrands allowed the Dane to use his speed and run at the goal. Nearing the danger area, he slipped the ball inside to de Boer whose finish this time (from the 18 yard line) would have graced the Nou Camp.

Although Rangers dominated the second period, Dundee continued to play quite well, without looking dangerous. Chances were few and far between. Eventually Alex McLeish substituted Caniggia and gave new signing Steven Thompson a chance to make a name for himself in the final thirty minutes. The early signs were promising as the new striker put himself about, harassing defenders, tackling as well as winning the ball in the air.

Rangers' efforts to get that vital third goal intensified when Michael Mols was replaced with 18 year old striker Steven MacLean. The youngster duly played a part in the killer goal which came ten minutes from the end. Lovenkrands, cutting in from the left wing, sent a pass to MacLean on the 18 yard line. He controlled the ball, turned slightly and delivered a great pass inside the full back and into the path of de Boer. The Dutchman then hit the ball first time across the six yard box where debutant Thompson (getting there before the defenders) expertly tapped it into the net. Scoring on his debut was definitely a bonus and a welcome one at that, avoiding any future concern over when that elusive first goal would materialise. Such headlines would obviously not apply to the new Ibrox striker when the league programme resumed.

With the points tied up, Rangers knew that they would be going into the winter break as league leaders but morale was further boosted when news filtered through from Pittodrie that Aberdeen (having lost 7-0 to Celtic in their previous encounter) had actually drawn 1-1 with the defending champions. So Rangers' lead at the top was increased to three points and maybe it was going to be a happy new year after all!

After the game, the focus was naturally on debutant Steven Thompson who kept a down-to-earth attitude that boded well for his future at Ibrox. "I could not have written a better script. It was great to start my Rangers career. The goal was from the range I like as well and I would not complain if I scored a barrow-load like that. It was a massive confidence-booster for me. All the lads have been very welcoming and I am looking forward to our trip to Dubai so we can bond some more. It takes time to settle in but I just want to get on with it. People will expect me to score goals because I am a striker and I will continue to do my best. Chances will come my way and, hopefully, I'll take them. You don't have to be a brain surgeon to work out you are going to get many chances playing for Rangers. I spoke to Billy Dodds before the game and he wished me all the best and so did Ally McCoist." As most fans would have expected, Dodds also scored on his debut (for Dundee United) the same day so maybe both clubs their transfer decision had been the correct one.

On summing up the squad's performance throughout the first part of the league programme, Alex McLeish said, "We have been tested with injuries and suspensions but they have coped and some have limped to the break. They deserve a rest and my message when they return will be 'look forward now'. Players have put the club before themselves. Peter Lovenkrands has been struggling, Claudio Caniggia toiling with injuries and Craig Moore had a stomach upset. He was nauseous before the game and physically sick during it but still played on."

The Rangers fans expect no less of their heroes.

The Rangers team: Klos, Ross, Moore, Amoruso, Muscat, Malcolm, Ferguson, de Boer, Caniggia, Mols and Lovenkrands.

At the winter break the top of the league looked like this:

	P	W	D	L	F	A	PTS
RANGERS	24	20	3	1	68	18	63
CELTIC	24	19	3	2	63	16	60
HEARTS	24	10	7	7	40	41	37
DUNFERMLINE	23	11	3	9	39	41	36
HIBS	24	10	4	10	36	36	34
KILMARNOCK	24	9	6	9	26	36	33

With the winter break coinciding with the opening of the transfer window, topics discussed in the newspapers included the various clubs' training trips abroad and which players might be coming or going at Ibrox and Parkhead. While Celtic headed for Florida to prepare for the second half of the season, Rangers went to Dubai, hoping that President Bush would not start a war in the region before their friendly match against German Bundesliga side Energie Cottbus had taken place. Combining this training exercise with their search for new players, Rangers invited two players to join them in Dubai.

Former French international left-back Jerome Bonnissel had only 6 months of his Bordeaux contract left and was out of the first team picture while Dan Eggen, veteran Norwegian central defender, was in a similar position with Alaves in Spain. Alex McLeish was looking for defensive cover with the left side a priority in view of both the Arthur Numan situation (he had missed the previous month's match) and the Michael Ball scenario as a date for the Englishman's return was still to be confirmed. With Rangers' finances being in such a parlous state, a loan or a short-term deal was being considered. Apparently, the training exercise went well and both trialists spent the week with Rangers in Dubai, playing against the German team. Reports suggested that Bonnissel, a 'buccaneering' left back, had impressed more with his forays up the left flank and dangerous crosses into the box catching the eye.

ARBROATH 0 RANGERS 3
(Moore, Ferguson, Arveladze)
Crowd: 4,125

At Ibrox, any transfer deals were put on the back-burner and the season re-started with the third round of the Scottish Cup. The holders faced an icy trip up to Arbroath - quite a contrast from their recent desert surroundings in Dubai. As usual, the newspapers tried to angle their reports and stir up some interest in this tie, wondering if a shock 'a la Berwick' might be on the cards. After 36 years, and a few successful cup visits to Berwick since that infamous 1-0 defeat, you would have thought that Celtic's recent and more disastrous cup exit (against Inverness Caley at Parkhead) would be the new benchmark when postulating about cup shocks - but not a bit of it!

Regaled with stories of how tight the pitch would be, how bad the surface could be, how enthusiastic the opposition players were certain to be (trying to emulate Berwick's draw of the previous season) and, inevitably, how a bitter gale-force wind would be blowing in from the North Sea, chilling the spirits of our 'fancy Dan' players! Despite most of the above scenario, Rangers had a comfortable victory, reminding everyone of how far they had come in the past year since that miserable draw at Berwick when too many of the players had, indeed, looked like 'fancy Dans'.

Although fit again, Mikel Arteta was wisely not risked while Steven Thompson and Peter Lovenkrands were out injured. With the strong wind at their backs, Rangers took charge of the match from the start. It was no surprise when skipper Ferguson opened the scoring in 27 minutes. After collecting a McCann corner on the right, he made his way in-field before unleashing a low drive that Shota Arveladze cleverly stepped over, fooling the home keeper who could only dive in vain as the ball entered the goal at his right hand post. If this did not exactly end any Arbroath giant-killing dreams, the second goal, 5 minutes later, surely did.

Again from a corner on the right (taken by Ricksen this time), the ball was floated into the box from where Craig Moore sent a looping header into the top corner of the net. The rest of the match saw Rangers play in a most professional manner, retaining the bulk of possession and ensuring that Arbroath could not mount a come-back.

The contest was over when Arthur Numan made a typical foraging burst down the left flank but infield from his usual beat. Running from his own half, he threaded a lovely pass between two defenders into the path of Arveladze. As the Georgian neared the penalty box, he back-heeled the ball and, spinning, turned the ball on to his other foot before sending a pass-like shot low into the corner of the net. It was a great finish, stemming from that tremendous run by Numan.

The one moment of concern for Rangers came 15 minutes from time when an unfortunate clash of heads between Amoruso and Ricksen saw both leaving the pitch with blood streaming. Amoruso was taken immediately to Ninewells Hospital in Dundee to be examined for concussion while Ricksen had four stitches put in his cut. The news the next day that Amoruso had had 13 stitches inserted in his face (suggesting that Amo's good looks would be only temporarily disfigured) and that he would probably miss at least the next two matches thus intensifying Rangers' efforts to find cover in central defence that had always been one of the main priorities.

'Man of the Match' Ferguson was pleased with his side's efforts. "I think people learned last year how difficult it can be at these grounds after what happened at Berwick Rangers. There was no doubt we got a shock there last year after believing that we just had to walk out and win the game. At Arbroath we applied ourselves correctly and got the job done. The gaffer had stressed to us to try and go out in the first 15 to 20 minutes and get a goal."

The Rangers team: Klos, Ross, Moore, Amoruso, Numan, Ricksen, de Boer, Ferguson, McCann, Mols and Arveladze.

By the start of the following week, Jerome Bonnissel had indeed been added to the Ibrox ranks. With no fee involved, Rangers signed the player until the end of the season with a view to offering him a 2 year contract. Meanwhile, on the Dan Eggen front, matters had stalled due to the fact that his club, Alaves, were now insisting a £40,000 fee from him to buy his way out of his contract. With less than a week until the transfer window closed, Rangers were not giving up on the player but a deal was looked increasingly unlikely. If Rangers eventually won the Championship, it would be with the players now on the books.

Wed. January 29, 2003
HIBS 0   RANGERS 2
(Ferguson, Caniggia)
Crowd: 13,686

The league title race began again with a match against Hibs at Easter Road. This was the third visit this season, having won the first two encounters 4-2 and 3-2. As usual, Rangers had vital players (the likes of Arteta, Amoruso, Lovenkrands, Thompson and Hughes) missing due to injury, a frustrating situation considering the fact that there had been a winter break of a month.

Not unexpectedly, Hibs threw everything at Rangers from the first whistle, intent on gaining revenge for their three 2002/03 defeats by the Ibrox club so far. As ever, this would turn out to be the club's hardest away fixture (after those trips to Parkhead and Pittodrie) and once again, Rangers would need to show all the determination and heart that they had found in the past year under Alex McLeish. Nobody exemplified this better than Barry Ferguson who once again was 'Man of the Match'.

In a scrappy first-half, the Light Blues never really hit their stride as the Easter Road outfit got stuck in, harassed and denied Rangers' creative players any space. Still, for all Hibs' energy and pressure, they failed to create any clear-cut chances

At half-time, there is no doubt that the home team would have been feeling more satisfied with the events of the forty-five. Rangers could only improve - and they did. After 8 minutes of the re-start, Ricksen made a great run up the right wing and passed inside to the supporting de Boer. Just outside the box, de Boer fooled his marker by making a 'Mols' turn and slipped the ball into the path of Barry Ferguson who had surged forward. His run took him into the penalty area where he held off defender Townsley before crashing the ball high into the top right hand corner. It was the type of strike that was fast becoming his trade-mark.

As might be expected, from then on, Hibs battled even fiercely for the equaliser but still could not carve out any real chances and the game was finished as a real contest (6 minutes from time) when Rangers scored their second. Cutting in from the left, McCann hit a pass to Arveladze in the box. With his back to goal, the Georgian cleverly held the ball up and, with perfect timing, cutely back-heeled the ball into the path of McCann who had continued his run and brushed past the full back. Taking the ball in his stride, the winger then sent the ball low across the face of the goal where substitute Caniggia had the easiest of chances, tapping into the empty net from a couple of yards out. Game over but not the drama.

In the final few minutes, Hibs defender Gary Smith was sent off - for the second time this season against Rangers. In fact, it was the fifth Hibs' dismissal in their last four meetings with Rangers at Easter Road. At least this showed that fight and commitment were not aspects lacking in their encounters with the Ibrox club.

Rangers maintained their three point lead at the top over Celtic who also won their (home) match against troubled Dundee United at the foot of the table and just about to sack their manager Paul Hegarty. New man Ian McCall (ex-Rangers player and Falkirk manager) would have to work miracles as his new team was due to meet Celtic again the following week in their CIS semi-final clash at Hampden.

Those in the Rangers' camp were pleased with their return to league action although caution was still the name of the game. Ronald de Boer summed it up: "I think we have proved so far this season we have a good spirit and mentality. We're happy to be three points clear at the moment with thirteen games to go. But we have to remember that there is a long way to go. The good thing is that we are going to get stronger in the next couple of weeks with three or four guys coming back from injury and Jerome Bonnissel added to the squad."

The Rangers team: Klos, Ross, Moore, Malcolm, Numan, Ricksen, de Boer, Ferguson, McCann, Mols and Arveladze.

A couple of days later Dan Eggen, the Norwegian central defender, passed a medical at Murray Park and signed a short-term contract to the end of the season. He was signed ostensibly as cover for Moore or Amoruso (currently injured) but the giant defender saw this as a chance to show Alex McLeish that he was good enough (and fit enough) to be in the Rangers side regardless. He saw the coming months as his chance to win a proper contract.

FEBRUARY

Sat. February 1, 2003
RANGERS 2 ABERDEEN 0
(Mols 2)
Crowd: 49,667

Eggen, nevertheless, was not included in the squad for the first game at Ibrox since the winter break although a place was found on the bench for Bonnissel. A few days ahead of their CIS Cup semi-final against Hearts at Hampden, Rangers could not have wished for tougher opposition (apart from Celtic) than Aberdeen who had drawn with them at Pittodrie when the clubs last met. Since then, they had replaced their manager, the laid-back Ebbe Skovdahl. Another player (Arveladze) was added to the injury list due to a hamstring injury picked-up at Easter Road the previous Wednesday.

On the plus side, the fans were excited at the return of Spanish sensation Mikel Arteta who had not played for a couple of months.

In the last game before the winter break, Aberdeen had done Rangers a favour by taking two points off Celtic so Rangers expected a tough game. Just how tough it was surprised even the most seasoned of Rangers fans with Aberdeen putting on their best performance at Ibrox in years!

From the outset, the visitors' tactics were evident. When their opponents were in possession, Aberdeen had everybody behind the ball and closed Rangers down quickly. Nothing new there then! However, this time, they combined determined and aggressive defending with quick and dangerous breaks at every opportunity. For once, an Aberdeen side had not come to Ibrox just to sit back, defend and hope to keep the score down. Indeed, on 2 occasions, the Dons could have scored but were defied by the quick reactions of Stefan Klos. Then, after a defensive mix-up almost resulted in a goal for the away side, some Bears started to growl.

Thankfully, a few minutes later, it was Rangers who scored the opening goal when Ricksen, on the left following a corner, sent over a right foot cross into the crowded area for Mols, of all people, to rise above the defence and head home despite the attentions of a defender on the goal-line. At half-time, the fans were reasonably happy with what they had witnessed.

The second-half began much the same way as the first with Rangers pressing but failing to increase the gap despite a great shot from de Boer which brought out yet another good stop from the keeper. Aberdeen, nevertheless, continued to play with spirit and never looked out of it. Indeed, their breaks out of defence were increasingly causing the Rangers defence some alarm.

The Rangers fans were becoming restless at the sight of the Dons actually putting pressure on their back four. With 15 minutes left, Tosh darted into the Rangers area, leaving players in his wake, and sent a tremendous swerving shot into the far corner giving Klos no chance. Even the most fervent 'follow-followers' had seen that coming and Rangers looked to be in trouble. Who knows what might have happened if Aberdeen had held on to their draw for more than a couple of minutes? But the fact is that they did not.

In a sweeping move from their own territory, Ferguson passed to de Boer, midway in the Dons' half. He then moved forward and sent a clever pass between two Dons defenders into the path of Claudio Caniggia (a substitute for the tiring Arteta) who was running down the left flank, inside the Dons' penalty area, and heading for the bye-line. But then he turned back sharply (beating Anderson who had slid in to block) and shot at goal. The keeper did well to stop his effort but the ball merely bounced out to Mols who, gleefully, volleyed it into the net off the leg of the defender on the goal-line.

For the final twelve minutes, the game continued much as before. Aberdeen began to surge forward with a new urgency, determined to get something for all their efforts whilst Rangers were looking for number three. The nearest they came was when a Maurice Ross volley was brilliantly saved by Preece. The biggest cheer in that final part of the game came when newcomer Bonnissel made his debut, coming on for Neil McCann. The fans could see promise in the lad as he raced down the left flank, showing not only great pace but the ability to produce dangerous left foot crosses. His coolness and passing also augured well for the rest of the season. With the final whistle went, came the realisation that, next to an Old Firm tussle, an Aberdeen clash was always going to be Rangers' hardest match.

One of the happiest Rangers players at the end of the match was Mikel Arteta, who had played for 68 minutes after being out for two months with a hamstring tear. "It was great to be back. I didn't have any matches with the second team and just went back in for my first game since December 1st and it was hard on the legs. I'm really looking forward to the rest of the season and hope that I can avoid any more injuries."

The Rangers team: Klos, Ross, Malcolm, Moore, Numan, Ricksen, Ferguson, Arteta, McCann, de Boer and Mols.

Tues. February 4, 2003
RANGERS 1   HEARTS 0
(de Boer)
Crowd: 31,609

The following Tuesday, on a bitterly cold night at Hampden, Rangers found Hearts barring their route to a successive CIS Cup Final. Alex McLeish even had the luxury of improving on the eleven that started the previous match against Aberdeen by including a fit-again Lorenzo Amoruso. Rangers had sold out most of their allocation of tickets but unfortunately only a few thousand Hearts fans had made it to Hampden to support their side. The crowd only just nudged 32,000.

However, from the start, it was the blue side of the National Stadium that was treated to some great attacking play. Rangers showed their intent immediately by pressing forward at every opportunity and denying Hearts possession. Indeed, the Edinburgh side could barely string three passes together and made no headway whatsoever in their opponents' half. On the few occasions that they got to within thirty yards of the Rangers' goal, their move was broken up by Amoruso who had begun brilliantly. Not only was he dominant in the air against the giant striker de Vries, his timing and strength in the tackle was winning applause from the fans. Even better was his distribution out of defence which started attacks and kept Hearts on the back foot. He was more than ably assisted by Craig Moore, also looking assured.

In that first-half, Rangers were virtually in total control (with the lion's share of possession) and swept towards the Hearts' goal with great passing and movement that usually originated from Amoruso or Numan, then Ferguson or Arteta. The only thing missing was that the final ball, too often, was not good enough with crosses being over-hit or intercepted by determined defenders. Hearts did well getting their entire team behind the ball when Rangers had possession thus the cup holders had to pass their way through a solid maroon barrier that started at the half-way line.

Then Numan, not for the first time, started a move from defence by driving up the left flank. At the right moment he slid the ball forward to Neil McCann whose pace took him past defender Maybury. For once, his cross to the back post was met by the unlikely figure of Ricksen who elected to send his header square across the face of the goal where fellow Dutchman de Boer headed it simply into the net. As in many games that season so far, Rangers spent the rest of the half trying (and failing) to get that killer second goal. Hearts' manager Craig Levein was no doubt praying for the half-time whistle without seeing any further damage being inflicted on his side. Rangers fans were hoping for a second-half much the same as the first - only with a few more goals.

Unfortunately, that is not how it turned out. Hearts played with even more commitment in the second period as they tried to muscle Rangers out of the game. They did succeed in interrupting the Ibrox side's rhythm and certainly had a greater share of possession in the Rangers' half but they did not really threaten Klos. Mostly, their attacks were broken down well outside the Rangers' area with several efforts coming in the shape of a hopeful punt into the box.

As the match wore on, it became a more towsy affair, as the pundits would say. Hearts' physical approach was allowed to continue by referee Mike McCurry who showed a great deal of leniency. His mercy, though, was short-lived and perhaps ill-advised as the bookings would soon start with Stamp, Ricksen, Arteta and Pressley all being noted. Rangers, though, were still managing to carve out more chances than their opponents and, although the second-half had been a bit of a toil, the result was all that mattered in the end.

Manager McLeish was obviously content with his side's performance in getting to another CIS Cup Final. He summed the match up realistically. "In the first half we really dominated, played some lovely stuff but we were only one goal up and I stressed that to the players at half time. I knew that Hearts would have to show some sort of reaction in the second half. They had a bit more pressure and we couldn't put them away at the other end. The resilience of our defence was good especially when you consider the physical presence of the Hearts team. Craig and Lorenzo started the game very well but the tempo of the whole team was impressive. The speed of the passing from our lads at the back was crucial to that. There was no hesitancy or dwelling on the ball. That allowed us to get going on wave after wave of attacks."

So, Rangers strode on to another final, the first of the season, and awaited the winner of the Celtic/Dundee United clash two days later. Alex McLeish, although barely a year in the job, knew the score. "The expectations at this club are that we win every single game; it's always a must-win situation for the players. We have to be in cup finals at Rangers. That is what the fans expect. That is the pressure that we all should be able to accept and then handle. For the fans, it's all about winning it again this year - and it has to be for us as well."

The Rangers team: Klos, Ross, Moore, Amoruso, Numan, Ricksen, Ferguson, Arteta, de Boer, Mols and McCann.

Sat. February 8, 2003
DUNFERMLINE 1 RANGERS 3
(McCann, Amoruso, Caniggia)
Crowd: 8,754

At East End Park, Alex McLeish only made one alteration to the side that defeated Hearts and, for a change, a voluntary one. Out went Michael Mols and in came fit-again Shota Arveladze. Once the match had started, however, the biggest surprise was the home team's formation and tactics. Normally Jimmy Calderwood was the adventurous type who would send his team out to win matches and have a real go. This time he played it more cautiously with a diamond formation in midfield, at the head of which was Stevie Crawford - the side's top scorer. With the country's third top-scorer withdrawn into midfield, a goal threat was sacrificed to help protect the defence. It soon became apparent that Crawford's remit was to occupy Barry Ferguson's space, preventing him from making runs and spraying passes into the danger area.

During the first-half, this tactic worked well and Fergie was not allowed to exert his usual influence. As a consequence, the Pars had the upper hand for most of the first 45 minutes with Rangers' attack virtually anonymous as the home side piled on the pressure. Just after the half hour mark, Rangers had to make an adjustment in their defence when Maurice Ross pulled a hamstring, later forcing him to withdraw from Scotland's friendly match against the Irish Republic the following Wednesday. Bob Malcolm came on to play in midfield with Ricksen reverting to right-back. This change was almost a turning point in the match as, from then on, Rangers had more of a grip in midfield and, especially in the second-half, took control once they started to play a better brand of football.

Only 4 minutes after that enforced change (having been inferior until that point), it was Rangers who opened the scoring...from a corner kick. Taken short on the right by Arteta, he simply tapped the ball to Neil McCann who sent the ball swirling into the far corner of the net as Arveladze jumped with the keeper, both trying to get to the ball first with neither succeeding. As the teams trooped in at the break, Dunfermline could have been forgiven for feeling hard done by, having dominated the first-half. At this rate it would be another 30 odd years before they managed to beat Rangers!

However, right at the start of the second period, the Pars were level when veteran striker Craig Brewster hit a powerful volley into the net from the edge of the box. This might have been the shock that Rangers needed and, from this point on, they played their best football of the match and took complete control. With this constant pressure, a goal was inevitable - although not from the expected source. McCann was awarded a foul by Hugh Dallas (in 71 minutes) about 22 yards from goal. As with the first goal, Arteta simply touched the ball to the side but this time for Lorenzo Amoruso who was lurking just outside the corner of the box. Normally, the fans in row Z of the stand behind the goal would have been quivering in their boots but, this time, his thundering strike fairly screamed into the postage stamp corner of the net. Amo's unstoppable shot deserved to win any game and, it has to be said, his team-mates probably celebrated as much in amazement as in joy.

From then on, Rangers looked distinctly more comfortable than they had in that first-half, refusing to let the home side fight their way back into the match while showing their superiority in terms of skill. The icing on the cake came in the final minutes when substitute Caniggia scored the third goal. It was the result of Rangers' best move of the game. Ferguson slipped a characteristically incisive pass through to the strong-running McCann whose inch-perfect cross was met on the six yard line by the unmarked Caniggia, ghosting past his marker to nod the ball simply into the gaping net. It was a neat finish to a match-clinching move. Rangers were right to feel satisfied with a good day's work completed in horrible weather conditions on a poor playing surface that denied players the opportunity to show their real skills. It had been a day for rolling up the sleeves and battling for the points and Alex McLeish's side had done this admirably.

Afterwards Neil McCann (who had been involved in all three goals to some extent) was pleased with his contribution. Injury had made it a difficult season so far but he was hoping that the corner had been turned. "The start of the season was a nightmare for me. I was coming in and contributing to goals but I wasn't finding that level of fitness you need. I've now played five games on the bounce and I'm going in the right direction but there is still more to come from me because I'm still getting tired towards the end of matches. Being injured gets you down but you look at the likes of Michael Ball and it puts things in perspective. I was pleased I managed to keep going until the end and set up Claudio Caniggia. That's the mark of a Championship-winning team - when you can get results without playing your best. It's going to be a very exciting run-in to the season and I want to play my part in it all."

McCann's mention of crocked star Michael Ball was opportune as his manager revealed later that the unlucky English defender had been training again for the past month with no ill effects, having been given the all clear to step up his rehabilitation by specialist surgeon Dr Steadman in America. Encouraging noises were now being made and maybe Ball would actually play in a match before the end of the season.

Substitute Bob Malcolm, who had done well during the match, was obviously in a confident frame of mind when he felt able to make a few cheeky comments about Lorenzo Amoruso's ability to take free kicks. He claimed, "The big man was due a turn. He's been so bad in training I think there's only three floodlights still working at Murray Park! He practises a lot but not many go in so I was delighted to see that one hit the net."

The Rangers team: Klos, Ross, Moore, Amoruso, Numan, Ricksen, Ferguson, Arteta, de Boer, Arveladze and McCann.

The next day Celtic returned to three points behind Rangers following a late 2-1 win at home against Livingston. However, Rangers' hopes of winning the title were boosted by the news that their ace striker Henrik Larsson had sustained a double fracture of the jaw that would keep him sidelined for up to 6 weeks, probably missing the two vital matches in March against Rangers - in the league at Parkhead and the CIS Cup Final at Hampden a week later. Although the absence of Larsson was an undoubted handicap for Celtic, many Rangers fans still realised that the team had to do the job of overcoming opposing outfits before seeing if the goal scoring talents of Hartson and Sutton would compensate for the missing Henrik.

The answer to this question was delayed when Celtic's game at Motherwell was postponed the following Saturday due to a frozen pitch. However, this unexpected cancellation gave Rangers the bonus of putting themselves 6 points ahead should they beat Hearts at Ibrox. Thanks to the international friendlies in midweek, Rangers lost two players who had been performing well - Craig Moore (hurt in Australia's win over England) and Neil McCann, injured in Scotland's dismal defeat against Ireland at Hampden. Also still out was Maurice Ross who had damaged a hamstring the week before at Dunfermline. To replace them, in came Muscat, Malcolm and Caniggia.

Bearing in mind the recent close match in the CIS Cup semi-final, the fans were expecting a tough game as Hearts would, naturally, be out to avenge that Hampden defeat. And that was indeed the case! As with so many of the visiting sides at Ibrox, Hearts seemed to have every man fighting for every ball, denying the Rangers' players the space and time for their fluent style of football. The 'commitment' of the Hearts players might be seen in the fact that they ended the game with 6 players booked, including every defender!

During the first half, Barry Ferguson was stamping his authority on the game as per usual but, even more heartening, was the fact that Mikel Arteta was looking more like his old self after a couple of months on the sidelines. Obviously it might take him a run of a few more games to get back his touch and rhythm, but the signs were there - not good news for the opposition. However, despite all the creative attacking play from midfield, too often the final pass or shot was disappointing and it looked as if the fans were in for another one of those matches where Rangers just could not convert their obvious superiority into goals.

Nevertheless, Rangers continued trying to break down the stubborn Hearts' defence although it took until 5 minutes from half-time before this actually happened. A run by Arteta was stopped by foul means out on the left touchline, maybe 30 yards from goal. The Spaniard took the free-kick himself, hitting a vicious in-swinging cross into the box with his right foot. As a clutch of players jumped to make contact, it was the unlucky Scott Severin whose head diverted the ball backwards, into his own goal.

The second-half continued in the same vein as the first with Rangers looking for a second goal to kill off the opposition. Where have we heard that before? Rangers continued to play some excellent, skillful, attacking football but the killer final pass or finish was missing. Although Hearts had slightly more possession than in the first-half, they were not really causing any problems, unlike, say, Aberdeen a couple of weeks earlier. Still, with only a one goal lead, the longer it remained, the more nervous the Rangers players and fans became. Their apprehension was justified as this game still had one stunning moment left that occurred in injury time with only seconds of the match remaining.

A Hearts' free-kick, just outside the centre circle, was punted deep into the box. By now, of course, the visitors had gambled everything and had 4 guys playing up front, one of whom was giant central defender Kevin McKenna. As a crowd of players jumped for the ball, it landed outside the 6 yard box and a scramble ensued with Amoruso, in the thick of things it, trying to get the ball away. As luck would have it, the ball squirted out to the side to Hearts' top striker de Vries. As he hit what would have been a certain equaliser, Amoruso, like a soldier throwing himself on a grenade, leapt and blocked it with his legs. The ball was then cleared to safety by Muscat and the whistle sounded for time up. That was how close Rangers had come to throwing away two invaluable points in the championship race. Amoruso was named 'Man of the Match' for his all-round brilliant display which included, of course, that match-winning tackle.

After the game, it emerged that, apparently, at both half-time and full-time, the Rangers players had engaged in heated arguments so much that the manager did not have to comment on where they had gone wrong. Alex McLeish saw this as a good sign. The fact that they were annoyed (with themselves and each other) for not killing the game, certainly confirmed the team spirit in the dressing room. As McLeish admitted, "They were battling with each other in the dressing room. I couldn't get a word in edgeways. That's fine by me. It shows they have a passion for their football and the club."

The Rangers team: Klos, Muscat, Malcolm, Amoruso, Numan, Ricksen, Ferguson, Arteta, Caniggia, Mols and de Boer.

The following week, in the run-up to the Scottish Cup tie away to Ayr United, most of the talk was about the players possibly leaving Ibrox in the summer. The good news was that Peter Lovenkrands seemed ready, at last, to sign an extension to his contract that had been the subject of negotiation for months. On the down side, Arthur Numan admitted that when his contract expired in the summer, he would not be staying at the club. Due to the financial climate, Rangers, like most clubs, had to cut their costs, the main element in this being the wage bill. Rangers had offered Numan a one year extension but (according to reports) with a massive reduction in his basic wage - reputedly £1 million a year. The club had offered him a much lower basic with bonuses for the number of matches played and other incentives. Numan decided that this drop in his income would be too great and opted not to accept the club's offer. So, after five years, he would be leaving in the summer.

Sat. February 22, 2003
AYR UTD 0 RANGERS 1
(de Boer)
Crowd: 9,608

On the Saturday, Rangers faced a tricky Scottish Cup tie with Ayr at Somerset Park minus Fernando Ricksen who had been suffering from flu. To balance that, Craig Moore returned after missing out the previous week. Still injured was Maurice Ross. The match turned out to be yet another one of those nervous affairs when missed chances meant that Rangers, despite their domination and superiority, were just one blunder away from disaster.

Rangers suffered a blow as early as the 21st minute when Arteta twisted his ankle on the poor playing surface and had to be replaced by Stephen Hughes. Until then, Rangers had controlled the play with the home team making little headway in threatening Klos' goal. The half continued with Rangers in complete control but failing to make many openings let alone actually score the decisive goal. Even the Ayr fans in the capacity 10,000 crowd must have thought that it was only a matter of time before their side fell behind.

Ayr manager Campbell Money must have read some stirring Burns to his players during the interval because in the second-half they were more in the game with the home side gaining greater possession and playing more passes. As the game wore on, with Rangers knowing that one slip could be calamitous, the best player on the park finally made his class tell and scored the decisive goal. Just 12 minutes from full time, Ronald de Boer netted his 15th of the season. Muscat sent a ball up the right hand channel that substitute Stephen Thompson did well to chase. Showing characteristic energy and enthusiasm, Thompson harried an opponent and gained possession. By now, the ball was right out at the touchline and the striker took on defender Lovering. From being seemingly boxed in by a couple of Ayr defenders, Thompson managed to gain that extra yard away from his immediate opponent, allowing him to swing over a dangerous cross - normally the type that he would have been supplied with. De Boer, lurking around the penalty spot, out-jumped his marker (having leapt early) and, appearing to hang in the air as the ball came to him, simply nodded it down, just inside the right hand post and against the balance of the keeper.

Ironically, now that Rangers had at last taken the lead, instead of looking more comfortable, they began to look more vulnerable as sloppy play crept into their game. For the final ten minutes, Ayr threw caution to the wind and had a real go. Having said this, the only two real chances they made came in the last five minutes and were caused by Rangers' errors. Klos rescued his team-mates the first time and, a wild blast over the bar by Grady, defused the second opportunity.

Rangers had sneaked somewhat uneasily into the quarter-final draw and, once again, missed chances could have cost them dearly. Afterwards, Alex McLeish conceded that his side hadn't played to their normal standards. "We made a few chances but it wasn't our best performance. In front of goal we were wasteful. We got into some great positions during the match but just couldn't put them away. We were in control but while it's 0-0, you're always only one slip away from an upset." On his verbal spat with Ronald de Boer, he said, "I thought Ronald had started slowly and we had a wee exchange midway through the first half. I think he was a bit angry. He got himself going and went on to have a great game. He is real quality. His touch and movement in those conditions were superb."

The other talked about 'spat' after the game was of a different kind. Ayr striker and (alleged) Celtic fan James Grady claimed that Lorenzo Amoruso had spat on him during the match after a tussle between them.

The Rangers team: Klos, Muscat, Moore, Amoruso, Numan, Malcolm, Ferguson, Arteta, McCann, de Boer and Arveladze.

By Monday, Amoruso was denying that he had deliberately spat at his opponent while Grady maintained the opposite point of view. The SFA Video Panel was called into action and that body would eventually decide Amoruso's innocence or guilt. If found guilty, a minimum suspension of two matches would be the customary punishment - not something that would be welcomed by Rangers at this crucial part of the season.

In Monday's draw for the Scottish Cup quarter-finals, Rangers were yet again drawn away, this time to the winner of the Hibs v Dunfermline replay. It had been over a year since Rangers had a home draw in any domestic cup competition. In the CIS Cup, Rangers had already beaten both teams away on their way to the final as well as beating both teams twice away in the league. This would be the fourth time this season that the Rangers would visit whichever side won the replay. It was also the only all-Premier league clash of the draw with both teams the only sides left, apart from the Old Firm, who were in the top six of the league table! If Rangers were to win the Treble, they were going to have to do it the hard way.

By the Thursday, the Video Review Panel had decided that Amoruso, indeed, had a case to answer and he would appear later in March to answer the allegations before the SFA Disciplinary Committee. Should he be found guilty, a 4 game ban (thanks to his accumulated points total) was apparently the punishment awaiting him! That evening, Celtic won through to the quarter-finals of the UEFA Cup to find Liverpool their next obstacle in the competition. As Martin O'Neill acknowledged, this, for once, might just be seen as good news for Rangers as Celtic would be playing them in a vital league match at Parkhead on Saturday 8th March, followed by Liverpool at home on the Thursday before the Old Firm CIS Cup Final at Hampden (Sunday) followed by a trip to Liverpool the following Thursday. With 4 crucial games in the space of 12 days, the pressure would really be on Celtic. Depending on results, this could be their best season since the Lisbon Lions of 1967!

MARCH

Sun. March 2, 2003
LIVINGSTON 1 RANGERS 2
(Amoruso, Arveladze)
Crowd: 10,004

For Rangers' trip to Livingston, one of only two domestic games lost since the arrival of Alex McLeish, changes had to be made due to the usual injury situation. Out were Numan and de Boer while Mikel Arteta had at least recovered from his injury sustained at Ayr. Jerome Bonnissel was given his first start while Muscat kept the other full back berth with Ross still unavailable. With Rangers' next match the Old Firm game at Celtic Park, it was vital that no points were dropped.

The game began comfortably for Rangers with the midfield taking control and the defence looking steady when the home side were in range of Stefan Klos. Nothing much happened of note until the opening goal which arrived in the 8th minute. Arteta took a corner from the right that found Lorenzo Amoruso leaping powerfully on the 6 yard line to bullet a header high into the centre of the goal with keeper Alan Main well beaten. Then, in the 13th minute, a poor offside decision cost Rangers a legitimate goal - not for the first time that season. Luckily, for the official, the second Rangers' goal was only delayed by a couple of minutes.

Ricksen won a tackle just inside his own half and the ball went to Arteta who beat his opponent and set off on a runs towards the Livingston goal. As he moved forward , he veered left and, from outside the box, passed to McCann on the wing. His subsequent, brilliant cross had real pace and went between two defenders and their keeper to be met by the diving Arveladze, running from the back post to nod simply into the net. With only 16 minutes on the clock, Rangers were two up and coasting. In fact, so comfortable were the visitors that it was not until the 40th minute that Livi made their first real chance of the match when a cross from the left found

Lovell at the back post but he miscued his shot and Klos saved with ease.

Into the second-half and, in the 53rd minute, Rangers had another chance when a tremendous pass from Ferguson found Arveladze running into the 6 yard box, having beaten the offside trap. The striker's cute flick, however, hit off the keeper and was cleared by a defender before it could reach the goal.

Ironically, the next great chance fell to Livingston as Zarate chased a cross into the box but Moore, who was there ahead of him, whacked the ball away. As the striker had gone down just before this, the referee decided that he had been tripped by Fernando Ricksen, running behind the forward. Replays were inconclusive but seemed to suggest that if Ricksen had caught the heels of Zarate it had been entirely accidental. Zarate took the spot kick himself and hit the ball straight down the middle. Klos dived to his right but, luckily for him, his legs managed to divert he ball away and it was eventually cleared upfield to safety. Maybe justice had been done after all.

The game continued as before with Rangers looking like the more likely side. After another chance had been spurned, however, the home side swept upfield. In the penalty area, on the left, Zarate was confronted by Craig Moore. The forward managed to get a vital half yard on the defender and clipped over a head high cross for Dadi (getting across his marker Jerome Bonnissel) to head in from a few yards out. It was a silly goal to lose with virtually the last kick of the ball. Still, another tricky away fixture had been successfully negotiated to keep Rangers 6 points ahead with only 9 matches of the campaign left.

'Man of the Match' Lorenzo Amoruso suffered a broken nose after a challenge with Eugene Dadi but shrugged it aside and confirmed that it would not stop him playing against Celtic in the next game. "My nose had already been broken in the UEFA Cup this season. We fixed it as best we could but it took another knock. We will wait until the end of the season now and see what we can do.

As for the Celtic match, it's a big, big game for us because it could be the game that gives us a big step forward to winning the league."

The Rangers team: Klos, Muscat, Moore, Amoruso, Bonnissel, Ricksen, Ferguson, Arteta, Mols, Arveladze and McCann.

Sat. March 8, 2003
CELTIC 1   RANGERS 0
Crowd: 58,787

For the vital Parkhead match, Rangers would be without the two influential Dutchmen who had missed the Livingston game - de Boer and Numan who had failed to recover from their injuries. Bonnissel was given his Old Firm debut and Peter Lovenkrands replaced Michael Mols from the previous game. Maurice Ross had, at least, recovered from his hamstring injury and he replaced Kevin Muscat who still had to feature in an Old Firm match, leading to speculation that Alex McLeish perhaps doubted the Australian's temperament for such a confrontation. Naturally, Rangers' rivals had fewer injury problems, being at full strength, apart from the still-injured Henrik Larsson.

Unusually, some amusement was caused before the game by a banner draped over the front of the Rangers' section of the stand that read 'Martin, we don't want to be here either.' The fans may have been alluding to all the furore about Mr O'Neill's new rolling contract but, by the end of the match, it could have been taken more literally after the disappointing Rangers' display.

The game started at the usual frantic pace with both sides nervous of making mistakes. Strangely, it was Rangers who seemed marginally more confident and they gained the upper hand in terms of possession. However,despite some neat midfield play (mainly from Arteta and Ferguson), they failed to create even a half chance thanks to a poor final ball or their strikers' inability to shake of the physical presence of Celtic's three strong men at the back. Gradually, Celtic began exerting some pressure in the opposition half of the field although they, too, failed to find an end product with Hartson missing a real chance from close-in.

Meanwhile, Rangers managed to threaten and a brilliant, sweeping move up the left flank saw Bonnissel find Arveladze (with his back to goal inside the box) who pushed the ball back to Arteta, just outside the area. The Spaniard hit the ball well past the defenders in front of him but, unfortunately, his effort screamed just inches past of Douglas' right hand post. This was Rangers' best effort in an unproductive first-half.

In the second-half, with renewed vigour, Celtic pounded the Rangers' goal. First Hartson missed a sitter that must have left him thinking that this just was not going to be his day. As usual, Celtic's main threat came from set pieces. As Amoruso was shepherding a bouncing ball behind for a goal kick, Sutton barged into his back, knocking him and the ball over the line. Instead of a foul, the referee gave a corner. From the resultant kick, Ross missed the ball and Hartson, unmarked, found himself with a free header on the 6 yard line. Luckily his effort went well wide of Klos' right hand post.

Then Rangers had their first shot on target. A brilliant pass from Arteta, using the pace of Lovenkrands, sent the Dane into the Celtic box with one defender ahead of him. With no support and from an acute angle, he fired a low shot that the diving Douglas managed to collect comfortably. This was only a brief respite, however, from the Celtic attacks and, ironically in a counter-attack, the home side managed to open the scoring in the 57th minute.

Arteta had surged deep into the Celtic half in a promising attacking move but, just outside the box, he was tackled by Valgaeren. The loose ball found its way to Lennon then Thompson. Craig Moore moved forward to close him down, leaving Hartson unmarked. Thompson then flighted a clever ball into the box (where Sutton was his target) with Amoruso tracking back to defend and Bonnissel behind the English striker. Nevertheless, it was Sutton who won the header, directing the ball down to the still unmarked Hartson. With plenty of time, he chested the ball down and smashed an unstoppable shot past Klos from 10 yards and thus obliterating the memory of his two other earlier misses.

After that, Rangers gained more and more ground as Celtic seemed content to hit on the break and Alex McLeish replaced Arteta and Bonnissel with two more attackers, Thompson and Caniggia. Rangers were having the best of the possession but it was not resulting in the creation of any real chances. Then, with the game drifting away, there was a final thrilling moment. A free-kick, well outside the Celtic box, was touched to the side for Amoruso to have a shot. His thunderous drive went past the Celtic wall and was bound for goal when Douglas, diving to his right, managed to get both hands to it and palm away to safety. If it had proved to be a last gasp equaliser then it would have been an injustice to Celtic.

For once, only the most biased of Rangers' fans could complain about the result. Celtic had looked to be the hungrier side and made the better chances. The referee, conditions or plain bad luck could not be blamed. It had just been a bad day at the office, as Ricky Gervais might have said. Ironically, statistics showed later that Rangers had slightly more possession than Celtic, had only one shot fewer at goal but more shots on target. But thanks to that most important of all statistics, the goal, Celtic found themselves only 3 points behind with a game in hand - against Motherwell at Fir Park, a venue where they had lost at earlier in the season.

As for Rangers, they had only a week to suffer before trying to rectify matters with a victory in the final of the CIS Cup. It was obvious, though, that the manager had been hurt by the lack of quality in his players' performance, resulting in his first defeat in an Old Firm match. McLeish said, "People can try and prepare you for losing but it's different when you're at the centre of it. You know that there is going to be a barrage of criticism. If you win, you're great and if you lose you're a dud - that's the bottom line with Old Firm games. I've never liked losing and at the cutting edge of working for Rangers, when you lose against your biggest rivals, you appreciate how hard it is to take."

Mikel Arteta, playing in only his second Old Firm game, was as disappointed as his manager. "I don't think there was a great deal between the teams. They had more corners and free-kicks and, of course, they scored a goal but that was about it. We just have to accept that defeat and move on. We still have a great chance to beat them in the CIS Cup Final and make up for that slip. People remember trophies and we are desperate to win that one. In a way, the league defeat will inspire the team on Sunday. The crowd will be split, the atmosphere will be fantastic and it will be an incredible experience."

At least Rangers, after the disappointment of losing at Parkhead, had the consolation of knowing that they were still top of the league and that the final Old Firm match of the season would be at Ibrox. That could still turn out to be the league decider.

The Rangers team: Klos, Ross, Moore, Amoruso, Bonnissel, Ricksen, Ferguson, Arteta, Arveladze, Lovenkrands and McCann.

The CIS Cup Final
Sun. March 16, 2003
CELTIC 1   RANGERS 2
(Caniggia, Lovenkrands)
Crowd: 52,000

The biggest surprise for the first cup final of the season was the fact that the newly-laid Hampden turf was bathed in sunshine with no wind or rain to spoil the prospect of a great game. All the pre-match talk of Celtic giving greater importance to their forthcoming second leg UEFA tie at Anfield was shown to be nonsense when Martin O'Neill fielded his strongest side, apart from the injured Agathe. More of a surprise was Alex McLeish's line up. With Arthur Numan still injured, Jerome Bonnissel continued at left back while Ross dropped to the bench, allowing Fernando Ricksen to play at right back. Re-instated were Caniggia and Mols with a fit again Ronald de Boer coming back into the team, to play behind them.

Although Celtic started the game more brightly, Rangers began to get more possession and take control of what was turning out to be an enthralling and even match with both sides showing the usual Old Firm commitment. Then Rangers scored in 23 minutes. Ricksen started the move with a cross-field pass to Barry Ferguson who then prodded forward to Ronald de Boer. The Dutchman did one of his familiar turns (that took him away from his marker Neil Lennon) before threading a perfect pass between Mjallby and Smith for Lovenkrands. Rab Douglas left his goal to narrow the angle at the corner of his 6 yard box and succeeded in partially blocking Lovenkrands' effort. However, the ball trundled across the 6 yard line where first Mols and then Valgaeren slipped in their attempts to get to the ball. All was not lost and Caniggia came swopping in from the back post to side foot the ball past the despairing lunge of Balde.

This spurred Celtic on and a few minutes later they had their best chance of the match. A punt from the right saw Sutton knocking the ball down to Larsson who chested it in front of him. Lorenzo Amoruso was alert to the danger and, as the Swede shot, he lunged forward to block the ball and send it well wide for a corner kick.

Rangers' second started with a long, low pass from Bonnissel on the left which found Michael Mols who had come deep to lose the giant Balde, his marker. Showing instant control, Mols did his trademark turn, releasing a deft pass between Celtic defenders into the path of the galloping Lovenkrands who had already left Mjallby for dead. As Douglas rushed out to narrow the angle, the Dane clipped the ball past him before continuing his run and celebrating with his trademark cartwheel.

Rangers were now in control of the match and, just before the interval, they could have gone three up when a Caniggia cut back was beautifully controlled by Mols with his back to goal. The striker held off his marker and laid the ball off to Ricksen whose shot was blocked by the arm of Valgaeren as he threw himself in front of it. A penalty? Referee Kenny Clark did not see it that way!

As the second-half began, if Rangers players and fans had hoped that Celtic's recent exertions would leave them short of energy and, perhaps more importantly, willpower, they were quickly disabused of this notion. Showing great determination and commitment, the Celtic players found new reserves of energy and began to pound away at Rangers' defences. Of course, as they moved forward en masse, they tended to leave themselves more exposed at the back than normal. So, despite more pressure and more long balls into the Rangers' penalty area, it was the Govan team who created the first real chances of the second-half although they came to nothing.

Then Celtic got a corner on the right and an inswinging cross was sent over by Thompson. Larsson managed to steal away from his marker Ricksen, and stooped low to head the ball in at the near post, off the face of Klos who had no chance of saving it. Game on! Only a few minutes later came the most controversial moment of the entire match - especially when those at the game saw the television replays later! The ball was given away cheaply in midfield by Arteta. As Celtic surged forward, Larsson swept past Amoruso and, with Hartson running on his left, he pushed the ball to the side leaving his striking partner with the simplest of chances to put the ball beyond Klos. To the relief of the Rangers players and fans, however, the Assistant Referee on the Main Stand side had already lifted his flag to indicate offside, much to the dismay of Martin O'Neill. The Celtic manager's disappointment would only increase after the match when he had seen the television replays - Hartson had, indeed, been onside when he 'scored'. If Hartson felt bad when he saw his goal chalked off, worse was in store at the tail end of the match.

In the final 25 minutes, Bonnissel, who seemed to have picked up a groin injury, was replaced by Maurice Ross and then Arteta was replaced by Bert Konterman as the manager decided to shore up a midfield under constant pressure from Celtic. Rangers' task was made somewhat easier when Chris Sutton was stretchered off with a broken wrist. For once, Rangers could not be blamed as the accident happened as a result of his team-mate Bobo Balde clashing with him in an aerial assault before landing on top of him.

The match continued as before with Celtic pressing for the equaliser and Rangers defending stoutly while trying to catch them on the break. Indeed, a couple of goals may have materialised but for timely interventions by Balde. Then, 5 minutes from the end, Neil Lennon was only booked for pushing Fernando Ricksen over, with the ball 10 yards away in Thompson's possession. Still, perhaps justice was done a couple of minutes later when Lennon walked after receiving his second yellow card. This time it was for a professional foul on Shota Arveladze who had beaten Mjallby before putting the ball past the Irishman and attempting to run round him. The Irishman, knowing that Arveladze would have a clear run into the Celtic half, simply stuck out both arms to obstruct him and brought him to the ground, richly earning his card - despite the later efforts of his manager to claim that he could not have got out of the way and had not deserved his dismissal!

Just when it looked all over, the Old Firm proved once again that nothing should be taken for granted in these matches. In the final minute of normal time, a penalty was awarded to Celtic. Petrov slid his pass to the 18 yard line where Balde was still lurking from a corner kick. He cleverly extended his long leg backwards, as if waiting to collect the pass but Amoruso, trying to get to the ball before it reached him, dived in and Balde fell forward into the box.

A penalty was awarded and, to the surprise of everyone in the stadium, it was not Larsson who stepped up to take it but John Hartson. The Welsh striker proved once again how easy and quick it is to go from hero to zero in Old Firm games. The week previously, he had been Celtic's match-winner but this time, he was going to end up a loser. He strode forward, hitting his penalty low to Klos' right and, although the keeper dived the wrong way, the ball went past the post by about a foot. While Hartson hung his head, the Rangers fans celebrated this unexpected miss with Amoruso (jumping in the air) no doubt thinking that he was the luckiest man in the Universe.

Everybody knew that the trophy was Ibrox bound for the second successive year and, after 5 minutes of injury time, the final whistle sounded. Nobody would have been happier than Michael Mols, winning his first cup medal. He explained beforehand how much it would mean to win a gong as he did not feel the League Championship medal had been really earned due to his injury-hit debut season at the club. Most fans would have disagreed with him there when they remembered how he had brightened up the first part of that title-winning season before his tragic injury in Munich. After the match, Mols' tears flowed as he held both the trophy and his three year old son. It was an emotional moment both for him and all friends of Rangers.

'Man of the Match' Claudio Caniggia was also celebrating a first - his first goal against Celtic. Winning his medal also helped relieve the pain of his last final appearance at Hampden when he was injured against Celtic in the Scottish Cup Final after only 17 minutes. "To play against Celtic and score my first goal against them is just the way to make up for the pain of being injured last season in the Cup Final. This time I only have good memories of Hampden and I know my goal will live with me for a long time to come as it was such a special moment. I have seen and done a lot in my career but these Old Firm games are amazing and I have always dreamed of scoring in one since I signed for Rangers."

As for Rangers' other goal scoring hero, Peter Lovenkrands, he was clearly delighted to have continued his impressive scoring record against Celtic, having scored twice against them in his previous Hampden appearance. "I enjoy Hampden. The pitch was very good and we were able to play good football and create a lot of chances. I'm just very happy that the team won, that's the most important thing although I'm very happy to have scored again. It's incredible that I keep scoring against Celtic. I felt good and the team played magnificently in the first half. Still, we must give Celtic a lot of credit because they've had a hard week with some tough games and today we took advantage of it."

Another satisfied man was Alex McLeish who had just savoured his third successive Hampden cup victory over Martin O'Neill and his third trophy as Ibrox boss. "It was a hard fought one, no doubt about that. In the second half we tried to protect our lead which was maybe human nature. Celtic came roaring back at us and you have to credit them for that. They are a very good side. Whether they upped a gear or we contributed to our own problems I don't know but we were under serious pressure."

The Rangers team: Klos, Ricksen, Moore, Amoruso, Bonnissel, de Boer, Ferguson, Arteta, Caniggia, Mols and Lovenkrands.

Before Rangers could play their postponed league match against Motherwell (at Ibrox on the following Wednesday), the SFA Disciplinary Committee made its decision regarding the charges against Lorenzo Amoruso that he had spat on James Grady in the cup tie at Somerset Park. The Rangers defender was found guilty by the panel and given a two game suspension with 12 points added to his discipline record which meant his aggregate of points would see him incur another two game ban. Rangers would have to cope without their in-form defender for the next four matches, starting with the Motherwell game.

Wed. March 19, 2003
RANGERS 2 MOTHERWELL 0
(Ferguson, Lovenkrands)
Crowd: 49,240

Apart from Amoruso, Rangers started the match without Arteta, Bonnissel and Caniggia. Malcolm replaced Amoruso while Ross returned at right-back leaving Muscat to fill the injury-hit left-back position. All three left-backs (Ball, Numan and Bonnissel, ironically brought as cover for the former two) were now injured. Steven

Thompson got a rare start in place of the veteran Argentinian.

Rangers (like the crowd) began in a rather subdued fashion with Motherwell looking eager to take the game to the home side. They started passing the ball about neatly, trying to threaten the Rangers' goal and, indeed, could have opened the scoring when Lehmann's shot was blocked by the chest of Klos.

That was the wake-up call and a fresher approach was evident as Rangers powered towards the Motherwell end of the park. This is not to say that the visitors sat back and defended in depth. At every opportunity, they attacked. Nevertheless, all the real pressure came from Rangers although no genuine chances were created by the home side. Then, in the 18th minute, Barry Ferguson scored his 17th goal of a tremendous season. Michael Mols was fouled from behind just outside the area, in a central position. Ferguson stepped up to take the kick and from 20 or so yards curled a beauty over the wall and into the top left hand corner. It was 'Beckham-esque' in its accuracy. From that point onwards, Fergie would produce a vintage performance which resulted in yet another 'Man of the Match' award.

Before half-time Ferguson almost grabbed a second goal when he fired a low shot just past the post. As usual, Rangers had been in control throughout most of the first-half but still had not managed that elusive second goal. Unusually, though, the fans did not have to wait long for this to happen - less than a minute, in fact. No sooner had the CIS Cup been paraded at the interval (and the second-half started) and the game was virtually over, thanks to a Lovenkrands goal.

A great spell of possession play in their own half saw the ball passed from Lovenkrands to Moore, then to Ferguson who fed Muscat on the wing. The Australian surged forward in a manner reminiscent of a typical Numan foray. As the first defender came towards him, he neatly side-stepped, kept going forward and, as another defender closed in, sent a deft pass between defenders into the path of Lovenkrands who was powering into the penalty area. With the ball, the Dane moved slightly to his left before smacking his shot low past the outstretched hand of keeper Dubourdeau who, earlier in the season, had 'the game of his life' against Rangers at Fir Park. There was to be no repeat of that. As the players swamped Muscat in congratulation, Lovenkrands acknowledged the tremendous part the Australian played in creating the goal.

After this, maybe inevitably, the match drifted to a tame conclusion with Rangers obviously delighted to secure the three points and go six ahead of Celtic who had two matches in hand. The league race was now entering its most critical phase with only 7 matches left for Rangers with 4 of them, including the Celtic game, at Ibrox.

Fernando Ricksen, afterwards, showed that his focus was firmly on the big prize. "That's us 6 points ahead of Celtic and although Celtic have two games in hand we already have the points so we are in a better position. It was nice to win the cup of course but the league for us is much more important so we know what we have to do. That's what we're trying to achieve and we're certainly on the right track. Every prize that I win is welcome and very much appreciated."

Barry Ferguson was also delighted to have gained the three precious points. "Sunday's game did take a lot out of the boys but the gaffer told us to go out and give it everything. In the last ten minutes we tired a bit but that was to be expected. I felt we commanded the game and totally deserved to win. I was happy to have scored - my first since the end of January but I haven't really been practising them. I don't train every day and spend a lot of time doing exercises to help my pelvic injury."

The Rangers team: Klos, Ross, Moore, Malcolm, Muscat, Ricksen, de Boer, Ferguson, Mols, Thompson and Lovenkrands.

DUNFERMLINE 1 RANGERS 1
(Caniggia)
Crowd: 9,875

Before Rangers' quarter-final cup tie at Dunfermline, it was announced that Alex McLeish had been named as the 'Manager of the Month' for February. Big Eck would probably have preferred the award of a clean bill of health for his first-team squad! Out of the Dunfermline tie were Numan and Bonnissel (still!) while Amoruso was suspended and new injuries had ruled out both Lovenkrands and Mols. Ross was relegated to the bench for this one allowing Ricksen to go to right-back with Konterman taking his place in midfield. At least Claudio Caniggia returned after having a midweek rest following his exertions in the CIS Cup Final.

It was quite an even affair for the first 20 minutes or so before Dunfermline opened the scoring. Mason, just inside the opposition half, headed a Rangers' clearance forward to Craig Brewster who looked yards offside, just outside the penalty box. As the Assistant Referee's flag stayed down, Brewster controlled the ball with his chest and laid it off to Grondin. The French midfielder took one touch as he surged forward and then sent a hard, low shot from 18 yards to Klos' left before Ferguson and Moore had the chance to close him down. It was the former Arsenal reserve's first goal for the Pars.

This, naturally, resulted in increased pressure from Rangers as they sought the equaliser which was not long in coming. In the 31st minute, Konterman, on the half-way line, passed the ball forward to de Boer who had come deep. He turned Gus McPherson (another ex-Ranger) and slipped a lovely pass through the middle and into the box for Caniggia who, in turn, clipped it past Stillie, watching it roll into the net just inside the right hand post. Both sides were probably quite happy to go in at half-time all square.

The second period started in much the same fashion as the first but what had been a competitive game seemed to become much tousier with the appearance of substitute Noel Hunt who had been signed from Shamrock Rovers. The young striker put himself about with obvious relish, intent on upsetting both defenders and any other opponent who came within range of him. The match continued in a slightly heated manner with too many players showing only effort and aggression rather than skill. Two exceptions were de Boer and McCann who continued to create openings.

Strangely, Neil McCann was substituted by Shota Arveladze whilst having perhaps his most productive spell of the entire match. With 15 minutes to go, keeper Stillie made the save of the match. A short Arteta corner was taken by the supporting Muscat who sent a pass into the box to de Boer. The classy striker then laid the ball back to Ferguson (some 22 yards out) who sent his shot fizzing towards glory only to see Stillie get strong hands on it and push it away from goal.

The final 10 minutes saw Rangers increase the pressure but Caniggia and then Arveladze missed absolute sitters. Then, right at the end, Ferguson was sent off. Hunt took possession near the half-way line, on the touchline. He was going nowhere but, with a rush of blood, Fergie lunged at him as he tried to run up the line with the ball. Although he did not actually make contact with his opponent, referee Underhill sent him off nevertheless.

After the match, one point of contention was the treatment of Mikel Arteta and the denial of an obvious penalty-kick. Alex McLeish defended his young midfielder. "Mikel tends to embellish things a bit but, at the end of the day, a foul is still a foul. Referees are maybe put off a bit but they have to recognise when a free kick is a free kick nonetheless. They can talk to him about the other thing, as I can. It's a foreign thing that we've seen over the years. I don't want him going down if he's not been touched. I don't condone that type of thing at all. But I think there were genuine infringements on certainly three or four occasions."

As for the game in general, McLeish recognised that a replay should not have been necessary. "We missed some real sitters in the second half. It's really gilt-edged stuff and we've got to be burying those. It was always going to be a game where we had to get the sleeves rolled up but I still felt we managed to play some decent stuff."

The Rangers team: Klos, Ricksen, Moore, Malcolm, Muscat, Ferguson, Konterman, Arteta, Caniggia, de Boer and McCann.

Apart from still being in the cup following a difficult away tie, Rangers were further cheered up later that day when First Division Inverness Caledonian Thistle repeated their shock elimination of Celtic from the cup by beating them 1-0. Also, if Rangers overcame Dunfermline in the replay at Ibrox, their opponents in the semi-final at Hampden would be Motherwell, a side rooted at the foot of the league. It augured well for successive Scottish Cup glory. This time, the final would see them taking on Inverness, Falkirk or Dundee - provided Rangers disposed of Dunfermline and Motherwell. With this incentive to reach the final (and end up with at least the two trophies from last season), the Treble was also becoming more of a possibility following the events in Inverness. The Rangers' fans could look forward to a tremendous climax to the season.

The next week it was announced that, for the Dunfermline replay, Barry Ferguson and Lorenzo Amoruso (currently suspended) were eligible to play. On the downside, Craig Moore, having picked up two cup bookings, would be suspended. Most fans dreaded the thought of Moore and Amoruso missing at the same time so the return of Amo was certainly a relief.

More good news later in the week when it was announced that Barry Ferguson had signed a 5 year extension to his contact that would see him play the best years of his career at Ibrox - until 2008. Critics like ex-Celt Davie Provan offered the opinion that Barry should have had more ambition and 'improve' his game by moving to a better league such as the English Premiership but the skipper stated that he was happy at Ibrox and that he could fulfil all his ambitions with the club. His extended contract, more than anything, was a signal of intent that Rangers were determined to be top dogs again in Scotland and make real progress in Europe in the coming years.

APRIL

Sat. April 5, 2003
RANGERS 2 PARTICK THISTLE 0
(Mols 2)
Crowd: 49,472

After a two week break when the Scotland team won at Hampden against Iceland (before going down to the mighty(!) Lithuanians in the Euro 2004 qualifiers) normal service was resumed when Rangers took on Partick Thistle at Ibrox. Having endured a torrid time before scraping a 2-1 win in their last meeting at Firhill, Rangers should have known that they were in for a tough match. Things were made even harder by the absence of some key players. Out, due to suspension, were Ferguson, Amoruso and Muscat while Numan and Bonnissel still had not recovered from their injuries received weeks before the break. Arveladze and Thompson were also struggling to regain full fitness although the Georgian striker was given a place on the bench. With four full-backs unavailable, Ricksen returned to the right-back slot while Maurice Ross had to play out of position at left-back.

From the start of the game it was obvious that Thistle had adopted the correct tactics by refusing to give their opponents time or space on the ball. Additionally, they tried to break forward themselves when the opportunity arose. When the ball was lost, every Thistle player seemed to get behind the ball, in their own half, meaning that the Light Blues had to play through the whole team in order to create a goal. It must be said that Thistle's energy and commitment were admirable as they harassed and harried at every turn.

Rangers, as usual, had the majority of possession and pressure but just could not create a clear-cut chance. Ironically, it took a

Ricksen tackle to deny Britton a probable Thistle goal. The half ended with no goals and the home crowd showing their displeasure at the lack of chances being created.

Within two minutes of the re-start, a chance was gifted to Thistle by Maurice Ross who, under no pressure, casually passed back to Klos but the ball was under hit and straight into the path of Burns. Thistle's top striker took the ball into the box, one on one with Klos. The German keeper, however, stood up well as the striker approached and his shot hit off the keeper's chest before being mopped up by Konterman. This scare seemed to breathe fresh life into Rangers and they started to power forward with more energy and creativity. A more attacking threat was supplied by Neil McCann who came on at left back for Ross. Indeed, it was a McCann free-kick from 20 odd yards that looked net-bound until it was tipped past by Arthur who deserved the congratulations of his team-mates.

With 20 minutes to go and the home crowd becoming ever more anxious, the deadlock was broken. A Ricksen throw on the right was headed out but only to the feet of Hughes, still inside the box. His first attempt to get past a defender failed but the ball fell kindly to him outside the box and he whipped in a brilliant cross that was met by Mols on the 6 yard line. His deft header flashed just inside Arthur's near post to the cheers of both relief and joy from the Rangers fans. Only another five minutes passed before the match was over as a contest when Mols, following a great series of passes that started with Malcolm just outside his own box, scored the second.

Thereafter, the only thing of note that happened came 5 minutes from time when Thistle should have scored. Lilley, on the wing, cut in and beat Craig Moore. He fired over a great cross that Rowsen, on the penalty spot, volleyed low towards goal. Fortunately Stefan Klos managed to block the effort by with his leg and the ball bounced out to Caniggia (of all people) who then took it for a walk upfield to clear the danger. With hardly anything to do throughout the game, Klos had brought off two great saves in the match. Such is the fate of the traditional Rangers goalkeeper!

After the final whistle, the home crowd left feeling satisfied that this hard-fought victory had seen the Ibrox men go 9 points clear of Celtic who, the following day, would play one of their three games in hand. As it turned out, Martin O'Neill's men only managed a draw against Dundee at Dens Park thus trailing Rangers by 8 points. With only one more match before the split in the league for the final 5 games, Rangers were now in an even stronger position.

Meanwhile, manager McLeish was rather downbeat but nevertheless pleased with the three points. He pointed out that missing players might have been a factor in the side's performance. "We were without Ferguson and I think it's fair to say that any team in the land would miss their best player. When I look at the complete picture, there were few in the team who didn't do themselves justice." Following praise for Michael Mols' two goal contribution, McLeish said, "So far as I am concerned, whoever keeps banging the ball into the net stays in the team. I think our former striker, Ally McCoist was a classic example of this rare ability of front players to impose themselves at any stage. He could be running about the park, doing little, for 89 minutes and then with seconds remaining he would score the winning goal."

How the fans wished they HAD a McCoist up front this season - the title would have been won by now!

The Rangers team: Klos, Ricksen, Malcolm, Moore, Ross, Hughes, Konterman, Arteta, de Boer, Mols and Lovenkrands.

The following evening saw the official Rangers 'Player of the Year' awards. Not surprisingly, Barry Ferguson was voted 'Player of the Year' as well as the 'Players' Player of the Year'. Equally predictable was the award for 'Young Player of the Year' which went to Mikel Arteta. Both footballers thoroughly deserved their accolades and, in the following game, showed why they had been honoured.

Wed. April 9, 2003
RANGERS 3   DUNFERMLINE 0
(Lovenkrands, Ferguson, Arteta,)
Crowd: 24,752

Rangers played their Scottish Cup quarter-final replay against Dunfermline at Ibrox in front of around 25,000 fans, the smallest crowd at the Stadium for years. Perhaps nobody should have been surprised as the match was being broadcast live on Sky and it was the 6th time that the sides had met that season, with one more match still to come at Ibrox. Familiarity obviously does breed contempt - or at least boredom!

Once again, Alex McLeish had to make team changes. Out was the suspended Craig Moore while Maurice Ross had not recovered in time from a foot injury. On the plus side, Barry Ferguson returned from 'league' suspension, having his final suspended game still to come the following Sunday. Likewise Lorenzo Amoruso's 4 game ban was 'lifted' for the cup although he had a one match ban still to be served. Even better, was the return of Arthur Numan after a 6 week lay-off .

Unusually, the game started with a great chance to open the scoring being offered to the visitors after only two minutes. Inside the box, Brewster sent a brilliantly timed pass through to Hampshire who, thankfully, missed the target. If the player had felt bad about his miss then, a few minutes later, he must have felt much worse as Rangers stormed into the lead.

Dunfermline keeper Derek Stillie tried to start an attack by throwing a long ball out to the right wing to defender Andreas Skerla but Peter Lovenkrands, showing great awareness, anticipated the move and bore down on the Lithuanian. Skerla had to take one touch to control the ball but, before he could take another one, Lovenkrands had swooped from behind him and taken the ball away from his boot. Zooming in on goal and from just outside the box, the Dane fired a tremendous shot low past the horrified Stillie. In such moments are matches decided. Instead of possibly being a goal up at Ibrox, the visitors found themselves a goal down after only a few minutes.

The second was supplied by Ferguson, his 18th goal of a most productive season. The midfield maestro started the move from just outside his own penalty box by running with the ball to almost the halfway line where he completed a nice one-two with de Boer. Then he flighted a pass out to the left-wing for Lovenkrands who deftly nodded the ball back to the supporting Numan. The Dutch defender carried the ball to the edge of the opposition box before sending over a dangerous swerving cross to the 6 yard line. Ferguson, having continued his drive into the box, burst between the defenders and, with a great diving header, sent the ball low into the net just inside the left hand post. With only 19 minutes on the clock, it already looked like game over.

Early in the second period, it was not long before the killer third goal arrived. De Boer was the creator when he sent a beautifully weighted pass into the box for Arteta. The Spaniard had been looking more like his old self throughout the match and the goal he scored at this point could only have boosted his confidence. As Stillie came out to narrow the angle, Arteta chipped the ball delicately over him and it went into the empty goal despite the vain clearance attempt of a couple of defenders on the line. After this, it resembled a training exercise with Rangers missing more chances.

Afterwards 'Man of the Match' Barry Ferguson stressed that it had been a good team display. "It isn't just about me, Amo or Arthur. It was a team performance and we carry a squad of 24 players so everyone is playing their part. The manager spoke to all of us and said he wanted us to make a good start and play better than we did at the weekend. He felt we'd been a little slack in some areas. We did make a great start and played some very good football after that. We took control of the game and it was nice to get on the scoresheet myself. That was my 18th goal of the season but I'm not setting myself any targets. The most important thing is we are in the next round of the competition."

Another Ranger who could feel good about his own display against Dunfermline was Mikel Arteta who showed something like his early season form before it was interrupted for 9 weeks by injury. The youngster admitted to the public as well as himself that he had not been showing the form he was capable of since his injury.

"I've had a couple of injury problems this season but I can't use them as an excuse. I know I haven't been playing like I was at the start. Now I have to work harder to get back to my best. I have spoken to the manager about it and told him I want to work very hard to get fully fit for the last 8 or 9 games of the season. I want to be the best I can be because it's such an important moment for the club, for me and my team-mates. I know I have to play my part."

The Rangers team: Klos, Ricksen, Malcolm, Amoruso, Numan, Ferguson, Konterman, Arteta, de Boer, Mols and Lovenkrands.

Before the next round of league games could be played, a bitter row broke out among the clubs or, to be more precise, between Celtic and the others in the SPL. Having reached the semi-final of the UEFA Cup, Celtic found themselves in the position of having to play in Portugal against Boavista on the Thursday before playing their first league game after the split on the Sunday. The SPL Board had decreed that they should play Rangers at Ibrox on that day. After the disgraceful events at Parkhead in 1999 when Rangers had clinched the Championship at the home of their old rivals, (leading to crowd misbehaviour among the Celtic fans), the SPL decided that never again would the final Old Fim match of the season be a 'league decider'. Apparently, the only date on which it was arithmetically impossible for the title to be clinched was the first date available and this was why that date had been chosen.

Celtic Chief Executive Iain MacLeod and manager Martin O'Neill were outraged and in the press complained about this being 'unfair' and 'unsporting'. O'Neill went further and said that it would never have happened to Rangers! Some pointed out that quite a few times in previous seasons, Rangers played in an Old Firm match after a vital European match days before. In 1993, when they were one goal away from a place in the Champions League Final, they played 8 matches in 25 days. In that spell, they even had to play a re-arranged league match on the Wednesday, a Scottish Cup semi-final on the Saturday against Hearts, followed by their trip to Marseilles on the Wednesday with another league game on the Saturday. Nobody then seemed to be talking about changing fixtures to 'help' Rangers do well in Europe!

Sun. April 13, 2003
DUNDEE UTD. 1 RANGERS 4
(De Boer 2, Arveladze 2)
Crowd: 10,271

This acrimonious dispute was put behind everyone when Rangers travelled to Tannadice to play a United side second from bottom but with a new manager (Ian McCall) who was determined to haul his team away from the relegation area. Once again, the visitors would be without their captain and former captain as Ferguson and Amoruso completed their suspensions. Michael Mols was also unwell and his place was taken by Shota Arveladze. When players saw the state of the pitch (reputedly the worst in the Premier League), maybe it was just as well that Ferguson, with his pelvic problem, was banned. The surface was hard, rutted and covered by sand in many places. No wonder it was the home of 'The Arabs'!

The home team started brightly enough, taking the game to Rangers when they could but failing to create anything in front of goal. After a few minutes, Rangers managed to exert some sustained pressure on the Tannadice side's defence and a sequence of play saw them win 5 or 6 consecutive corners as United failed to clear their lines. From the final corner, Arteta's attempted cross was blocked but the loose ball eventually found its way to Numan who passed to Lovenkrands on the left touchline.

The Dane's cross, into the penalty area, was missed by Gary Bollan who had de Boer lurking behind him. The striker chested the ball down before drilling a low shot past keeper Gallacher into the left side of the goal.

Rangers' second goal came in the 17th minute after more sustained pressure. Arteta sent his pass left to Numan who slipped it forward to Konterman who made a simple pass to de Boer hovering on the left hand edge of the penalty area. With Duff blocking his way, de Boer made just enough space for himself to cross with plenty of pace. Arveladze, having stolen in from the back post ahead of a defender, headed home from only a few yards out and, even at this point, it looked like game over.

It took until the 40th minute before Dundee United seriously threatened for the first time in the game. The ball arrived at the feet of Wilson who took a stride forward before unleashing a great effort at Klos' goal from the edge of the penalty area. With the German beaten, the ball smacked off the bar and bounced away to almost the corner flag where it was eventually cleared.

In injury time, Arteta drove forward towards the penalty area with three defenders in front of him. Spotting de Boer's clever run, the Spaniard threaded the ball through the defenders into the path of the striker who dinked the ball over the keeper who had left his line to narrow the angle. This sublime finish was a fitting climax to a first half in which de Boer had given a real Dutch master class, despite the dreadful playing surface.

Credit, though, must be given to the home side for their spirited start to the second period. For the first 15 minutes, they showed that they had not given up on this game. Of course with a three goal lead, Rangers would have taken their foot off the gas but nevertheless United plugged away, trying to get a goal that could have been the basis of a comeback. Ex- Ranger Billy Dodds, who had come on as a substitute, showed that there was no room for sentiment in his book when he managed to catch Craig Moore under the eye with the palm of his hand as he rushed at the unlucky defender. Blood was drawn and the Aussie had to go off for attention.

Ironically, instead of pulling a goal back, United went further behind shortly after this. Muscat sent the ball out to the right touchline where it was controlled by de Boer. He cut inside (evading Bollan) then shrugged off another two opponents before splitting the United defence with a pass to Arveladze running just outside the box. His first touch took him into the area but the ball seemed to get caught, momentarily, under his feet. Still, with great aplomb, he managed to blast his shot high into the net leaving the keeper with no chance.

United, however, refused to lie down and were rewarded with a consolation goal when Dodds bundled the ball in a couple of minutes later. After this, the Rangers players seemed content just to avoid any possible injury on the difficult surface for they knew that the 'crunch time' was just ahead, starting with a Scottish Cup semi-final next against Motherwell at Hampden.

'Man of the Match' Ronald de Boer was modest in his assessment of the game and the side's form in the league. "This isn't just about me. It's all about a squad effort. That's what's brought us to this position. Of course, it's nice when you play well and the fans sing your name but for me the most important thing always is helping the team to the result. Bringing success to Rangers is all that is on my mind but you don't do that by yourself. We are in a fantastic position now with only 5 games to go in the league and we simply have to keep telling each other to take one game at a time and stay focused."

Looking back on the United game, the Dutch ace said, "I was pleased with the goals. The first one was quite early on and that always settles you in an away game. I felt we played some great football in the first half on what was a very tough surface. You didn't know what the ball was really going to do at times so to score four goals and win like that is very pleasing."

The Rangers team: Klos, Muscat, Malcolm, Moore, Numan, Ricksen, Konterman, Arteta, de Boer, Arveladze and Lovenkrands.

When the league split - with only 5 matches remaining - the table looked like this:

	P	W	D	L	F	A	PTS
RANGERS	33	28	3	2	86	23	87
CELTIC	31	25	4	2	76	20	79
HEARTS	32	15	9	8	53	46	54
KILMARNOCK	33	14	8	11	43	46	50
DUNFERMLINE	33	13	5	15	48	56	44
DUNDEE	33	10	12	11	44	48	42
HIBS	33	11	6	16	46	58	39
ABERDEEN	33	9	10	14	32	48	37
LIVINGSTON	33	8	8	17	41	50	32
PARTICK THISTLE	33	6	11	16	29	50	29
DUNDEE UNITED	33	5	10	18	29	61	25
MOTHERWELL	32	6	6	20	35	56	24

Before the resumption of league hostilities could take place, there was the little matter of a Scottish Cup semi-final. Despite the fact that it was top of the table against bottom (with a 63 point gap between the sides), nobody expected this match to be a formality - cup semis never are!

Sat. April 19, 2003
RANGERS 4 MOTHERWELL 3
(Konterman, Mols, Amoruso, Partridge og)
Crowd: 29,352

Motherwell's chances of causing an upset increased when, days before, Ronald de Boer ('Man of the Match' in his last outing) Mikel Arteta, Peter Lovenkrands and Claudio Caniggia were all ruled out, either injured or ill. The fans, however, seemed unperturbed as they knew that the manager had more than capable substitutes able to handle the Motherwell challenge.

The fans' confidence seemed to have been justified when

Rangers scored in the second minute with the first real action of
the game. A sweeping move saw Numan sensibly slotting his pass
through to Barry Ferguson, just outside the opposition box.
Crowded by defenders, he was pushed towards the left touchline
with no place, seemingly, to go. However, in a nice reversal of
direction, he turned inside and released a pass into the middle just
outside the penalty area. Konterman, rushing towards it, feinted as
if to shoot (fooling a defender) and then, having made a yard of
space, cracked a scorcher high into the goal from about 22 yards
out. It was not quite a replica of Bert's finest hour when he scored
against Celtic in the CIS Cup semi the previous season but it was
sensational enough to be remembered for quite some time.
Hampden seemed to agree with the big Dutchman.

At that point, most spectators thought that the match had been
already won and were guessing how many Rangers would score.
Unfortunately, perhaps, so did the players. It was Motherwell who
now took a grip of the game and proceeded to press forward,
playing with a liveliness and skill that belied their position at the foot
of the league table. But, despite some fluid play, it was 9 minutes
before their first shot at goal and that was a long-distance effort
from Adams that flew well over the bar.

Motherwell then equalised just a couple of minutes after
Konterman had squandered a good chance. Amoruso, cleaning up
in defence, was put under pressure on the left flank as he tried to
send his pass upfield to Neil McCann. It was well intercepted,
though, by Corrigan who pounced near the half-way line. He drove
forward and passed to Clarkson whose great cut-back was clipped
over the diving Klos and into the net by Craig.

Then, in the 27th minute, Motherwell sensationally took the
lead. After some scrappy play, Pearson did a neat one-two with
Clarkson and, just inside the penalty box, got a foot to the ball
before Amoruso could whack it to safety. It was touched to the right
to McFadden and, with tremendous vision and skill, he curled a left
foot shot high into the far corner of Klos' goal. It was an exquisite

finish that showed what the youngster was capable of and why the rumours persisted that he would be playing in the English Premiership the following season - if not at Ibrox or Celtic Park!

Just three minutes before half-time, a second-half 'mountain to climb' was nearly on the cards but Motherwell's young striker Clarkson missed a great chance to put his side 3-1 up. Funnily enough, just after this, it could have been all square. Just inside the Motherwell half, Barry Ferguson sent a brilliant pass through the middle to Mols. As the striker raced into the box (with Vaughan chasing), Dubourdeau came out to dive at the Dutchman's feet. Mols managed to round the keeper but stumbled over his outstretched hands and, falling, tried to shoot into the empty net. Unfortunately, he was totally off balance and his shot hit the side netting.

Rangers' intentions were clear as the teams came out for the second half. Alex McLeish had decided to replace the ineffectual Arveladze with Steven Thompson whose strength and energy were obviously needed to combat the battling Motherwell team.

On the half-way line, Ricksen intercepted a stray Motherwell header and his first time pass found Thompson. He surged forward and took it to the side of Partridge before releasing a perfectly-weighted pass into the stride of Mols on his left whose controlled shot, from about 8 yards out, did the business. Only five minutes later and business was booming as the Gers went into the lead. McCann had been fouled way out on the left touchline and Ricksen elected to take the free-kick. His kick was flighted into the middle of the box where Amoruso, losing his marker, rose unchallenged to send a powerful header high into the net. What a turnaround in fortunes!

The match, as a contest, seemed over as Rangers scored their fourth goal when a Muscat cross was headed into his own goal by Partridge. At last, it looked as if the Motherwell challenge was over. The final 20 minutes might have seen Rangers in control of the match but Motherwell certainly had not given up. Then, three minutes into injury time (with practically the last kick of the game), Motherwell got a consolation goal for their perseverance. With the match ending 4-3, most observers were in agreement that, unlike many nervy, boring semi-finals, this had been a really entertaining match. Credit went to Motherwell and their young players but, in the end, the honours went to Rangers.

If a cup final appearance was a satisfactory result for the Ibrox men, even better was to follow. Later in the day, Hearts (with a last minute goal) beat Celtic 2-1 at Tynecastle meaning that Rangers were still 8 points ahead of their league rivals who now only had one game in hand. It looked as if the final Old Firm game at Ibrox really would determine the destination of the Championship.

Having survived a scary first forty-five, manager McLeish was satisfied with the end result and that second-half performance. "At half time, it looked like it wasn't going to be our day. We were 2-1 down and it's always difficult to come back against a team that was as well motivated as Motherwell. We didn't take our foot off the gas after the early goal. They simply gave everything and scored two excellent goals. It would be unfair not to give credit to Motherwell. I never thought that this game would be a cakewalk or that 'Well would turn up and crumble. They never gave us a minute and during the interval I told my players I wanted to see more hunger and desire from them. I made it clear to the players that I wasn't pleased with the way we had been out fought by the other team in the first half."

The Rangers team: Klos, Muscat, Moore, Amoruso, Numan; Ricksen, Ferguson, Konterman, Mols, Arveladze and McCann.

RANGERS 1   CELTIC 2
(de Boer)
Crowd: 49,740

After all the furore about the actual date of the final Old Firm
match of the season, it duly went ahead on 27th April with the
Celtic players showing no signs of tiredness whatsoever after
having beaten Boavista in Portugal on the Thursday to reach the
final of the UEFA Cup. Indeed, it was the home players who looked,
for the most part, out of sorts, after a great opening 20 minutes in
which they should have scored three times.

Of the two main injury doubts before the game, Ronald de Boer
made it into the side but Mikel Arteta could only find a place on the
bench. Bert Konterman was the player keeping the Spaniard out of
the team. Also, Shota Arveladze could not even get a place among
the substitutes so disappointing had his form been of late.

Martin O'Neill sprang a surprise by ditching his regular 3-5-2
formation for a 4-4-2 one, no doubt due to injuries to Mjallby and
Lambert. Thus, McNamara was at right-back and Laursen came
in at left-back. This way, Celtic hoped to cope with the two
Rangers wingers who, as it turned out, were destined to be
ineffectual anyway.

The game actually started brightly enough for the home side.
After a neat Ricksen tackle robbed Larsson (moving into a
menacing position), Rangers should have opened the scoring
in the second minute. From just inside the Celtic half, a perfectly
placed chip over the heads of the Celtic defence by de Boer found
Caniggia, in the clear, bearing down on keeper Rab Douglas.
The ball bounced up beautifully for him and he lobbed it over the
advancing keeper. Unfortunately, it went over Douglas but was off
target and went past the right hand post by a yard. What a let-off
for Celtic! Even this early, the Ibrox faithful wondered if this sitter
would prove costly.

Only a few minutes later, the home side had another chance to take the lead. Arteta took a corner on the left which was met by Amoruso, 6 yards out and totally unmarked. The big Italian's header, however, flashed over the bar.

After only 8 minutes, Douglas had to be replaced due to an injured thigh and former Livingston goalkeeper Broto took his place between the posts. Calls for pressure to be put on the Old Firm debutant were soon answered. A free kick, just outside the box and in a central position, was blasted against the wall by Barry Ferguson. The ball, somehow, managed to squirm behind the Celtic barrier where Michael Mols attempted a shot. Laursen's foot, however, blocked his effort. Mols then had another go that was blocked again. This time, the ball bounced out to de Boer but his snatched shot went through a ruck of players and fizzed just past the post. The Rangers' fans could have been forgiven for thinking that it was going to be just one of those days,

As if to confirm this, in the 29th minute, referee Dallas awarded Celtic a penalty. Larsson had swept the ball, from the left channel over to the right side of the pitch, to Hartson just outside the box. The big Welshman took the ball forward into box at its junction when Amoruso, barring his way to goal, decided to try and get a touch before Hartson's next could take the ball past him. Unfortunately, he was a split second too late and Hartson touched the ball before he did. The striker then went over Amoruso's outstretched leg and Hugh Dallas awarded the obvious penalty kick. As both Larsson and Hartson had missed vital penalties in recent weeks, the task of converting this one fell to Alan Thompson who scored.

Worse was to follow a few minutes before the interval when Celtic claimed their second. Agathe set off on a run down the wing in anticipation of the return ball from Hartson which duly happened. Lovenkrands had been slow to react and had to chase the Celtic winger. He attempted a sliding tackle but missed ball (and player), leaving Agathe to chase the ball to the bye-line. With Amoruso bearing down on him, Agathe cut back for Larsson who cleverly flicked the ball further in the middle and Hartson (between Numan and Ricksen) side-footed into the corner of the net. It was a real body blow to Rangers' hopes of winning this match and Celtic seemed to know that they had fired themselves back into the Championship race.

As the second-half began, the home fans hoped that Arteta (replacing Konterman) could ignite a spark of revival and give Rangers a chance of snatching at least a draw from the jaws of defeat. The change seemed to work initially as Barry Ferguson began to get more freedom in midfield. Ferguson, who would be given the accolade 'Players' Player of the Year' later that evening, had been one of the better performers. As in the first-half, Rangers created three chances early-on but failed to take any of them.

The threatened goal eventually arrived in the 57th minute with de Boer chalking up his 18th of the season. Numan, infield and just inside his own half, fed the ball out to Lovenkrands who then slotted a great pass down the line for the overlapping Numan. Reaching it ahead of Agathe, Numan delivered a brilliant cross on the run and de Boer, unmarked and 8 yards out, powered a controlled header into the left side of the goal with Broto rooted to his line.

Unfortunately, instead of the next 15 or so minutes galvanising Rangers, it merely seemed to increase Celtic's doggedness and resolve to hold on to their lead while trying to score on the break. In the final half-hour, Rangers had the bulk of possession and pressure without really creating any clear-cut chances. Indeed, it was Celtic who managed to carve out two of the best opportunities but Klos saved both with the match finally fizzling out disappointingly.

All those connected with Rangers felt that they had lost a golden chance to virtually tie up the title. Making it even worse was the fact that this was Rangers' first defeat at Ibrox in 18 months with Celtic being the last winners there. In fact, this undefeated home run had stretched to 38 matches including, latterly, a 21 game winning streak with all 16 of their home league matches won until the Celtic game. On the positive side, Rangers still had a 2 point lead over their rivals at the top even if Celtic won their game in hand atFir Park. The destination of the league flag was still in the hands of the Ibrox men - 4 wins out of 4 in the final matches (2 home and 2 away) would see Rangers crowned Champions in May.

If it was possible, Arthur Numan, playing in his last Old Firm game, was even more disappointed than his manager. "I have said before that I want to leave Rangers on a high - and that has to be winning the title. It was my final game against Celtic and it's not a nice memory to have lost it. I've gone through all the highs and lows of Old Firm games in my time here. It's the type of fixture where there's not a lot between the teams. It was very disappointing that we didn't get going in the second half after we made it 2-1. We missed three good chances in the first 15 minutes and, if we had taken one of them, it would have shaped the game differently. Celtic have proved they are a strong side and it's always going to be hard to get back from 2-0 against them. But we had over half an hour to try for an equaliser but we just couldn't play the way we had to."

With 4 matches left, Rangers were still in the driving seat but it looked as if there could still be potholes to be negotiated on the road ahead before the Premier League trophy could be lifted by Barry Ferguson.

The Rangers team: Klos, Ricksen, Moore, Amoruso, Numan, de Boer, Ferguson, Konterman, Caniggia, Mols and Lovenkrands.

MAY

Sun. May 5, 2003
DUNDEE 2   RANGERS 2
(Wilkie og Arteta)
Crowd: 9,195

Unfortunately, that first pothole would appear on the road to Dundee the following Sunday! With 4 hurdles left to regain the Championship, Rangers fell at the first. Due to injury, Lorenzo

Amoruso was out with Bob Malcolm replacing him while Muscat came back in at right-back. Rangers got off to their best start of the league campaign with a goal in just 35 seconds, thanks to Dundee's Lee Wilkie. Arteta collected the ball and, from just outside the penalty area, pushed a neat pass out to the left-wing for Numan. The Dutch defender hit a first time cross into the 6 yard box where the Scottish international defender reached it before his own keeper, with Ronald de lurking behind him. Wilkie's very long, outstretched leg managed to toe-poke the ball into his own net and Rangers fans started to think that maybe this would not be such a difficult fixture after all.

How wrong! For the next 15 minutes Rangers dominated the play and had a few chances to get that vital second goal but failed. Such misses were to prove costly when Dundee equalised.

Craig Moore, out on the left flank, intercepted the ball and beat his man to move forward. As he was about to pass, a tackle from behind put him under pressure and his pass went astray. The ball eventually ended up with Caballero, 20 yards from goal. With Malcolm a yard off him (blocking his way), the Argentinian side-stepped to open up a shooting opportunity and fired the ball into the goal off Klos' right-hand post. Rangers knew they had a real game on their hands.

As if things were not going badly enough at this point, the home side actually took the lead in 27 minutes. Having repelled an attack, Khizanishvili played the ball out to Caballero, in acres of space and just inside the Rangers' half. He then proceeded to head straight towards the Rangers' goal with Moore and Malcolm backing off and allowing him to make progress unimpeded. As he neared the penalty area, the two Rangers were unsure whether to close him down or cover the two supporting Dundee forwards to either side. It became a moot point as Caballero smacked in a tremendous shot from all of 20 yards (again!) despite Klos getting a hand to the ball.

In desperation, Rangers drove forward in search of an equaliser before the interval. A couple of minutes before the whistle, Rangers thought they had scored but the goal disallowed for off-side. Just when it looked like Rangers were not going to get a break, they did - thanks to that man Wilkie again. Ricksen threaded a brilliant pass between two defenders into the box for Mols who was being covered by Wilkie. As Mols characteristically held the ball up, trying to turn, the big defender, in a rush of blood to the head, committed what can only be described as a rugby tackle. It was an obvious penalty and it looked as if Wilkie had both begun and ended the half by gifting Rangers a goal.

Barry Ferguson stepped up to take the vital kick. After a bit of gamesmanship from Dundee players insisting that the ball be further back on the penalty spot, Ferguson hit his penalty well, sending the keeper the wrong way. Unfortunately, the ball crashed off the underside of the bar and, as it bounced out, was cleared away before the referee blew to signal half-time.

In the second period, Rangers dominated the proceedings even more as the home side set out its stall to defend in depth and hit Rangers on the break, finishing them off with a third goal. Subsequently, Rangers had the lion's share of both play and pressure without ever really creating gilt-edged chances.

Despite taking the game to Dundee, Rangers just could not set up any real chances for themselves and, as for the home side, even when they broke away, they did not create anything either. They seemed content to let Rangers play their way through the whole team. Too often Rangers' play was simply too elaborate when a quicker, more direct approach was needed. Then, with time running out, Rangers were awarded their second penalty of the match in 82 minutes. A hopeful Ricksen punt from deep was beyond substitute Arevladze but, nevertheless, the Georgian chased the ball although Wilkie was ahead of him, ushering it back to his goalkeeper. At the last second Wilkie seemed to panic, thinking that the Ranger might just get to the ball first so he let the ball run on and blatantly barged Arveladze to the side. Another stonewall penalty!

Once again, Ferguson assumed the responsibility. Unlike his first penalty attempt, he hit this one low but his shot was too weak and too near to the diving Speroni, enabling him to divert the ball for a corner kick. Amazingly, before either side had time to consider the consequences of the penalty miss, another one was awarded from the resultant corner. As the ball came into the area, Dundee defender McKay jumped up and used his hand to hit the ball away from Malcolm, jumping behind him. Again, there could be no dispute about the award. This time, however, Mikel Arteta decided that he would have a go from the spot. Most suspected that there would not have been too much of an argument from the disconsolate Ferguson.

With their third penalty, Rangers finally managed to equalise when Arteta sent the Speroni the wrong way and smashed a shot (not unlike Ferguson's first failed attempt) high into the net. Although Rangers pressed forward with renewed vigour in the dying minutes of the game, the only shot of note came from substitute Hughes whose effort from 20 yards was well held. Thus the game ended with Rangers dropping two precious points, opening the door for Celtic to equal their total by winning their game in hand at Motherwell the following Wednesday.

Dutchman Michael Mols was equally disappointed and determined. "Can we still win it? Yes, we have to believe that we can. We're obviously disappointed to have let things slip a bit. We know that only three points are good enough at this stage, with Celtic winning at Dunfermline. But we have three hard games to come and Celtic have four hard matches to play. It's maybe going to come down to who makes the next mistake. All we can do is keep our heads. We have to make sure that we beat Kilmarnock at Ibrox on Sunday and just take it one match at a time."

Afterwards, manager Alex McLeish admitted that the Dens experience had been one of his most nail-biting experiences as a Rangers manager. "There's no doubt that this is the type of game that puts years on you. I still felt the players showed a lot of fantastic spirit to keep fighting after we went behind to two fantastic strikes from Caballero. It's going to be about bottle now and I believe that both teams have got the mental strength to handle what faces them in the weeks ahead. I think that when any team wins the league, the best side will have done it. If it's us or Celtic, the best team will have won. Now we have to try and keep our nerve for the run-in."

The Rangers team: Klos, Muscat, Malcolm, Moore, Numan, Ricksen, Ferguson, Arteta, de Boer, Mols and Lovenkrands.

The news for Rangers later in the week seemed to suggest that the title could be decided on goal difference. When Celtic played their game in hand at Fir Park the following Wednesday, they knew that they needed to win by 4 goals to leapfrog Rangers at the top - for the first time in 5 months. They duly did, helped by the fact that they were playing against ten men for 2/3 of the match after Adams of Motherwell had been sent off in the first-half. With three games left, each half of the Old Firm had two home and one away game to play. The position at the top of the league table had never been tighter with only one goal separating the sides.

	P	W	D	L	F	A	GD	PTS
CELTIC	35	28	4	3	87	24	+63	88
RANGERS	35	28	4	3	89	27	+62	88

Sun, May 11, 2003
RANGERS 4 KILMARNOCK 0
(Mols 2, Arveladze, Caniggia)
Crowd: 49,036

By the time of Rangers' next home game against Kilmarnock, Celtic had increased their lead at the top to 3 points (and a 2 goal advantage) thanks to beating Hearts 1-0, courtesy of a penalty, at Parkhead the day before. Alex McLeish knew that he needed goals as well as the points so, with a full squad to choose from, he put Ricksen at right-back and Hughes in midfield. As Celtic had, apparently, performed very nervously against Hearts, many of the pundits were expecting the same from Rangers especially after dropping points in both their previous games. The word 'bottle' was being bandied about with many questioning whether Rangers had it or not.

Within 5 minutes of the match starting, the doubters seemed to be answered and Rangers proceeded to turn on one their best displays of the season. Although it ended in a 4 goal win, it was really going on 20! In the most one-sided match seen at Ibrox all season, Stefan Klos did not have one save to make. Indeed, he barely had a passback to deal with. This was a team performance that had everything - apart from another half dozen goals! Every player showed great desire and a determination to win by as many goals as possible. Not once did they allow Kilmarnock to control the game even for a few minutes. The passing and movement was sublime with the skill factor evident throughout the side. The Ibrox crowd, willing the players to succeed, also played a major part by making more noise than at any other time during the season. Space forbids a description all of the goal-scoring chances but Rangers' creativity around and inside the penalty area, even when many opportunities went a begging, was thrilling to behold.

The pattern of the match was established in the very first minute. Kilmarnock kicked-off but gave away possession immediately. First Numan got the ball, then Lovenkrands who knocked it inside to Ferguson. His chip upfield was headed on by Mols into the path of Lovenkrands whose first-time cross bounced on the penalty spot, going over the head of defender Shields who then slipped. Ronald de Boer pounced on it but, from a few yards out and with only the keeper to beat, he blasted wildly over the bar when it seemed as if a tap-in was all that was necessary. With only 15 seconds on the clock, Rangers should have been ahead.

However, before any "one of those games" mutterings from the crowd, the home side did open the scoring. Mikel Arteta collected the ball out on the right touchline and, with de Boer and Ricksen, kept possession with some neat triangular play. As the Spaniard received the ball back just outside the corner of the penalty area, he tricked the Kilmarnock defence by sending a clever reverse pass into the box for Mols. The striker had timed his run perfectly to stay onside and dispatched the ball low into the far corner of the goal. The Dutchman's joy, however, would be doubled a minute later when he scored an even better goal.

In fact, it was Mols who started the move himself. He passed the ball back to Barry Ferguson, standing just outside the centre circle. The skipper looked up and spotted de Boer running through the middle. His exquisite chip over the defence (in front of de Boer) meant that keeper Marshall had to come to the edge of his area to block but the ball bounced off Marshall landed straight at the feet of Michael Mols, almost 30 yards from goal. With great perception and skill, Mols hit the loose ball first time and lofted it over everyone into the net. It was a reminder of the 'old' Mols and what he was capable of in that first season at Ibrox before his terrible injury.

Kilmarnock fans, hoping that this would be a typical game of two halves, were be mightily disappointed. The second-half followed the same pattern as the first, with perhaps even more chances being squandered by the men in blue.

Nothing improved as far as the visitors were concerned, illustrated in the 54th minute when they had a triple escape with the worst miss by Arveladze from a few yards out. However, the Georgian striker made up for this sitter a few minutes later when he did score Rangers' third goal...and from a much more difficult position.

It started with Mols, in the centre circle, sending his pass out to the left-wing for Arveladze. The striker moved forward and cut inside. Then, from outside the junction of the penalty area, he looked up and sent a superlative shot into the top right corner of Marshall's goal. Rangers were now top of the league by a one goal margin! The final goal of the game was scored by second substitute

Caniggia. De Boer took a free-kick quickly from his own half, having spotted the run of Caniggia, keeping onside. Clear of the Kilmarnock defence, the veteran got to the ball (just outside the penalty area) before Marshall and, with his first touch, took it past the ex-Celt. He ran on and side-footed the ball into the empty net before the angle became too acute.

So the match ended with a 4 goal victory and three points that enabled Rangers to overtake Celtic at the top of the table, thanks to a better goal difference of two.

A delighted 'Man of the Match' Michael Mols said after the game, "That was as good as we've played all season. And we're going to need two more performances like that if we are to give ourselves a chance of winning the title. I think everyone could see the hunger. We knew what we had to do and we did it. Everyone talks about pressure and bottle and that is obviously there when it gets as close as this. And, we're also having to play after Celtic but at least you know what you have to do. However, we know that anything less than that type of effort, commitment and performance level will not be good enough. It's a case of getting the heads down, not bothering about what anyone else is doing and getting our heads focussed on what will be a very hard game at Hearts next."

Mols also paid tribute to the fans who have always supported him through the good and the bad times of his Ibrox career. "You could sense among the fans that they were up for it and behind us. The noise was unbelievable. The place was going mad when I scored those two goals and the support was incredible. We are all in it together and that just makes the players all the more determined to win this championship."

A delighted Alex McLeish felt that his side had made recent critics eat their words. "Celtic put pressure on us by beating Hearts and now we have managed to put the pressure back on them. We have two games to negotiate - Hearts at Tynecastle and Dunfermline at home. This kind of performance, the one we witnessed here, must give the players confidence. Over the past month or so I've had to chop and change the personnel within the team mostly because of injuries. Against Kilmarnock, though, it all came together."

The Rangers team: Klos, Ricksen, Moore, Amoruso, Numan, Hughes, Ferguson, Arteta, de Boer, Mols and Lovenkrands.

The top of the table now looked like this:

	P	W	D	L	F	A	PTS	G/D
RANGERS	36	29	4	3	93	27	91	+66
CELTIC	36	29	4	3	88	24	91	+64

The following week, Barry Ferguson added to his honours when he was voted the Scottish Football Writers' 'Player of the Year' to accompany his earlier award of Players' 'Player of the Year'. He was the youngest player ever to have won this accolade twice. His awards were all the more remarkable considering that he had played through the pain barrier for most of the season and could not remember when he was last been fully fit thanks to his painful pelvic injury. "It has been very frustrating but I will get it sorted at the end of the season. All I want is to feel 100% fit again. I'm sick to death of taking injections and painkillers. They have become part of my life and I'm just fed up with it now. I've lost count of the jabs I've taken and now I have to take medicine to line my stomach to stop me being sick from the tablets. That's what it has come to for me and I don't want to go through all that to play football. This has been a massive season and I was willing to do it once - but I won't do it again. I can't even remember the last time I was fully fit. But I know what is wrong with me and I know it will be sorted now."

The see-saw nature of the title tussle was again evident that midweek as Celtic took on Dundee at Parkhead in a game re-arranged to allow Celtic longer to prepare for their UEFA Cup Final a week later. Celtic duly thrashed the men from Dens 6-2 thus overtaking Rangers at the top of the table by three points and, crucially, two goals. Cue a rush of paranoia from some fans who flooded the various radio phone-in shows to say that Dundee had not exactly exerted themselves against Celtic especially having left out top striker Lovell, Cabalerro (scorer of two goals recently against Rangers) and prized asset Khizanishvili, a reputed signing target for the Ibrox club. Saner fans noted, however, that the scorer of the second Dundee goal in the final minute was ex-Celt Barry Smith and that this goal could yet prove to be crucial at the end of the season. The closeness of this title race was obviously getting to the fans.

Sun. May 18, 2003
HEARTS 0   RANGERS 2
(de Boer, Lovenkrands)
Crowd: 15,632

When Rangers took the field at Tynecastle, they knew what they had to do. Anything other than a win would surely signal the end of their challenge for the Championship even if arithmetically there would still be a chance on the final day. As usual, the pundits trotted out the statistics - it had been almost 5 years since Hearts had defeated Rangers, a run taking in 18 matches. Indeed, that last defeat had been at Tynecastle in Dick Advocaat's first league game. Despite this series of unbeaten games, everybody connected with the club knew that this would be a very difficult match. The only change in the Rangers' ranks was that Lovenkrands dropped out to be replaced on the left flank by Arveladze.

From the beginning, Rangers passed the ball about alright and their movement was good but failed to create any real openings. This was mainly due to the organisation of the home side with players back in numbers and fighting to close Rangers down at the earliest opportunity. Fierce tackling also reminded Rangers that they would have to fight hard for victory. Unlike the previous game against Kilmarnock at Ibrox, Rangers good play came to nothing when they reached the final third of the pitch.

Ironically, near half-time, the visitors had Klos to thank after Hearts' striker de Vries tried to run at the Rangers' defence. He barged between Moore and Ricksen and the ball broke to him as it bounced off first Moore and then Ricksen's foot. The big man's left foot shot from 8 yards looked a winner until the diving Klos managed to divert it past the far post with the tip of his fingers. What a save from one of the players of the season.

When the second-half started, it was obvious Alex McLeish had decided that Rangers had to go for victory with more attacking power so he changed his formation to 4-2-4. The ineffective Arteta was replaced by Lovenkrands with Arveladze moving over to the right flank. This meant a front line of Arveladze, de Boer, Mols and Lovenkrands with only Hughes and Ferguson in midfield. Despite this, or maybe because of this, it was Hearts who began the second half in the ascendancy showing renewed vigour and determination.

However, Rangers withstood the Hearts' pressure and gradually started to get a grip of the game again. Then, in the 62nd minute they got a break at last. An Arveladze corner from the right was headed on by de Boer. As Amoruso jumped for it, de Vries, for some reason, hit it away with his hand and the referee, only a few feet away, awarded a clear-cut penalty. The only problem for Rangers was who should take it. Ferguson had missed 2 at Dens Park two weeks previously and Arteta (who had scored with his side's third penalty in the same game) was no longer on the field. Shota Arveladze stepped up to do the necessary but he made the mistake of trying to side-foot the ball into the net - a method that infuriates fans when it fails. His effort was too weak and too near to Moilanen in goal, who dived to his left and palmed the ball on to the post before it was cleared.

Luckily for the Rangers' players, before the possible consequences of such an opportunity spurned could prey on their minds, they got the opening goal. Even better, it was penalty culprit Arveladze who made up for his miss by playing an instrumental part in the goal. In the 65th minute (from a Rangers' corner), Hearts broke upfield but just outside the penalty area, Valois was superbly tackled by Moore. The ball broke to Hughes who galloped towards the other end and, as he neared the penalty box, slipped the ball to the supporting Arveladze (confronted by Neilson) who made just enough space to get his cross in. As the ball reached the 6 yard line, Pressley stepped out to play offside but his timing was fractionally wrong and de Boer's subsequent near post header fairly zoomed into the net despite the keeper getting a hand to it.

The relief of the travelling fans was matched by that of the management team on the bench. Not long after, the second goal arrived. This time, an Amoruso defensive header from his own half was bulleted upfield. De Boer, onside, latched on to it and ran into the box until he was near the by-line. Showing great awareness, he looked up and sent a tremendous cut-back into the path of Lovenkrands who, from 8 yards, side-footed the ball past the goalkeeper. The Dane's traditional cartwheel of celebration just about summed it - this goal had put Rangers back on top of the table, having scored one more goal than Celtic.

On the final day of the league season, Rangers would have the advantage of being at home (to Dunfermline) whilst Celtic would have to travel to Rugby Park and face Kilmarnock. Provided both teams won, the Championship would go to the side that won by the bigger margin. Thanks to that extra goal scored, Rangers knew that they just had to match Celtic in order to win the title.

Afterwards, one of the quiet men of Ibrox found himself in the spotlight. A relieved Stefan Klos said, "Obviously there is going to be a big focus now on strikers rather than goalkeepers. I know I still have an important job to do because losing just one goal could be a disaster. But we need to go out and give it everything against Dunfermline, try to win the game and score as many as we can. There is no point worrying about what is going on at Kilmarnock although I'm sure the crowd will tell us. We have been strong at Ibrox all season and I'm sure we can give it one more massive effort. We have scored a lot of goals but we need to dig out one more display and try to push ourselves over the line."

Looking back at the Hearts match, the stopper said, "It was important for us not to lose the first goal and I knew that Hearts would have a go. We didn't play as well as we can in the first half, maybe we were a bit anxious because we knew that if we lost it was all over. But the gaffer told us at half time that we still had 45 minutes to get the win and we would have settled for 1-0. The heads maybe dropped a bit when we missed the penalty but after we scored a couple of minutes later we never looked back. It's been an amazing few weeks."

Regarding the final league match, manager Alex McLeish said, "The energy of the Rangers fans behind us will be a big, big factor. They showed against Killie last week what an influence they can have. I don't want to make any wild boasts about ramming in goals because that would be disrespectful to Jimmy Calderwood and his players. But we've given ourselves a great chance if we give the same performance as we gave at Tynecastle."

The Rangers team: Klos, Ricksen, Moore, Amoruso, Numan, Hughes, Ferguson, Arteta, de Boer, Mols and Arveladze.

With one match left, the top of the league looked like this:

	P	W	D	L	F	A	PTS	G/D
RANGERS	37	30	4	3	95	27	94	+68
CELTIC	37	30	4	3	94	26	94	+68

Sun. May 25, 2003
RANGERS 6   DUNFERMLINE 1
(Mols, Caniggia, Arveladze, De Boer, Thompson, Arteta)
Crowd: 49,731

After what seemed like an eternity to Rangers fans, the Super Sunday Showdown finally arrived. It had been different for Celtic fans with the final of the UEFA Cup in Spain to distract their thoughts until the Thursday morning. While Rangers had a clear week, working towards the climax to their season at Murray Park, their great rivals had been losing to Porto by 3 goals to 2, after extra-time in Seville. Many wondered if the Celtic players' midweek exertions (and huge disappointment at losing the biggest game of their careers) would have an effect their game at Kilmarnock. Maybe the pendulum had swung in favour of Rangers again. Thousands of Rangers fans responded to those earlier jibes that they would be watching 'The Bill' (while Celtic played in Seville) by wearing policemen's helmets for the day.

As the teams emerged at a packed Ibrox, the Rangers players knew that they had to win (and probably win by a large margin) to ensure that the title returned to Ibrox for a world record 50th time. Once again, due to injuries, Alex McLeish had to make changes. Out of the side that finished against Hearts were Peter Lovenkrands and Stephen Hughes to be replaced by Claudio Caniggia and Mikel Arteta. For some players, who were maybe making a final Ibrox appearance, it was an extra special occasion. Stars such as Amoruso, Mols, Numan and Caniggia looked to be moving on to pastures new so winning the Championship would be the ideal way to take their leave.

In the May sunshine, a vibrant Ibrox was awash with red, white, blue and orange tops, scarves and flags. The noise and singing, even before the emergence of the teams, confirmed that, as Alex McLeish had hoped, the fans were indeed up for the occasion and ready to play their part by inspiring the team to make history. It seemed as if the volume had been cranked up even more since the previous home match. If a crowd could influence a game, this one would!

As it was, Rangers got off to a dream start. In the 2nd minute, the Dunfermline defence was breached. Inside his own half, Amoruso sent an accurate pass up the middle to de Boer who controlled it instantly, wheeled away from his marker and slipped the ball to Caniggia, running on to the 18 yard line. In turn, he sent a delicate pass between two defenders for Mols in the area. It was slightly behind the Dutchman but he showed marvellous control with his first touch and then, with a slight swivel, managed a shot in the opposite direction from that expected by everyone around him. It trundled past the outstretched hands of the diving Stillie, hit his right-hand post and spun into the net. Ibrox went bonkers!

One minute later, the Rangers fans really would have been in wonderland if de Boer had not missed an absolute sitter. The Dutch ace started the move by swinging a pass out to the right for Caniggia who, reaching the bye-line, supplied a great cross to the 6 yard line where the unmarked de Boer (on the 6 yard line with the goal at his mercy) met it with a diving header. Incredibly, the ball flashed past the left-hand post, to the frustration of both fans and players.

The tension increased considerably when Dunfermline equalised in the 11th minute. Striker Stevie Crawford sent his pass out to the right flank where Lee Bullen volleyed the ball immediately into the centre for Brewster (on the 18 yard line) who cleverly laid the ball back to Jason Dair. His subsequent 22 yarder fairly screamed beyond Klos into the net. With no score in the Celtic game at this stage, Rangers had to start all over and the fans had to raise the volume once more.

Just 5 minutes later, Rangers regained the lead when Amoruso, in the centre circle, casually passed the ball out to the right wing to Ricksen. He attempted a one-two with de Boer but the return pass looked to have been covered by a defender. Ricksen, however, did not give it up and slid in to the tackle to see the ball rebound to Caniggia only 8 yards from goal. With great calm and skill, he passed the ball into the net....and Ibrox went crazy yet again. Although he had put Rangers one goal ahead of Celtic on goal difference, it was back to square one when Sutton gave his side the lead at Rugby Park, one minute later.

Then, in the 29th minute, a third goal arrived. Moore launched a speculative cross up from deep but the ball flew over Amoruso's head. The big Italian refused to be beaten and chased after the ball, keeping it in play. On the left, he turned near the corner flag but, instead of passing it back down the wing as many expected, swung over a great cross to the 6 yard line where Arveladze (having lost his marker at the near post) dived forward and glanced his header into the far corner. Once again Rangers were a goal better-off than their table-top rivals.

With the news that Sutton had put Celtic 2-0 up, the Old Firm were tied again on goal difference although Gers were ahead in terms of the number of goals scored. Neither game saw any more scoring before half-time.

In the first 10 minutes of the second period, Rangers had two or three chances that came to nothing but the substitution of McCann for Caniggia looked as if it could pay off big time. Meanwhile at Rugby Park, in the 54th minute, Celtic were awarded a penalty and Thompson converted to put Celtic in the title driving seat for the first time that day. Rangers knew they needed another goal. Ironically, just after Celtic's penalty, Rangers were denied a good shout for one due to handball but referee Dougal refused to listen.

Five minutes later, the moment that might just have kept Rangers in the title race. At the end of a quick (and rare) Dunfermline breakaway, a cross ball was laid off by Dair back to Brewster 22 yards out from goal. The striker's shot was heading high into the net when Klos, diving to his right, got both hands to it and palmed it away. It was his first and only save of the match but it might have helped win the league title. As so often happens in football, within a minute, Rangers went further ahead. Out on the left, Neil McCann took a free kick with such curl and pace that it was a striker's dream. That man Ronald de Boer ran on to it and headed brilliantly past Stillie. Funnily enough, at almost the same moment in Rugby Park, Larsson was hitting the post when a goal looked certain. That Old Firm goal difference was now the same again.

Within a minute, it looked as if the pendulum had really swung in favour of Rangers when a 5th goal was poked past Stillie. Another great dribbling run from McCann ended with a low cut back a few yards from goal where Bullen's attempted clearance hit off Steven Thompson and squirted into the net. Delirium in the stands. Not only had this goal put Rangers ahead in terms of goal difference but it was also the 100th league goal. As Rangers' dominance of the match continued (with other chances being missed), the fans began to believe that the title was coming home. Then, doubts re-emerged when Celtic were awarded a second penalty against Killie. The roar that echoed round Ibrox when Thompson missed that one was a mixture of relief and joy. However, just 3 more minutes later, Petrov scored Celtic's fourth. Now, with only 6 minutes to go, all the fans knew that if Celtic scored one more goal the title would be theirs - snatched from Rangers in the dying minutes of the season.

To make sure, Rangers needed one more goal and it nearly came when a Thompson header hit off the junction of the post and the bar. Then the same player fired a shot which Stillie gathered at the second attempt, before McCann could pounce. As the match moved into injury time, the tension was almost unbearable. Then, a minute from the end, it was Rangers' opportunity to settle the matter once and for all. A brilliant run and wall pass from McCann to Thompson and back saw the winger race into the area. He was brought down from behind and this time the referee could not refuse the penalty. But who would take it?

With Ferguson and Arveladze both having missed with their last efforts, it was Mikel Arteta who stepped forward this time. Of course, the fans had not forgotten how the young Spaniard, three weeks earlier, salvaged a point at Dens Park in the dying minutes - now he stood up to seal the Championship for Rangers. Everybody knew that if he scored, Celtic would have to score twice in the final two minutes of their game. Players such as Klos and de Boer turned their backs as they just could not bear to watch. The resounding roar they heard confirmed that Arteta had done his job properly. Under the greatest of pressure, the young man had stroked the ball low into the right-hand corner of the goal having sent the keeper the wrong way. At that point, everybody inside Ibrox knew the title was secure.

However, when the final whistle was blown half a minute later, the roar was not one of unbridled joy as the game at Rugby Park still had a minute to play. Rangers had at least done their job and as the players shook hands with each other, that one minute seemed to last an eternity. Then, the thousands of radios in the stadium sent out the news that Celtic had (only) won 4-0 making Rangers the Champions by one goal. What a fairy tale end to the league campaign, grabbing the crown from their greatest rivals in the final minute of the final league game. What a way to win a world record 50th Championship! Many pundits had suggested that Rangers would fail to take the title as they did not have an out-and-out scorer in the mould of Larsson. However, this final match emphasised a different type of strength as all 6 goals were scored by different players - a feature of the play throughout the season. They did not have to rely on one player in particular to get the vital goals and had out-scored their rivals and won the Championship after all. Meanwhile, at the other end of the park, Stefan Klos had played his part, appearing in every minute of every game of this memorable season.

The Rangers team: Klos, Ricksen, Moore, Amoruso, Numan, de Boer, Ferguson, Arteta, Caniggia, Mols and Arveladze.

AFTERMATH

After the trophy had been presented and the laps of honour (wearing a variety of obligatory silly headgear) been completed, the Rangers players could reflect on the incredible end to a long, hard slog that had been their league campaign. Skipper Barry Ferguson was perhaps more delighted than any other having grown up supporting the club. "There were a few nerves out there - I began to feel them the night before. The tension was unbelievable. When the gaffer shouted to me that Celtic had scored their third goal it was

the worst I've ever felt, to be honest. But we showed what
tremendous spirit this team has and we managed to go up the park
and get another couple of goals. Mikel was trying to tell me what
was happening at Rugby Park but his English isn't that good and
I didn't understand him. It wasn't until Fernando came across that
I realised what the score was. I knew then that I had to drive the
team forward to get more goals. They responded magnificently
and did that."

Ferguson relished the achievement of his boyhood dream to
captain Rangers to the Championship. "Winning the league is
something I've always dreamed about and to do it as skipper is
unbelievable. This means the world to me. But, fair play to Celtic,
I watched them on Wednesday night and they were superb as they
have been throughout the season. They are a good team and
deserve a lot of credit. Still, if we'd beaten them at Ibrox a few weeks
ago it would have been all over. People keep asking what the
difference is between this season and last. I don't know. Maybe it's
Alex McLeish because he's been great. We were 18 points behind
Celtic last season so that tells you we have come on leaps and bounds."

Unlike some of his team-mates, Fernando Ricksen was
celebrating his first Championship medal. "I have never been
involved in anything like that. It was just incredible. It's the best day
of my life, a day that players live for! At one stage I felt the title had
gone. I was the closest player to the gaffer in the second half so
I was the one getting all the updates of what was happening with
Celtic. He told me to get the message across that Celtic were 3-0
up and we had to get more goals. We got two quick ones to go 5-1
up but even then Celtic scored again. Even when Mikel scored the
6th we still didn't know. It was the longest minute of my life at the
end when we had to wait for the final whistle from the Celtic game.
It was crazy. I don't think I would ever want to go through that again
on the last day. It might have been exciting for everyone not
involved with both teams but for us it was scary. Losing on the last
day would have destroyed me. But now I am a champion and it

feels so, so good. We have lost just three matches all season and scored over 100 goals - that is the form of a team that deserves to win the league."

Manager Alex McLeish was also feeling good as it was his first Championship as a manager. He was also a relieved man. "It was turmoil out there. Things were swinging one way then the other and it produced an amazing afternoon. With the season Celtic has had I knew we could never rule them out until the final whistle at both grounds. But I hope that that experience is something that will serve me well in the future. I have to thank the players and the fans because they never gave up and we got the rewards in the end. My thanks also go to Andy Watson and Jan Wouters for all their tremendous work throughout the season.

It's a fantastic feeling for me and I know how much it means to the Rangers fans. When you sample that yesterday, you wonder if it gets any better. But I know that Rangers is all about winning and that's what we'll keep trying to do. Dick Advocaat brought most of these players here and he's shown he's a shrewd judge of a player. I got a bit more out of them and I think Dick recognised that. I think if you are big enough to make that decision, it doesn't make you less of a man - it makes you more of a man. I was guided by Dick and David Murray and we got the players back to having the spirit again. The aggression of the team, the positive energy of the players was just incredible yesterday as they went after it. When we lost to Celtic a few weeks back, there was a question mark over our bottle, suggestions we'd drop points in the run-in and crash. But the players showed fantastic resilience and strength of character to respond to that. You have to give credit to Celtic for coming back at us but we stood up to it."

The final task at the end of such a tremendous season would be the Scottish Cup Final against Dundee and, with victory, would come the Treble.

THE FINAL SPL TABLE

	P	W	D	L	F	A	PTS	GD
RANGERS	38	31	4	3	101	28	97	+73
CELTIC	38	31	4	3	98	26	97	+72
HEARTS	38	18	9	11	57	51	63	+6
KILMARNOCK	38	16	9	13	47	56	57	-9
DUNFERMLINE	38	13	7	18	54	71	46	-17
DUNDEE	38	10	14	14	50	60	44	-10
HIBS	38	15	6	17	56	64	51	-8
ABERDEEN	38	13	10	15	41	54	49	-13
LIVINGSTON	38	9	8	21	48	62	35	-14
PARTICK	38	8	11	19	37	58	35	-21
DUNDEE UTD	38	7	11	20	35	68	32	-33
MOTHERWELL	38	7	7	24	45	71	28	-26

Sat. May 31, 2003
THE SCOTTISH CUP FINAL
RANGERS 1 DUNDEE 0
(Amoruso)
CROWD: 47,136

After the unforgettable finale to the league campaign, it was maybe inevitable that the Scottish Cup Final would be something of an anti-climax, regardless of the result. It was not that it was a poor game or a one-sided affair with the under-dogs, Dundee, being outclassed. In fact, the Dens Park outfit played as well as they were capable of without really creating any clear-cut chances. This should not have surprised students of the season as Dundee had only managed to win 10 of their 38 league matches, finishing 6th in the table. Playing attractive, attacking football was their strong point but scoring goals was not.

As for Rangers, the adjective that best sums up their performance was 'lacklustre'. They dominated the match and played the ball around competently on the ground, keeping possession but, just like the other finalists, there was a lack of creativity in opening up the opposition defence. Compared to the previous game against Dunfermline, there was a distinct lack of energy and urgency although this was maybe expected after the side's exertions of the previous weeks and the emotion of winning the title in such dramatic fashion. While there was a lot of neat passing and movement (with a lack of biting tackles or aggression), the game was not one to thrill the Hampden crowd.

Rangers' cause had not been helped by the fact that, once again, 4 players had been injured in the run up to this Hampden occasion. Out were Arteta, Lovenkrands, Caniggia and Hughes giving Bob Malcolm the chance to play 90 minutes in a cup final as a holding midfielder. Rangers, as usual, played a very attacking formation with only Ferguson and Malcolm in midfield, assisted, when necessary, by McCann and Arveladze on either flank. To their credit, Dundee also lined up with an adventurous system (4-3-3) and were determined not just to sit back.

Despite this, the OPTA statistics at the end of the game showed that Rangers had 62% of the possession as opposed to Dundee's 38%. However, this belied the fact that Dundee played well and threatened Rangers with quick breaks. Indeed, in the last 15 minutes of play, many Rangers players looked dead on their feet and could scarcely raise a gallop, even Steven Thompson who had only played for the final half-hour. Having used all his subs, Alex McLeish could not even replace a limping and strapped Neil McCann who bravely played on, trying to remain a 'nuisance' to Dundee as he later put it.

The match almost started with a shock and produced the shot that came nearest to a goal for Dundee. In the 4th minute, Rae picked the ball up on the right side of midfield and ran at the Rangers defence. He was allowed to drive into the penalty area, side-stepping Moore before Amoruso charged out to block his shot. The ball rebounded out of the box, straight to Smith who fired a great shot at goal. Fortunately, with the diving Klos looking beaten, the ball whacked off his left-hand post and was promptly cleared to safety.

After this, Rangers started to build up a head of steam and, several minutes later, a tremendous cross from Neil McCann was headed past by de Boer at the back post. Then, in the 14th minute, McCann, on the right this time, took a great free kick that went into the crowded 6 yard box where Michael Mols saw his header cannon off the crossbar before keeper Speroni was fouled by Moore, attempting to take advantage of the rebound.

In the 24th minute, Rangers best move saw Ferguson gather the ball in his own half, moved forward to the half-way line and send a 20 yard forward pass up the middle to de Boer. The Dutch ace typically controlled and turned in one movement, leaving his marker Khizanishvili for dead. De Boer zeroed in on goal with Khizanishvili and two defenders chasing him. From just outside the box, he shot but the defender managed to get his foot across and the ball was deflected a foot past for a corner-kick. It was the most skillfully created chance of the match.

Between then and half-time, very little of note took place at either end. The second-half was virtually a carbon-copy of the first with created chances just non-existent. Then, in the 65th minute, came the breakthrough for Rangers. It began with defender Khizanishvili (arguably Dundee's best player) barging substitute Steven Thompson off the ball near the corner flag on the right. McCann stepped up to take the free-kick and a magnificent in-swinging cross with pace was sent into the area where Amoruso had stolen a march on his marker, the same Khizanishvili. His glancing header whizzed into the net and the fairy tale ending to Amo's Ibrox career looked a distinct possibility. It was the big man's 6th goal of the season and probably his most vital one.

With a slender lead, Rangers continued to play a possession game, hoping that the Dundee players would run out of steam in the muggy heat of the Hampden bowl. Ironically, Dundee only grew stronger and it was the Ibrox side that started to wilt, looking as if they were running on empty. In the final 15 minutes, a couple of chances presented themselves to Dundee and, had they taken even one, they would surely have become favourites to go on and win the cup. In the final minutes, the tired Rangers players tried to kill the game by keeping possession and taking the ball into the corner at the Dundee end of the park. It worked. When Kenny Clark's whistle signalled the end of the match, the cheers were probably more of relief (that the Treble had been completed) than elation regarding the day's victory.

A season that started out more in hope than expectation ended with the club winning its 7th Treble while great rivals Celtic could only boast a losing appearance in a UEFA Cup Final. There was no doubt which one the Rangers fans preferred as they celebrated the presentation of the Scottish Cup for the 31st time - equalling Celtic's record number of wins. Add that world record 50th Championship and it was easy to understand why it had been such a tremendous season for Teddy Bears everywhere.

The Rangers team: Klos, Ricksen, Moore, Amoruso, Numan, Malcolm, de Boer, Ferguson, Arveladze, Mols and McCann.

As usual, the post-match comments were full of the delight to be expected in winning the Treble although for some Rangers players this would be mixed with regret as it could be their final match for the club.

One such player was Arthur Numan who was definitely moving on to pastures new. He had started his career at Ibrox with a Treble and had now ended it in the same manner, much to his great satisfaction. On leaving the club, Numan said, "The simple fact was that we couldn't agree a deal for me to stay at Rangers but I will never say anything negative about the club. I have been treated really well since the day I came in 1998. I've had five fabulous years at Rangers winning two Trebles and two doubles. When I left Holland, I had a good feeling from the moment I talked with

Rangers. I was proved right and have no regrets about the move. The atmosphere when we won the league at Ibrox will stay with me forever - without doubt it was the best I've experienced in my career. I'm just happy that I could go out as a Treble winner and have the chance to enjoy a final goodbye with the Rangers fans."

His fellow Dutchman, Michael Mols, appreciated that he too might have played his last game for Rangers. "I don't really know what I want but everything is still possible. I just want to go away on holiday and relax before making a decision. The likes of Arthur leaving will have some effect on my thoughts. He made this a pleasant stay for me but there are so many plusses and minuses to weigh up. Arthur and I have already discussed what we will do if I end up leaving with him. We are going to set up our own tours so that you can see the game then go out in Glasgow afterwards. We'll put together a whole package that you can book. It won't be about making money though. It will be more a reason to come back to Glasgow."

Another, more emotional, member of the side who looked as if he would be leaving was Lorenzo Amoruso. Rangers had accepted an offer of £1.5 million for him and, at the age of 32 (with only a year left on his contract), it seemed a sensible move by the club. The need to reduce a crippling wage bill was also a prime factor in letting one of the club's highest earners leave, even if he was willing to accept a pay cut to stay. As had become traditional, a tearful Amoruso was last up to collect his winner's medal and hold the trophy aloft, courtesy of Alex McLeish who went just ahead of him in order that the Italian's final moment of Rangers glory would not be diminished. It was a typically generous gesture by the manager who had just joined the ranks of an elite band of Rangers managers by winning the Treble.

Amoruso certainly appreciated the qualities of his manager. He said, "It was a nice gesture. But I've always had a good relationship with Alex. He is a great manager and a great person. When he took over, I was in Italy because I was suspended. Within three hours of being appointed, he phoned me and asked, "Hey, big man, you alright?" I asked "Who's that?" and he replied "Your manager!" It just shows you the person he is. Dick Advocaat wouldn't have done that!"

When asked about this season's achievements, Amoruso declared, "This was definitely the best because it was the most difficult to win. The feeling I had after the game was fantastic - it will be in my heart forever. The players were exhausted but after last week's thrilling last day this was brilliant. If it turns out to be my last game, what a way to end my Rangers career. I was a little emotional afterwards. The fans were great to me. People in Scotland don't realise how amazing they are because they are probably used to it. But it was brilliant. I hope the supporters can keep this good memory in their heart because I know I will."

For Barry Ferguson, he was living the cliché - a dream come true. He had watched his elder brother Derek win medals for Rangers years before and here he was actually captaining a side to the Treble. Like many of his team-mates, he urged the Rangers Board to extend the manager's contract as soon as possible before predators (from the likes of English clubs) could lure him away from Ibrox. "Big clubs in England might come looking for him now so it's important we get him tied up. I hope he does sign a new contract because he has been great for me and great for the team. He has helped me in many ways, even though I can't really speak about some of them. On the field, though, he has added goals to my game and told me to go forward when the chance is there. He is more important to Rangers than any player. He has to keep everyone in the squad on their toes. He gets very upset if we don't perform in training and he's brought a special mentality to the club."

Ferguson was as much relieved as elated that he had managed to finish the season at all, let alone on such a high note. On the Monday after the final, he was scheduled to have his long-awaited operation to cure the pelvic problem that had been plaguing him for most of the season. One man who knows how much Rangers need Ferguson is Alex McLeish. "If we can get him fully fit then I can't wait to see him next year. But he's been a great captain and he goes down in history now as the guy who captained the club to a Treble."

On the emotional end to his first full season in charge at Ibrox, he said, "I feel totally drained. It's been a hard season. Everything has been so close and the measure of our bottle is that we've gone the extra mile when required in major games. Now we've done it I don't know if I can face a night out with the exhaustion I'm feeling."

On the Cup Final itself, the manager said, "I was worried the players would be unable to go back to the highs of last weekend. They were tired and lacked spark and Dundee were excellent - so there were many times when I thought it wasn't going to be our day. In the dressing-room at half-time I tried to raise them. It was the usual clichéd stuff but there were some rousing Braveheart shouts just before we went back out. We showed great steel and resilience to see it through and make it over that last hurdle. As for Lorenzo, it was as if the script was written for him. I had a feeling he'd pop up with a goal after all the speculation. If he leaves, he has signed off in great style."

C.I.S CUP

Third Round	HIBS 2	RANGERS 3
Quarter-final	DUNFERMLINE 0	RANGERS 1
Semi-final	HEARTS 0	RANGERS 1
Final	CELTIC 1	RANGERS 2

SCOTTISH CUP

Third Round	ARBROATH 0	RANGERS 3
Fourth Round	AYR UTD 0	RANGERS 1
Quarter-final	DUNFERMLINE 1	RANGERS 1
Replay	RANGERS 3	DUNFERMLINE 0
Semi-final	RANGERS 4	MOTHERWELL 3
FINAL	RANGERS 1	DUNDEE 0